YOUR ACTIONS DEFINE YOUR EXISTENCE

How becoming accountable could make your existence better

NEELKAMAL KASHYAP

Copyright © 2025 Neelkamal Kashyap

This is a work of nonfiction. The events and the incidents mentioned in the book are true and real. However, some names and characteristics have been changed, some events have been compressed, and some dialogues have been recreated.

All Rights Reserved.

First Edition: April 2025
Printed in India

Printed at Gapmeta Ventures Private Limited, Navi Mumbai
Typeset in Adobe Garamond Pro

ISBN : 978-93-6070-947-1

Cover Design: Prajakta Sawant

Publisher: StoryMirror Infotech Pvt. Ltd.
               Unit No-F/705, 7th Floor, Kailas Corporate Lounge,
               Veer Savarkar Road, Vikhroli Park Site, Vikhroli West,
               Mumbai-400079, Maharashtra.

Web: storymirror.com
Facebook: @storymirror
Instagram: @storymirror
Twitter: @story_mirror
Contact Us: marketing@storymirror.com

No part of this book may be reproduced, or stored in a retrieval system, or transmitted in any form or by any means, electronic, mechanical, photocopying, recording, or otherwise, without the express written permission of the author.

"If you make yourself more than just a man,
If you devote yourself to an ideal,
and if they can't stop you,
then you become something else entirely
: A Legend"

Ra's Al Ghul

Dedication

I would like to thank my family (Mother, Father and Sister).

I would like to thank my Dog (Yuvi) for teaching me how to love and how to get over things.

I would like to thank my school and college friends for always believing in me.

My school and college teachers who always believed in me.

My Physiotherapist for always keeping my body together.

My mental Therapist for always keeping my mind together.

Both of your contributions have been immense in keeping me together as an individual.

I would also like to thank all those individuals who have come and helped me incredibly well and have been there for me at crucial times.

Thank you to all of you for turning me into the man that I am today and making my second book a reality.

And lastly thank you to all the haters, narcissists in my life, without your hate I would be nothing, so thank you.

Your contributions will never be forgotten.

"The Road to heaven feels like Hell.
The Road to Hell feels like Heaven."

Index

Introduction

Life, with all its intricate layers and complications, shapes us into the individuals we become. The journey through life is laden with a complex mix of joy, suffering, generosity, hatred, love, and countless blessings. These elements intertwine to create an experience that is uniquely ours, sometimes uplifting and at other times overwhelming. Life's abundance of highs and lows makes it captivating yet simultaneously daunting. It's a curious paradox—an experience both exhilarating and painful—that keeps us constantly seeking meaning and understanding. One of the central questions that permeate our existence is our constant "pursuit of happiness". How do we simplify our lives and make them more fulfilling, more peaceful, and less cluttered? How do we make it filled with more purpose? How do we make it feel more in sync with what we want? How do we embrace solitude? These inquiries often plague our minds, leaving us with endless thoughts and possibilities. Amid this internal chaos, we search for meaning in a world that offers little clarity about life. There is so much to offer, and yet we aren't able to figure out what we should relish, and that is what makes our lives complicated and complex and makes us question our "time in this world" and "Our existence".

Even as we recognise the fragility of our existence—that we are here only temporarily and could leave this world at any moment—we still find ourselves consumed by our daily worries. We obsess over our problems as though the universe revolves around them, making life far more complicated than it needs to be. In doing so, we risk losing the essence of what makes life a gift: its unpredictability, challenges, and moments of beauty.

Most of the time, these things make our lives both a blessing and a curse. There are moments when we celebrate its wonders, and there are times when we curse its hardships. However, this balance between joy and suffering makes the beautiful moments even more precious. This book has been written to explore that balance—how we can navigate life's complexities and make it less burdensome, as most of us share the quest for a simpler, more meaningful life. We often go to great lengths in search of answers to the questions that have eluded us for so long. It is during these times of uncertainty that we begin to question everything we know, everything we do, and everything we observe around us. Yet, we must realise that life was never meant to be fully figured out. If it were, we would lose the excitement, the curiosity, and the wonder that makes life worth living. Life is not merely a series of problems to be solved but a journey to be experienced in its entirety—both the struggles and the triumphs.

We must remember to live when we focus solely on solving life's problems. We overlook the richness that comes from embracing life's challenges and growing from them. Instead of avoiding difficulties, we must accept them as part of the human experience. Doing so makes us more resilient, grounded, and ultimately more capable of enjoying the peace and fulfilment we seek. We

    Your Actions Define Your Existence

must understand that often, the solutions to our sufferings, our impending issues, and our being overwhelmed or underwhelmed by something or someone lie within the periphery of our vision. Yet, our human nature leads us to ignore the obvious, to deny the truth, and to resist change. In doing so, we remain trapped in patterns of misery and discontent. This book is meant to provide you with a solution for solving only some of life's problems. I am not here to present a one-size-fits-all solution to your complexities. What this book offers, however, is a framework for understanding the underlying issues that contribute to your difficulties. By clarifying these root causes, you will be better equipped to chart a path forward.

A roadmap, even a simple one, makes the journey more manageable. Wandering with no direction only leads to more significant confusion and suffering. But when you have a guiding route—a strategy for growth and self-improvement—life becomes more purposeful and less overwhelming. Especially in today's fast-paced world, where peace and sanity are more complex, finding that sense of purpose is more important than ever. And because we are now living in a world where people can gather information about an endless number of maps that may take them to a place of happiness and fulfilment but unfortunately, having so many options, so many ideas, and so many roads are only making us feel more and more miserable as we are clueless on which path to choose, as instead of that we should be trusting our instincts and choose the path that we believe in, especially when we know the other side will be a version of ourselves who is so much at peace with all the fantastic things and the not so amazing things in our lives, and once you do that you end up becoming a person who is secure in their skin that it would motivate anybody to follow you but the first step you need to take is choose that particular path, and that would only happen when you end up becoming self-aware and start understanding yourself more than anybody else.

By taking the time to understand ourselves—our strengths, weaknesses, desires, and fears—we unlock the potential for personal growth and fulfilment. This book aims to guide you on that journey of self-discovery, helping you appreciate your life and make the most of its opportunities. Believing in your instincts, being grateful for your circumstances, and acknowledging the reality of your situation separate those who thrive from those who remain stuck in denial. The person who can accept life's trials and tribulations rather than resist them is the one who will emerge stronger, wiser, and more resilient. As we all know, accepting our drawbacks is and will never be easy, and often doing so often bruises our ego. But in the long run, this process of introspection and acceptance leads to a more fulfilling life that is less complicated and more attuned to the things that truly matter. This book will delve into the various aspects of life that contribute to its complexity. Examining these elements will uncover ways to make life simpler, more peaceful, and more joyful. The goal is not to eliminate life's challenges but to find healthier, more productive ways of facing them. Once you understand the dynamics, you will be empowered to make choices that lead to greater happiness and fulfilment.

So, as you embark on this journey through life's complexities, I encourage you to remain open-minded and curious. Embrace the lessons, hardships, and triumphs that life has to offer. The road ahead may be difficult, but with the right mindset and the willingness to grow, you will find that life's complexities can be navigated—and even celebrated.

  Your Actions Define Your Existence

Accepting unpredictability in life's richness is what makes it so much better. It is in the unexpected turns, the challenges, and the moments of wonder that we truly discover who we are and what we are capable of.

This book invites you to explore those depths, confront life's uncertainties, and develop a deeper understanding of yourself and the world around you. And when you do that, you will realise that life, in all its complexity, is a journey worth taking. We will talk in-depth about how no matter what we do and how much we work to improve our lives, life always finds a way to make our lives difficult and filled with challenges and obstacles. But what life never tells us is what these things are meant to do, and then when we go deeper and start exploring and start facing these issues, we realise on the other side is a person we so dearly wanted to become but weren't able to become simply because we were scared to take the plunge. The moment we hear the word suffering, we always interpret it to be something that would make us worse than we are right now, which is true in many ways, but what people don't realise is what lies on the other side, and very few are willing to take that journey. But that's not anybody's fault, as we live in a world where anybody or everybody would want those trophies and those laurels some of the incredible ones may have received. Still, only some want to take that path that has led them to become capable enough to be the beholder of those trophies. The only way we could become that person and be the ones holding that trophy is by being scared or suffering yet willing to take on that plunge; what else would you do?

The very fabric of human society has been kept alive by the unity and the interconnectedness we have often shared. Still, as times have changed, we as individuals have started deviating from the tribes we once were and started becoming solitary in our natures, even though, at the same time, we realised how no matter how much we grow, we will always need the help of a fellow human being to do and finish our tasks as nobody has ever been born or neither will be born capable enough to take on the world alone (unless of course if you are superman). Due to that, the way we are connected in today's day and age is way different than what it used to be. Still, the problem with the modern-day way of interconnectedness, which we call "globalisation" or the "social media era", is a simple fact that more and more individuals are getting increasingly depressed and resentful as they are chasing individual validation they might not even know. Further, social media has also allowed individuals to hurt each other without being accountable for their actions. With times, these very platforms, which were meant to become ways and platforms through which our lives get more accessible, have become messengers of doom. As all it has done is make individuals addicted to a virtual world that doesn't exist while on the other allowed the powerful elites to control the masses based on their whims and wishes, as with time more and more individuals are falling into that crevasse of desperation and resentment, whereas these very devices and platforms were once meant to be the source of our salvations and guide as an inspiration to the rest of mankind, but seems like everything has gone for a toss and we are now living in a world filled with individuals who have everything yet want what the other individual has for that is what has led to our lives being intertwined into a web of invisible complexities that none of us had expected, but has come, and the only way we could free ourselves from the clutches of this web is by making ourselves willing to make our lives better and by the willingness to make

     Your Actions Define Your Existence

our lives less miserable and make our existence an experience where we wake up to a grateful morning rather than a cursed night of what awaits tomorrow, and that is no way to live our lives and make something out of our existence.

We must understand the true transactional nature of the world. When we do that, we will start accepting the things that are and there and how we should go about our business to make our lives far less complicated than they already are, and that is only possible when we are willing to understand how the world works in general and what that would make us realise, is the fact that everything in the world has a value because we have assigned it to it, as without that even a diamond is as useless as a piece of stone. Still, because specific individuals assigned certain values to that particular stone, we now get what we get and how we get it.

We will discuss in depth most of the things that have made our lives so much worse than we could have ever imagined and how we could all deal with those things.

We will discuss the harshness and crude nature of our lives and how we could deal with it. When we do that, we become individuals who are far better equipped to deal with the issues of the world, especially the ones that involve us and are willing to make our lives the way they are. So, let's dive into the details of all these aspects and find out how we could make our lives so much more than we have been able to do until now.

At the end of the day, what we all want is to wake up to a morning where we no longer question our existence but rather appreciate it for the way it is. When we are able to do that, we can fill our lives with certain amounts of peace and zeal, and that would mean we have reached our goal.

What you are going to learn through this book is how to navigate the various complexities of your lives and reach a place where you have become strong enough to handle them and, at the same time, make your time on this planet a far better experience than what you have been used to until now. You will learn how often, even though things are simple and smooth, we tend to make our lives complicated with our own choices. When we end up doing that, we have no right to expect stability in our lives, as that's not what our actions are showing up for. You will learn how there is a thin line between protecting somebody's life and invading their everyday existence. You will learn how making ourselves bulletproof (mentally) makes us individuals who start regarding our presence in our lives far more helpful than wishing somebody to add value to their lives. In short, you will learn how certain troubles in our lives are bound to happen, whereas certain things could be avoided, and even if not, they could be handled much better. And how there is no magic place; instead, all our glories and defeats are meant to be cherished, lived and crucified in this very existence. And how knowing all of these can lead to a life that looks so much more content than most of us are used to living.

One of the critical points I have expressed in detail is that we constantly focus on all the negatives and worst possible outcomes, and most of the time, the narrative continues dominating our lives. Too often, we dwell on problems, setbacks, and disappointments—things that make life feel more complex and, at times, even unbearable. This focus on the negative can cloud our vision, preventing us from seeing the beauty, joy, and possibilities surrounding us. Life as a whole is way more prosperous than we could ever fathom, and due to that, it can present us with countless opportunities to experience joy, create memories, and find fulfilment. However, if we constantly fixate on what's wrong, we miss out on these moments of happiness. It's as though we are blind to the good because we are consumed by the bad. This book encourages readers to ask themselves: What if I focused on what makes me happy rather than sad? What if I concentrated on what I can control instead of what is outside my grasp? In asking these questions, we can see life through a more positive and empowering lens, realising that we have more control over our internal world than we might initially believe.

The book further explains how acceptance is not about resignation or giving up. Instead, it is about embracing reality with grace, even when painful. Acceptance allows us to reclaim our power because once we stop fighting against what we cannot change, we can direct our energy toward what we can change— our perspective, attitude, and actions. Through acceptance, we learn to face challenges with resilience rather than avoidance. We begin to see life not as a series of problems but as a journey that includes highs and lows. This mindset shift helps us focus on life aspects that bring meaning, joy, and satisfaction, even in the face of adversity. In this way, acceptance becomes a tool for personal growth and fulfilment. And in that way, I urge the readers to focus on what truly matters and to recognise the things that make life memorable.

Most importantly, it teaches the invaluable lesson that acceptance is always a better option than denial, no matter how difficult. While denial may offer temporary comfort, it only leads to more pain in the long run. On the other hand, acceptance allows us to live in harmony with reality, and in doing so, we free ourselves from unnecessary suffering. Through this book, readers will understand that the path to a fulfilling life begins with the choice to accept rather than deny.

Specific stories about suffering and misery will make you understand how you could make your lives better. If they already are, they will allow you to feel grateful and honoured for your life rather than the imaginary and dreamy world you always envisioned for yourself. Differentiation and gratefulness happen only when we end up losing all of it. Still, there are far better ways and better things that you could do to make your lives better before losing all the incredible things that life has bestowed upon you.

You will learn, in detail, how society shapes our thoughts, ideals, and desires, moulding us into a version of ourselves that fits neatly into predefined roles and structures. Often, this vision is different from our true selves, and it becomes essential to recognise that the life you want to lead could be vastly different from the one others envisioned for you. The key, however, lies in cultivating the courage to break free from these societal expectations. It's easy to go along with what is imposed, but actual growth happens when you question these imposed narratives.

This book challenges you to think deeply about your beliefs and societies. It asks you to identify which beliefs genuinely belong to you and which are inherited, unquestioned, or forced upon you. Once you gain this clarity, you can begin reshaping your world, carving out a reality that resonates with your authentic self. You may not always be free to change external circumstances, but by aligning with your inner beliefs, you can create a version of life that feels more meaningful and fulfilling. What you have to

   Your Actions Define Your Existence

understand is the simple fact that life often throws unpredictable events in our way, and the unfortunate part is we do not always get to choose our wins or losses. However, we always have a choice in how we respond to these outcomes. This book emphasises that we are not defined by what happens to us but rather by what we choose to make of those experiences.

When you start seeing wins and losses as opportunities for growth, a new perspective emerges—not driven by jealousy, envy, or a sense of inadequacy. Instead, you learn to accept every outcome with grace. Losing doesn't mean failure, and winning doesn't necessarily mean success. How you interpret these events and allow them to shape your character truly matters.

So, get ready, and let's dive deep into what's meant to fill your lives with a vision of our benevolence and gratitude!

ONE

Humankind and Its Complexities

As humans, we are complex individuals. We can come up with any rational explanation to defend our actions. Those actions may have led to catastrophic consequences that ended several individuals, but accepting defeat and being honest takes courage, and it is courage that most of us lack. Due to this, most of us fall into the species of Dream Killers, while the ones who do fall into the category of "Achievers."

Like the dream killers, the Achievers are blessed with the same physical and biological features. They have the same amount of time in the world as the ones who aren't pursuing anything worthwhile, yet only a select few can stride while most of us can't get out of the mud. WHY?

Well, it comes to various factors such as **our situation and how we handle that particular situation, the cost of saying yes to everyone else and saying No to ourselves, unwillingness to do what is suitable for ourselves, inability to negate people's point of view, unable to stop desiring validation, treating our parents as Gods and not humans, the failure to fulfil our tasks** as not doing them is much easier than not doing them, as doing requires us to take responsibility but not doing abstains us from responsibility and that's the very reason we are hell-bent of defending even the worse of our actions, as most of us are hesitant in taking responsibility, as being responsible means being able to own up to our actions and being who we are and yet most of us often refrain from being who we are as that gives us comfort.

I called the human species complex because of our inability to become who we are based on what we think or feel about ourselves. But rather than that, most of our identity and belongingness in the world is based on what an outsider tells us, and that's where we lack the edge and willingness to accept ourselves as we are far more concentrated on those opinions that I call Outside noise, to prove ourselves. Our body, mind, thoughts, health, and everything else are under our control, and most of the time, we can choose what to do with them, yet we surrender that control to an outsider and give power to that particular individual. The reason for that specific surrender is, once again, our inability to take responsibility, even for ourselves.

Having control and power is how the elites and the politicians rule us, and most of us often dream of having it. Still, it's such a passionate human paradox in which we usually deem ourselves capable enough to rule our district, rule our state or maybe rule our country, when at the same time, we aren't able to rule our minds and point them towards the direction we want it to be.

Different situations call for various requirements; for instance, when we join the armed forces, we are often taught to learn and understand how to prioritize our country's well-being. And yet the essential thing that we usually end up missing is the fact that when we are in the army or any other defence force, first it comes down to us how we make ourselves mentally and physically capable enough to stand among those men, as once we are capable enough to hold our weight, we can go around and dream of carrying the weight of our society and our dear ones, and to

 Your Actions Define Your Existence

maintain the weight of ourselves, we have to take responsibility and be capable enough to control ourselves in the way we consider to make ourselves as humans. And that's an insensitive thing to do, as it might mean becoming the person we had never imagined we could become, it might mean changing ourselves to others' dislikes while moulding ourselves to our liking, and trust me, that's a tricky thing to do but is one of the most rewarding things to do. It means becoming the true self of our self.

At the same time, becoming the person who might be at odds with our current group of friends, family or colleagues, but becoming the person who attracts individuals who are similar to our way of life, a life where taking responsibility is of utmost concern, a life where we exercise control over ourselves, a life where we point ourselves to the direction that those "Achievers" have always indicated. Still, we could not, as being beside the dream killers gave us comfort, peace and belonging to a larger group. But it is the path of smaller groups and taking up the responsibility that genuinely allows us to stride and become the men/women of our dreams. It's a tough place to be, for there are constant battles. Still, it's much better battling and using the sword when we are secure in our skin that we are no longer doing things to please people (friends, family, colleagues, partners) but rather doing things to please ourselves, and that's a much better place to be, for it is here that growth, discipline, focus, accomplishment, tears and loneliness meets, and in some cases it is these things that end up giving us the much-needed solitude, patience and calmness in our lives that we do dearly desired when we were in the company of the Dream killers.

Now, let's discuss in detail the situations I outlined above regarding the reasons for our inability to do things we desire or deem correct for our growth.

Our situations and how we handle that particular situation

> *"Although you may not always be able to avoid difficult situations, you can modify the extent to which you can suffer by how you choose to respond to that situation."*
>
> ***Dalai Lama***

 Your Actions Define Your Existence

We live in a world where we are often meant to face situations that none of us had ever hoped for. The trials and tribulations we all thought we were strong enough to face suddenly become overwhelming, and we can't escape them.

Well, these words sum up how we often feel in life, how that particular situation has broken us to the precipice, and during such times, it becomes crucial that we usually take the next step towards what we feel is the right choice. The right choice could have and should have a different meaning and context for everyone around us, but what matters is the willingness to make the right choice in the face of pressure to stay where we are. Now, this pressure could come from corners we had least expected; it could be coming from our dear and loving parents who are too jealous and insecure, thinking that their child's success and willingness to change might end up demeaning their power of that particular child, as once the child takes the path of growth, responsibility and greater awareness, they could no longer treat that child as the pawn they so desperately wanted them to be.

It could also come from your friends who loved you so dearly and had such incredible and unforgettable memories throughout your lives. Still, your decision to grow makes them uncomfortable, as that would mean they have been left alone in the sun. At the same time, you are busy learning and eventually building the roof that would cover all of them. But for that friend of yours, it would also mean staying under a roof constructed by you and visiting with people who would appreciate your courage to build that roof while at the same demeaning your friend for never having the courage to do something that incredible or maybe not unbelievable, but for simply lacking the willpower to do something worthwhile and noticeable.

It could also come from your partner/wife, who is too afraid and scared of who you might become. They fear you becoming unrecognisable once you start taking up these tasks. You would no longer be one among the many; instead, by taking this new path, you could become one among the few, or if you are willing to lose it all, you could become the one, but to become the "One" is a much more challenging task then being the "One among the Few" and is an almost impossible task for the "One among them all".

Your partner would be scared that you would no longer be willing to spend as much time and energy with them, as now you have taken the greater responsibility of setting yourself in order and making yourself the Man many would have never imagined. They are scared that now you would become simply too desirable for their liking, and that would make them uncomfortable.

It could come from your colleagues who are scared that the same individual who used to go out for smoke breaks or have a snack after office hours has started going to the gym. Once you take up these activities, you aren't doing anything to offend them; instead, your willingness to do something for yourself, take control of your life and take on responsibility is simply making them uncomfortable, as the more you start doing those things, the more they would feel lesser about themselves. Very few of them would ask you how you did it and would strive to move up with you. Still, most of them would decide to stay where they are, as it makes them comfortable and allows them to abstain from responsibility and, simultaneously, join the group they once were a part of, The "Dream Killers".

Let me share an example to explain the situation and how we could handle it.

Let's call my friend Cris and his father, Bane.

     Your Actions Define Your Existence

So, Bane was the father to two of his children, Cris and his elder sister, Jennifer. As a man, Bane was one of the most cruel, gruesome and monstrous individuals I had ever encountered. Bane used to beat his wife almost every day for nearly 30 years. Sometimes, it could have been a slap, or sometimes, it was an all-out total physical assault for more than 1 hour. There would be moments when Cris's mother would faint after getting beaten, and his father would turn towards him and his elder sister. And when his mother would slightly recover, he would sprinkle some water on her, and when she woke up, he would once again start beating her. He would beat her with iron rods and curtain roads and even went to the extent of beating her with a used hot iron. Cris's mother would often come and tell my mother how Bane would usually sleep around with his employees as he had a business of hospitals.

One day when I was acting of sleeping, as during those days my mother would forcefully make me sleep, Cris's mother came to my mother and told her how their household worker had fled, as the night before Bane had raped her. She then goes on to say to me how Bane even raped her elder sister's daughter. Hearing all of these horrific stories traumatised me and made me so angry and it made me feel so sorry for Cris, as I could never imagine the pain and agony his family had been going through.

But then, one fine day, Cris lost his cool and charged towards his father as he was about to beat his mother. In such an instance, Bane left the house soon after. He started staying in an apartment he had built for himself, a place where he illegitimately slept around with all of his employees, especially a woman named Tara, who had been working in the hospital since ages and is still working there.

Once his evil father left, Cris and his entire family were left to fend for themselves. And then disaster struck. When Cris was studying in college, his family got the news that Cris's father had married somebody else and even given birth to two daughters. By this time, his father's age was around 55, which shows how much of a sex addict he is. This broke Cris's mother completely, but Cris didn't lose hope. Cris also knew that his father had married somebody else without divorcing his mother, so they would win the case if he had decided to go legal. But Cris decided that at this age, going through all the legal procedures without any finances to back them up would mean they may win the case but lose everything they had. Cris decided he had to wait and work on himself, and when the time came right, he would decide what to do.

Seven years later, Cris got a call from his father, who apologised and asked Cris to join the family business. He also confessed that what he had done to him and his mother was inhuman, and all he wanted to do was make things right. Cris asked his mother, who told him to trust his instinct and work with his father, and also because Cris's mother by now had become seriously ill. She needed him by his side, so joining the family business was the only option; otherwise, he got good job offers outside India. Still, he supported his parents by ignoring those fantastic offers and putting the past behind him.

In the beginning, once Cris joined, he realised his father had changed, or thought so, as he was now so understanding of his needs that it would never stop him from doing anything, as he was taking the hospitals in the right direction. Also, their family business has gone through many downs recently due to endless controversies, so Cris took it upon himself to steady the ship. And so, things were going well until disaster struck.

     Your Actions Define Your Existence

Cris's father slowly and steadily started becoming his old self; he would overtake Cris's authority and repeatedly humiliate him in front of his employees. One fine day, he called Cris to his office and scolded him in front of all the employees. Soon, even the employees started undermining him, and due to that, he grew very frustrated but never lost hope. His father even went to the extent of retaking control and took away any financial control he had. Due to this, all of his planning came to a permanent halt, and it directly caused the hospitals to suffer, but his father didn't care, as all he cared about was to win and dominate his son to submission. In an extreme and unexpected situation, His father went to the extent of telling him that he could not use any of his cars and also told him in case he ever made his mother sit in any of the vehicles that he had given him, use, he would take away those cars as well.

These things affected Cris, but as usual, he usually took these attacks with a pinch of salt and continued to work.

By this time, Cris had developed a love for writing as he realised his family's story and the countless things he had faced were worthy of being documented. So, Cris started writing columns in various newspapers. During this time, he had also been approached by a publisher to write a book, to which Cris agreed and soon published his book. Soon, he started getting invited to various regional and national podcasts and got multiple awards due to his writings. Meanwhile, he also started his retail clothing brand with his best friend, which pushed him to the next level. Any other individual in their place would be submitted and bogged down to his father's assault. Cris used up all of this negative energy as fuel and propelled himself to the next level.

He was getting praised while doing all these things to propel himself to the next level. People even told him how soon he would trump his father if he continued to work himself to greater heights in a disciplined and immaculate way. But while people from every corner noted his strides and appreciated them, someone was burning from inside and wanted to rattle him. It was none other than his father.

One fine day, when we both were chilling at a café discussing our life ahead, discussing who my current favourite supermodel is, and debating about the political events around the world, Cris received a call from his father. And let me tell you, that phone call changed the entire mood in the café. Cris's father started yelling at him, telling him how he has been incompetent at work, how he has used up all the work time to concentrate on his writing and about how he funded his new clothing business by siphoning the hospital money and for the first time in my life I saw Cris lose his cool and yell at his father as well as he had enough. His father even told him that Cris had been funding all his foreign trips and the trips he had taken his mother to were all used up by stealing money from the hospitals. He even stated that it was a show whenever Cris took his mother for any medical checkup, as all Cris and his mother did was splash his money after stealing it. Trust me, I was an indirect witness to most things happening, as my cousin also works in the same hospital through my friend's graciousness.

All of these things stated by his father and all of these inconsistent behaviours demonstrated by his father proved my analogy that his father was an absolute narcissistic animal who wanted to put Cris off his radar as he was jealous of the things he had started to accomplish even after his repeated attacks and his plans to sabotage his own son's future. And soon after the phone call, he broke into tears and fell into my arms. I hugged him tightly, and all he did was cry as if he was howling like a wolf.

    Your Actions Define Your Existence

And I told him, "Cris, you deserve better", and he took my advice, and within the next 2 months, he published his second book, which became a bestseller. In the next month, his company reached the 6-figure sales mark, meaning he was an established entrepreneur and well-renowned author.

These accomplishments completely changed the game, and so within 3 months after the verbal diarrhoea he had heard from his father, he quit his family business and became way more accomplished than he could have ever imagined.

Today 5, years later, he is looking after his mother, who is now fitter than ever. He has a beautiful family with his wife and his daughter and son, and he has no contact at all with his father, due to which he has completely healed from the trauma his father had imposed upon his family. For his father, well, he has now lost the plot as he has sold his primary hospital (The one Cris was looking after) and even for the other ones, they have garnered a terrible reputation, as there is no clear direction in the future, as none of them has any capable individual to handle them, as he is too old now to handle them. His second wife barely looks after him, and his two daughters are way more spoiled than anybody could have imagined.

The things that we could learn from this story are fundamental and straightforward.

Cris used all the negative energy his father had spewed on him and turned it into positive fuel to make him a better and stronger individual. He never gave his father a response to any of the insults that were thrown towards him, as he was well aware of the fact that those insults weren't meant to tell him about his shortcomings. Instead, those insults were meant to hide his own insecurity for the very fact that his son had started to overshadow him. Any secure man would have loved to see their children prosper. Still, for a insecure and selfish men like Cris's father, none mattered, as somebody else prospering meant divided recognition, which an evil man like his father could have never tolerated. In the face of crisis, Cris never said no to responsibility, as that is what made him different from his father, and that's why he continued to turn up for work no matter what, as that's what a man with discipline does.

Cris should also be considered a highly calm and strategic individual, as he left his business only when he reached the stage where his company had taken off. His writing had started getting incredible recognition. He didn't make any impulsive decisions by keeping his ego at the forefront and quit the day he had his verbal fight or the many months his father humiliated him. Instead, he bided time and left once he knew he had established himself and could live on his terms. He had reached that stage, financially and mentally, where he knew he had become capable enough to live his life in a way where his father's toxicity was something that could be avoided.

We could also learn that even when Cris was going through everything he was going through, rather than whining and complaining about how miserable his life was, he continued to work on himself. His writing, business ventures, and even taking up MMA classes to channel his energies are some strategies he used to level up each day. While his father thought his son was good for nothing, he was making himself capable of doing almost anything, and that's what we all should aspire to do.

Revolting without considering all consequences and its after facts is an impulsive decision, but revolting once we have become more potent than the revolter is what every individual should do, as that puts victory well within our sight. Victory has a different meaning in every situation, and in this situation, leaving his

   Your Actions Define Your Existence

family business and finding his path was a more significant victory than fighting his father to defeat him, as once he left his father, his defeat became inevitable, as his son was his best soldier, and rather than trusting him, he kept on fighting his men, all to satisfy his frail and fragile ego.

Bane and how he handles Cris are all important life lessons. Had Bane left Cris to his elements, today, Bane's legacy would have been far more significant than he could have ever imagined. All the incredible things he is doing today through his writing and other ventures could have been with his hospitals, but instead, he kept attacking his son to win a war that never had any winner but had a loser, and it was him, Bane, Himself. He knew his son's importance but stopped him at every turn, fearing that he would overshadow him.

Had he accepted that his time was up and all he needed to do was guide his son to take his legacy forward, today, Bane would have been a legend in his field. He would have seen his son take his hard work to the next level and make him proud. Instead, he wanted to dominate his son, and even at such a later age, he tried to pull his son down, not knowing that every time he pulled his son down, he was indirectly pulling his own hard-earned business down. Still, such wisdom is beyond any ego-centric, narcissistic and insecure man. It eventually led to his downfall and the inevitable rise of his son, which he vehemently opposed, but that's the order of life.

Accepting our current situation and accepting reality takes courage. That is something Cris had, and that's why he tolerated his father while the attacks continued. He knew he wasn't strong enough financially to be well off without his father. And in regards to his father, had he accepted that he couldn't ride the ship at such an old age and let his son take guard with his guidance, we would have seen a different ending. But that's what life is about, as unpredictability is the true nature of our lives, and all we can do is either cower down to it or make ourselves stronger and prepare ourselves for it.

Remember, Complaints are what the weak do, whining is what the cowards do, sabotage is what the insecure do, guidance is what the leaders do, dominate is what dictators do, and acceptance of reality and pursuing their goals irrespective of what the odds are is what the courageous do.

We are all at fault for being either of them at some point in our lives (except the courageous part) for that's what makes us human, but it's about what we choose to be for most of our lives, as that's what defines us.

So make your choice, for your choices define your lives and your reality.

And that reality is the one you should be willing to fight for, for once you get it done, you will be able to cherish life with all its trials, victories and tribulations with far more content and peace in your mind.

 Your Actions Define Your Existence

Saying No to others and saying Yes to Yourself

> *"When you say yes to others,*
> *ensure you are not saying no to yourselves."*
>
> **Paulo Coelho**

This statement from Paulo Coelho pretty much sums up what I have been saying. Saying yes to yourself means having the courage to take responsibility for our actions and say yes to our needs and benevolent desires.

In our childhood, we were unaware of what our friends might have been doing until and unless we called them up to have a pleasant conversation or were informed about their current whereabouts through a particular neighbour, friend or colleague. But in today's day and age, it feels like we live in a non-stop documentary of ourselves. Through this documentary, we can convince everyone worldwide that we are having the best time. We are always smiling; we are always partying in the biggest of clubs; we are always holidaying in the best of destinations; we are always chilling with the most scantily clad women; we are constantly driving the most incredible cars; we are always chilling with our best of friends, so, in a nutshell, we are portraying ourself as living a life that any individual would envy, due to which we are getting more and more sad about the current state of their lives.

Most of us aspire to be wealthy, not necessarily billionaires. Most of us want a happy and abundant life where we are content with ourselves and our loved ones around us. And through the constant barrage of crap that we constantly see on the various social media platforms, we are made to believe that such a life is possible if we splurge and do whatever those influencers are doing.

But we must understand that everyone is meant to have a different life journey. They must prioritise their health and mental and physical well-being to realise the path and journey. That is only possible if we start saying "yes" to our own needs and say "no" to the needs of others. Now when we talk about saying Yes to ourselves, I am not necessarily talking about saying No to almost

   Your Actions Define Your Existence

every single request of assistance thrown towards us, but I am simply stating that how we could all benefit if we merely muster up the courage to prioritise our goals and tasks, rather than doing things for the benefit and likeliness of others, all in the hope that everybody would like us, but let me give you a piece of advice- no matter what you do, no matter what you sacrifice, no matter how much you make time for your dear ones, there will always be somebody who would be disappointed with you, there would always be someone who regards you as permanently unavailable, there would always be someone who regards you as arrogant, there would always be someone who regards you as unhelpful, there would always be someone who regards you as weak, there would always be someone who regards you as caring and accommodating, and there would always be someone who regards you as super busy and unavailable all the time.

So, what do you do in such an instance?

Well, the easier choice is to continue to live life on other people's terms and do things you don't feel like doing, or you can take control over your own decisions and start living life on your terms without causing any harm to anybody. You can help people you want to help, skip plans when you want to sleep in and prioritise things you love and feel are essential.

Let me explain this with a true story of one of my closest relatives.

Let's call her Gisele.

So, Gisele is the woman my family and I have known for almost 20 years; her son and I are the best of friends, and she has been one of my biggest supporters ever since I have known her. She always appreciates me when I have done something right, never forgets to scold me whenever she feels I messed it up at that time, and always explains how doing that specific thing will only cause me more harm than good. And so, based on the particular guidance I received from her and my parents, life has been a much better experience, and had I not heeded their advice, it could have been a lot worse. But somewhere down the line, I noticed that Gisele is never pleased about her own life and is often anxious and borderline depressed in many ways. The reason is her inability to say "No" to anybody.

Gisele's entire family takes advantage of her due to her inability to say "No". Her family often ignores her advice whenever she gives them any for their well-being. But once they have messed up their lives due to that particular situation, they would come back running to her. Whenever any of her family members needed any help financially, they would come up to Gisele; whenever any of her family members had a serious family situation, they would come to Gisele; even her neighbours would come up to her whenever they needed any financial help. If someone is sick, they would come running to Gisele for assistance. So, in many ways, she is everybody's saviour; that's what it looks like from the outside.

But the sad part is that nobody can be found whenever she needs any of those things. She is left to fend for it all by herself. Her husband bruised and battered her for more than 15 years, and none of her family members showed up. Her husband did all sorts of evil things to her, and yet nobody showed up. Her family members duped her of money, and when she went to ask them back for the money, they would throw insults at her. But the moment they needed help, they would again turn towards her, and guess what? She happily obliged and helped them even more, as she always stated that it was God's job to judge and decide what should be done to them, not hers. I couldn't comprehend it, but I felt sorry for her that such an innocent and benevolent creature was still living in such a dark age of humanity, and trust me, she was not alone. There are millions of people all over the world who are willing to cut themselves to pieces to fix somebody else. Still, the moment it's their turn, they have nobody they can turn to and live a life of despair and hope and barely hope arrives for such people, as such people are often taken advantage of by the vultures that rule the world. The cruel and selfish group of individuals take advantage of them, willing to sacrifice anybody for their victory.

So, the larger question is how an individual escapes such a situation.

Well, to start, say No.

This could be easier said than done, but you must start somewhere. The best way to do that is by saying "**No**" to those you feel don't matter in a few months, as they are the individuals who least expected you to turn up at their birthday or their prescribed party. When you say "No" to them, it signifies that you have better things to do (could be completing your sleep or any other random task). It simply sets out the message and impression that you aren't always available.

Once you have overcome the first obstacle, you go towards your office colleagues with whom you have been chilling for a large part of your time in that particular workplace. You often go out together for cigarette breaks; you guys usually have chaat or bhelpuri (Indian street snack) once the office is over, or maybe even have a few drinks in a nearby bar once your office is over. But since you have recently decided to go the gym, lose some weight, and get fitter, you say no to them, and at first, they push you to come with them. Still, in those 2-3 seconds, you made the decision that could enable you to take the next step or fall back into the trap. Both of these decisions are difficult and rewarding in their ways, so you must choose the reward. The reward you get by hanging out with them is having good food, a nice laugh, and a good time. Although once these moments are over, you are going to feel miserable about your action and how you once again messed up and feel back into the trap, while if you decide to say "**Yes**" to yourself and choose to hit the gym and can convey those things to your colleagues with conviction, and are able to back your words with action trust me, you will feel like the king of the world, and once you finish your workout, you are going to feel like a new individual. An individual who has finally broken the shackles and is now willing to take responsibility and has the courage to make yourself better and a much more robust version of yourself is where growth happens.

Once your colleagues have been conquered, you go towards your closest friends. Things get a bit tougher here, as these friends comprise individuals you call your closest circle. These individuals have stayed with you through thick and thin and been there for you when nobody else was there. These individuals have helped you and, in some cases, have done incredible things for you that you can never repay, as it was such an astonishing gesture. And so, in between all of these, what do you do? Well, you find a middle ground.

Remember that a few months back, you used to say yes to even an outsider you had just met, but today, you are no longer an individual who cares much about their opinions. Similarly, you could also distance yourself from your office colleagues, and now you are facing up to your friends.

Saying "No" is like climbing a hilltop. Initially, the hill looks relatively easy, as the first few terrains aren't that difficult. Still, once you continue to climb, you realise that the hilltop is a rugged terrain, and the higher you climb, the more challenging it gets.

Similarly, your friends and colleagues fall into the easy terrain mark. The difficulty starts once you reach the moderate/difficult terrain mark, as this is where your closest friends live. For these friends of yours, you must tread very carefully, and you should be aware that if you take one wrong step, you could fall steeply. Similarly, when dealing with these friends of yours, you have to know which plans you could skip and which ones you can't. And trust me, once you start staying away from those plans you realised could be skipped, your friends will get annoyed. Then they would get even more irritated the next time, but once they see you do incredibly well and surpass their expectations about you, they will start admiring and respecting you. Once they start doing that, they will no longer force you to be a part of their plans, they will understand what's essential for you and what's not, and in time even the group among your close friends will get smaller. In the process, you will be able to find out who your real friends are. And these individuals would one day ask you how you did it and would get inspired by you.

This has become possible only because of one action: **"Your ability to say yes to yourself and no to others."**

After conquering this terrain, you will come to the precipice of reaching the top, the most challenging terrain of the mountain—your parents and your partners (wife/husband, girlfriend/boyfriend).

Indeed, your parents would matter to you much more if you are unmarried or single, (although that might not be true in every situation for many individuals continue to share the same relationship with their parents even after they get married, but those instances are very rare) so how do you deal with these people, knowing that this is undoubtedly the core group of your life? As your parents knew you way before anybody else, the most significant challenge regarding them is that you will always be a naïve and immature child in their eyes. You may have climbed Mt Everest or won the world championships, but in their eyes, you are still a kid who never says no to the elders. This is where you need to pull the plug and start having boundaries between each other; you have to make them understand that you can't adhere to all their demands and, at certain times, you need solitude. Your parents can't take you for granted, and the only way you can do this, is by having honest conversations about how you can't be accessible to them all the time; you need to tell them that you love, respect and adore them as your parents but that doesn't mean that they can take you for a ride all the time. Now, I am not expecting a 14-year-old to say these things to their parents; but unfortunately, I have seen 30-year-olds having difficulty setting realistic expectations for their parents. The only reason for that is that they could never say no for fear of disrespecting their parents, but in the process, they are disrespecting themselves, and that's one hell of a miserable life to live.

The same attitude is what they have towards their partners.

Remember that just because you love, respect and adore someone doesn't mean they can take you for a ride; that could be anybody. Your wife or boyfriend should know that there are certain things they can't say or make you do about it, and the only way that could happen is if you start speaking up. Now, I am not necessarily asking you for a whole-out confrontation or a fistfight, as that would be utterly contrary to the results you would want.

Still, an argument and disappointment are quite the opposite reaction, especially when somebody they have never heard of speaking for themselves suddenly starts speaking up, and that is where they will try to pull you down. It is your utmost responsibility to stay true to what you regard as the right course

   Your Actions Define Your Existence

of action for yourself and move ahead, as that's the only way to avoid a life filled with misery and regret. Along the way, you will miss out on many things and lose out on many people, but by learning to say "**No**," you will gain new friends. New people who love you for who you are, and that's a life worth living, as these people can make even your worst days light up, and you can access such people only when you start realising your true priorities in life.

So, wake up tomorrow morning and start "Yes" to yourself and "No" to others, as that is where you will grow and become the person you were meant to be.

Unwillingness to do what is right for ourselves

Instant gratification, people pleasing, pursuing a perfect world, not being honest about our intentions, staying with people who suck the energy out of us. These are some of the reasons why most of us aren't able to do what is suitable for ourselves.

Our minds are in a constant state of war, wherein we are constantly imagining and contemplating wild, pathetic, and fanatical scenarios regarding how, if we do what is right or what we feel is correct, we might get judged or called out. We are scared to be someone willing to be an anomaly or an outcast, all in the pursuit of striving and reaching for excellence. Most of the time, we aren't able to take the extra step because of our fear of judgement. A judgment that prevents us from taking the steps that would enable us to leave the dungeons of loneliness embraced through the distaste of civilised society. There is a vast difference between an individual who takes the path of loneliness to embrace greatness and one who embraces loneliness through sheer hate and rejection.

The one who has embraced greatness is willing to be called an outcast to achieve his world-conquering goals. These individuals are driven by the sheer will to be the best in their fields. These individuals regard talent as a by-product of someone willing to put in the hard hours behind the scenes. These individuals are monsters in the proper sense, as victory tastes and smells like oxygen for them. They strive only to be the best, win everything, and defeat everybody in the way possible. None of them are enemies of society. Instead, these true champions decorate the world with their impeccable work ethic and sheer drive to prove everyone wrong, conquer the top, and stay at the top for as long as possible. Their presence is enough to deter opponents and shift them to plan B. Individuals such as Cristiano Ronaldo, Conor Mcgregor, Donald Trump, Virat Kohli, Michael Jordan, Novak

Djokovic and many more such individuals are present in our world who want to be the best from morning to night; they want to defeat everyone; as for them the 2nd place is a loss, and yet they are celebrated all over the world.

Why? Because they inspired Billions around the world, made them do what is suitable for themselves, and never fear judgement, as they are aware of the human mind and its potential. Through their sheer will, they stay on top and continue to live on their terms, making their lives way more worthwhile than they ever could be. And that's the reason they are champions, and that's the reason they are great.

The other half of individuals who embraced loneliness due to their distaste for human society and unwillingness to embrace humanity are a hazardous species. As these individuals have given up hope in themselves, they believe the world is a dark and tragic place for them. They don't want to accept people the way they are, and soon, they are blamed as outcasts and individuals who can't conform to the general human consensus. These individuals always succeed in satisfying human civilisations as some of the most notorious murderers, shooters, rapists, and criminals are all formed through this group.

This group of individuals have taken rejection in an entirely malevolent way. While the former group used that rejection and drive to make themselves stand out, this group did not care about the crowd. Had it been upon them, no crowd would have ever existed, as for them, everybody is an enemy, and the traumas of their evil childhood have pushed them down the dangerous and cruel path. And, unfortunately, there is no saving. They don't want to prove anything; life is a non-existent crisis, and they doubt their existence. They are some of the most resentful, pathetic and sorrowful human beings who could never celebrate

 Your Actions Define Your Existence

the beauty of human life. As for them, such riches are beyond their understanding. The pain and suffering they faced are simply tools they are now looking to pass on to whoever they can and by any means. They would inflict it upon themselves if they didn't do that due to the lack of courage to do Evil.

The former group came from the dungeons and made themselves worthy to live among the clouds while inspiring others to do that. Still, the latter group only seeks to send more and more individuals to the dungeons as that is what they have embraced, and that's what they want others to embrace as well, for who doesn't like the company of fellow human beings, especially when it makes you feel better, no matter how miserable your existence might be, you want more and more individuals to feel your pain, and that's how they make sure nobody is doing what is righteous and rather doing what they despise.

Let me share a real-life example to explain the story to you better.

Let's call him Ronnie.

So, Ronnie and I go back a long way; he is an individual who has known my family even before I was born, as he is 15 years older than me. He used to visit my mother even before my sister was born. Back then, our family barely survived as both my Mom and Dad came from a low-income family background, so it took a lot of time before our family could reach this far. And so, Ronnie knows our entire family story and has seen my Mom and Dad's rags-to-riches story with his bare eyes. But I always had one question in my mind: why the hell did Ronnie chill with us during our entire childhood? He used to play cricket with us and act just like us; he would do relatively immature and ordinary things for a boy older than us. And then I heard his story from my mother.

So, from his young days, Ronnie was very reserved and shy. He didn't have any mental condition, but some say he owned the darkness even before anybody was aware of it. Until we grew up, he often sat and chilled inside the house. He wouldn't talk much with anybody and would usually sacrifice what he wanted to do with his life to please people. If he got any pocket money from his parents, he would instantly plan to save it for himself and buy something he had dreamt of for ages. Still, if anybody knows that Ronnie possesses some reasonable finances, those friends or people of his would be quick to exploit his people-pleasing nature. They would make sure that those plans and wishes of his remain unfulfilled as they want their plans to come to fruition. In this way, Ronnie kept getting exploited and harassed by individuals all year round, and soon, when he tried to do something that would make him happy, he realised he had nothing to show for. And then, when he approached those who have always enjoyed at his expense, they would shun him away. They often told Ronnie they expected him to be much more mature and thoughtful when spending his money. Still, when Ronnie would explain that it was them that he finished all his money on, they would tell him that he should have been more competent and that it is his responsibility to stand up for himself and do what is right for himself.

But guess what? The next time those same individuals turned up towards Ronnie needing help, he would happily oblige, and when he went towards them, they would shun him away. This circle continued his entire life, up until the point that even during our childhood, we used to see Ronnie getting exploited day and night. And then disaster struck.

Ronnie's mother passed away, and ever since then, he has never been the same.

His mother, a high-ranking official in a renowned government sector office, was his source of strength, joy, and unlimited finances. She never questioned her son's life choices or spending habits, no matter how much of a failure or incompetent he was. For her, he was simply the most immense joy of her life, something most mothers could relate to. And so, once she died, he had no answers for all the questions that life had thrown upon him.

At 33, he was unemployed and had no savings to his name. His little sister had just been married, and her husband had occupied their house. Based on what I see every day, his brother-in-law runs the household.

Ronnie's friends had abandoned him, and the money they used him for disappeared. Ronnie was broke, and his brother-in-law was the new king of the house. Ronnie, being the kind of guy he is, is incapable of putting up a fight. Neither did he have anybody he loved, as having a partner during such tough and troubled times often makes our suffering lesser. But Ronnie had none of it, so he became increasingly resentful as time passed. He started being ignored by everybody, and he soon became known as Mr. Useless in our entire community, as the very same guy who used to help everyone once and spend money as if it was always in abundant supply suddenly found himself with nothing to fall back on.

Things became so bleak that his sister and her husband somehow conspired to ensure that her mother's entire pension money, divided among her son and daughter, would now be received entirely by her daughter. Thus, he had to turn to his sister whenever Ronnie needed money, even for personal use.

Due to such a bleak and helpless scenario, Ronnie became increasingly resentful and saw nothing to look forward to.

In between, Ronnie would often think about himself and plan to get married, as he is a human and a man, and we all need someone to talk to and share about ourselves, and we look forward to having an able and supportive partner. This situation applies to even the most broken and strong personalities, for we humans are incredibly social creatures, and a capable and responsible individual can often pick us from the darkest of holes, take us to safety and give us hope for a better future.

So, when my mother was made aware of his willingness to get married, she and several other women in our neighbourhood decided to take this upon themselves and approach the woman Ronnie had fallen in love with. This is the way arranged marriages take place in India. When individuals of the opposite sex are attracted to a particular individual and are interested in marrying them, the family members of the interested party reach out to them and approach them for marriage. And since Ronnie had never fallen in love or gotten involved in any romantic relationship, he approached my mother for help.

After some discussions, the women's family members agree to marry Ronnie with their daughter, and so do Ronnie and the girl. But every time it is concluded that everything is done now and Ronnie will soon be married, his sister plays the trick.

His sister meets the girl on the false pretext of knowing her and than she ends up destroying the marriage. She then comes home and tells everyone how she was insulted by the girl's family members. Had this happened once, it could have been believed, but this same thing keeps happening repeatedly, and if my counts are correct, it has happened almost 6-7 times. Recently, when the same situation happened again, it became so bad that my mother asked me to intervene, and it was there at that moment, that his sister blurred out the truth. She said, "**Ronnie is useless**

 Your Actions Define Your Existence

and has no right to the property, and once he has a wife, she will demand 50%, and 50% is enough for me, but that's not enough for my son." As soon as I heard these word's I couldn't believe what I had just heard. So, a sister is willing to make sure her brother gets screwed over, and his life is wasted all because she wants the entire property to her name and her son's. Once she said these things, I looked at Ronnie, and that measly coward of a creature said, **"I stand with my sister; we have to think about her son. I am hopeful he will look after me when I am old, I am willing to give up everything for him"**. As soon as he yelled out that word, I felt like taking off my shoes and hitting him as hard as possible. To the readers, pardon me for my language, but this has gone beyond being good. This has entered the territory of foolishness to the extent that we are willing to let go of something that we dearly love and are not willing to fight for. That's not what you would expect a man to do.

Ronnie has given up every bit of a right to be called a man, as he couldn't stand up for his rights, muster the courage for his about-to-be wife, and not take responsibility for his decisions and actions. Due to that, he will live a life of regret, desperation, and what could have been scenarios playing around in his head. Every time I meet him, I feel like I am meeting an individual who is already dead on the inside but is simply waiting for his outside to give up, and once that happens, he will no longer be able to go back and correct the wrongs he has done to himself.

Now, this story is one of the most incredible real-life stories I have ever witnessed, and we can learn a tremendous amount if we carefully read it and imagine ourselves in the same situations.

One of the most crucial lessons from this incredible story is how fast life slips away and how we could destroy our own lives if we abstain from the courage to take responsibility for ourselves.

We are in many ways only in control of what we can do; the outcome, whether it's positive or negative, is never in our control, and when we abstain from doing what we can do, we are in many ways labelling ourselves as incompetent and cowardly and simply lacking the responsibility to do what is suitable for ourselves.

Imagine a scenario where Ronnie had stood up for himself and said I love the woman, and I will bring her home, and I will make sure she stands for what is right, and we will make sure that you(sister) get what you belong to you. At that moment, there might have been an argument or a quarrel. Still, in time, he would have felt proud that he stood up for himself and laid down how bringing someone would not signal a shift in the power structure but would rather mean shared power, and unfortunately, that's what most humans hate, as why share a pie when we can consume the whole. But sharing the pie means we can fight longer and safeguard our legacy. Although it will depend on what kind of a person you share that pie with, it's worth taking that risk. In unity, we became superior and invincible in our short mortal lifespan.

We could also learn from his sister's behaviour how having a selfish attitude can often close our eyes to our proper responsibility. His sister knew that Ronnie was incapable of standing up for himself, and at that time, she should have stood up for him and given him what he wanted; instead, she chose what an individual with evil intentions would do. Due to her selfish nature, her brother will pay the price for his life. A life he has no interest to enjoy any further, as pain is all it has given him until now.

It is through responsibility and courage that we get to do what we want to do. We should strive to get our hands dirty at the present moment to ensure that they remain clean in the future. Unfortunately, Ronnie never had it in himself to fight for such

   Your Actions Define Your Existence

an ideal and make himself a better man. Instead, all he did was bottle up and keep himself where he was through his inability to fight for himself.

This story provides us with a blueprint for how we get massacred when we cannot stand up for ourselves for things we believe in. And getting massacred physically and dying is much easier than being massacred mentally and being made to live our lives without a proper purpose and a soul that's crying to die. **Any individual who goes through such a scenario has nowhere to hide but everywhere to die**. Unfortunately, such individuals even lack the essential courage to die, and for that purpose, their lives get withered away as if waves are sweeping away the sand.

It's upon us to decide how we choose to do our things and live our lives, as it is our moral responsibility to trust our instincts and do what is truly right. In that process of doing what we feel is correct, we may make mistakes, but in that process of trying and failing, we will grow. For growth rarely happens with failure. Courage and responsibility are the most expensive things once we have grown. Things that can't be bought but developed with a leap of faith. And that leap of faith is enough to make us the best version of ourselves. And that's a life worth living, for once we learn to own up to our successess and failures, we are able to take full responsibility for ourselves.

Negate People's point of view

> *"Be strong enough to ignore people's negative opinions so that your positive spirit can illuminate your true unique colour."*
>
> **Edmond Mbiaka**

If I do this, I am scared of what people might think. They will laugh at me, think I am crazy, believe my dreams are too lofty, and think I am too ambitious!

These things often come to our minds when we plan on doing something we dearly believe in and cannot do because of **fear of judgment.** This fear paralyses us and makes us timid and too cowardly to push through something we know we are capable of. It makes us question even the best of things that we have dreamt about ourselves. As a result, we remain stuck, unable to take the next step that could move us closer to becoming the person we deeply desire and aspire to be.

Let me explain this better by sharing an example of someone I have known for quite some time. Someone who stayed where she was because of people's opinions, and her fear of judgement allowed her to stayed where she is today. The story will also explain, how these decisions are killing her, could kill us, and how she has become far more resentful than anybody could have imagined, and how any of us could go down that path if we make decision similar to hers.

Let's call her Shalom.

Shalom is a bright 29-year-old who grew up with great care and love. She was lucky to have a father who always said yes to all her demands and never said no to anything she demanded or wanted to do. He would also give her things he could have never afforded, yet he gave them to her because she meant the world to him. For that reason, he never kept her away from any treasures.

But unfortunately Shalom turned out to be a big-time people pleaser and an individual who always wanted to stay in the good books of all her family members and individuals she knew, due to which she could never really make herself useful in anything she did. Every time she planned or did something, she announced that grand plan in an incredibly public way. She often started talking about her plans during family gatherings as she wanted people to admire her for having such bold and big dreams. There would be times when, in between public gatherings, I would often bring her to my side and tell her how happy I am to see that she has become capable enough to dream so big even after coming from such humble beginnings. Still, for them to become a reality, she has to stop announcing them randomly everywhere, as many people would often prevent her from pursuing them, for that's what we humans do. We are the masters of projecting our fears and insecurities onto someone else, for who wants to be alone in hell and be alone while being miserable and resentful?

So, even after my advice, she never really listened to me and kept on saying everything she dreamt of or thought about, as she felt she needed their admiration to prove to others that what she was doing was insane and incredible and all those sorts of things that would give her a fantastic amount of validation.

Luckily, she even started a few projects, but most of the things she had ever planned never came to fruition and never really took off. And trust me, some of the ideas were fantastic. Had some of those ideas come to fruition, she would have reached the next level, but they have yet to come to reality. In a particular instance, one of her idea was absolutely terrific, but she couldn't do anything about it and had to shelve the plan, all because a friend of hers had stated that it was not a rational plan.

Fast forward to today, that friend of hers who asked her not to pursue that plan has now implemented it herself, and she has been doing incredibly well and had recently quit her job as she realised the true potential of that new project of hers.

And while this happened, all Shalom could do was see her friend succeed at something she could have succeeded. She is seeing her

   Your Actions Define Your Existence

friend enjoy the accolades that she could have been enjoying. She is seeing her friend earn incredible money through something she could have done and earned, but it didn't happen.

Why? Because she was foolish enough to accept somebody else's viewpoint, make it her reality, and implement it in her life without having second thoughts.

There have been moments when her family members told her to stop dreaming, and that she should not start these businesses, as they were not worthwhile or necessary, and somehow, they managed to persuade her to give up those dreams of hers. And guess what? Today, she is marrying a guy who is one of the most orthodox individuals I have ever met. He has already restricted her life in such unfortunate ways that I can't stop thinking and say, **'What could have been?'**

It was understandable had Shalom's family had been very restrictive and constrained, but She had a father who always wanted her to aim for the stars, which she did throughout her life. Still, she could never take off, as she paid too much attention to what people spoke about her, and she paid too much attention to what they felt was right or wrong. Due to her habit of paying too much attention to people's voices, opinions, and viewpoints, she is about to marry a guy neither she loves nor finds attractive. Still, she is simply doing it because her aunt and her mother persuaded her to do so.

Even though her father is against her marriage, Shalom tells him she would be happy in it, even though she knows it is impossible.

With her marriage looming over her head, she stays home and feeds her cats and dog. She has recently learned to cook and tells me she doesn't want to disappoint her husband. I am like, "What the hell is wrong with you?"

There have been moments when I have been extremely angry with her and have told her about it, but she tells me that we are young and too naïve to do things on our own, so we should always follow what our elders and our friends tell us. I told her maybe that's why her friend is now earning riches with her ideas while she is feeding cats. I stormed out of the room, and she kept crying, saying I offended her.

Shalom's story can teach us incredible things, and these things eventually allow us to avoid making the mistakes that she did.

We all live in a society where we should behave in a civilized manner, but that is no reason to trust people for anything they say. It comes down to us and our willingness to trust our instincts and beliefs and tell ourselves, "Maybe this time I am right, and they are wrong."

Here are some ways we could negate people's viewpoints and do things we fully believe in.

Negate distractions—We live in a society where distractions are everywhere. Everybody is partying in the best clubs and travelling in the best countries. But we rarely get to know what they are doing, and even more rarely do we know them. Instead, we judge them based on the lenses given to us by social media. We so dearly believe they are living the best of lives or enjoying their lives to the fullest. But very rarely do we know the backstory behind their current reality.

At that moment, we have to decide and ask ourselves the all-important question of trusting our accurate instincts, really believing in ourselves, and genuinely keeping these distractions away from the vision of our eyes and being focused on what we believe is true and what we think would work. And when we can do that, we can segregate between the things that could be

   Your Actions Define Your Existence

labelled as distractions and the things that could be labelled as requirements for us to pursue our goals. And when we can make that differentiation, we have a jump start, which is what most people don't get in their lives. Still, the fact that we have got it is what matters, and soon we are doing things and spending time working on things that we had only hoped for, and slowly, we become the person we could have only dreamt of, and that's a hell of a lot better than scrolling down other people's lives.

Believing in our abilities- Our abilities make us who we are and could be. If I can lift 100 kg on the squat rack, I am capable enough to lift such enormous and incredible amounts of weight. I could tell people how to make their bodies lift such enormous and incredible amounts of weight. And that serves or showcases my ability to make my body do great things and, at the same time, motivate others to do amazing things as well. On the other hand, If I am not able to lift even a 5kg weight, all because I am too scared of lifting weights and would rather sit on the sofa and cry about how unfair the world is, then that would serve as a mirror of my abilities and my beliefs in that process. So, everything we do and every action we take, intentionally or unintentionally, showcases what we are capable and incapable of doing, mirroring every individual's ability, for it is through our abilities that we can define our existence. Even our ability to not do anything and waste our life and take it for granted shows our ability to be ignorant and never take responsibility for ourselves. For that purpose, it becomes imperative that we make ourselves capable enough to do things that would make our existence worthwhile and put our beliefs in it, for it is our beliefs in our abilities that make us who we are.

Any individual who truly believes in his abilities can make his life the way he wants it to be. If he believes in the actions that he can undertake to make his life better, then he will be able to do so. He must understand that the path to achieving that will be filled with obstacles and potholes, and only if he embraces them will he achieve what his mind has pushed him to and set out to achieve.

Taking a leap of faith- In life, our faith primarily allows us to make sense of the realities that exist in the world. Our faith that we will live another day will enable us to plan for the day ahead for months and years. My faith that my mom will be alright when I go to work allows me to go to work and earn some bread and butter for my family. Our faith that we won't be struck by an accident when we take the car out for a drive to work or any other place allows us to drive the vehicle.

So, everything we do is bounded and formulated by the faith we consider to have in ourselves and our lives. And yet, we can't take that leap of faith and do what is suitable for ourselves.

We get scared that what I am trying to undertake will fail and we won't get the desired results. I would be mocked and harassed by everybody for failing. Similarly, most of us are often scared that we may go bankrupt and have nothing to fall back on if we decide to quit our jobs and start our businesses.

Well, the sad part about life is that everything that we plan on doing and everything we have done has every possibility that it could fail and put us on the streets, but do you have anything else to do? Well, the answer should be Yes! But it could also be No if you plan on giving up that plan as you realise taking risks means taking the responsibility to choose to be courageous and challenge the general norm, and that's the path most people don't want to go to, for it brings a lot of loneliness, misery, suffering and also being labelled as an outcast. Still, unfortunately, that's where your mental fortitude is challenged, and that's where you grow.

 Your Actions Define Your Existence

What is essential and crucial to understand is the fundamental fact that every device and everything that we are surrounded by today was once an idea that came into someone's mind and was termed impossible or impractical. But here we are today, and the individuals who were then termed delusional are today known as geniuses. Their very ideas, which were impractical or foolish, are known as engineering marvels.

To better explain what I am talking about, let me share an example from one of my favourite movies, **"Man of Steel", released as Superman**.

So, Henry Cavil is known as Clarke Kent in this movie. He plays the role of Superman and sits in a church contemplating what he should do next. As a fellow army general known as General Zod from his home plan, Krypton (now destroyed) comes to Earth and warns the people of Earth to hand over Clarke Kent to him. The general wants him because Clarke is the answer to their plan of reviving their planet, so he wants Clarke by any means. The people of our planet started feeling scared as they knew that Zod's technology was superior and that he could inflict incredible damage on Earth. Due to this, the people of Earth are afraid, and the government is ensuring everything possible to find Clarke and hand him over. At this time, Clarke needs clarification, as he needs to know whether handing him over to the government is the best idea or handing him over to General Zod is better, as he doesn't trust either one. Once he decides he can't find an answer, he gets up from the church, and just as he is about to leave, the father of the church asks him what is troubling him. He reveals his identity to the father and tells his problems. The father pauses, as he is both fearful and courageous enough to stand next to him, and then gives him a line that sums up the situation; he tells him.

"Sometimes you need to leap of faith; trust comes later."

At this moment, Clarke decides to surrender to the humans and later surrenders to General Zod.

This story tells us that Clarke knew Zod could end his life or he could be outcasted by the humans as well. Yet he takes the risk of exposing himself to both, and that is something we should all learn from.

Sometimes, we have no idea what to do next in life, as the situation is too overwhelming for us, and we are scared of how even a single misstep could prove catastrophic. We decide not to take any more steps, so we stay where we are. In these moments, we should take the step we believe in and have that faith in ourselves. If that step gives us positive results, we will be ecstatic; if it provides negative results, we will learn and grow. Either way, we have much to gain and miles to go, depending on what we choose to do when the stakes are high and the margin for error is low, for that's where we become the person of our dreams.

These are some ways we could ignore people's points of view and stride towards things we strongly believe in. It's not just imperative; instead, it becomes necessary that we push ourselves, believe in ourselves, and have that inclination and faint voice in our heads that assures us that "maybe they are wrong" and "maybe I am right." This faint voice genuinely allows us to become and strive towards the person we dearly wish to be.

You must understand that there will always be someone who disregards your plans as too far stretched, terms you as too ambitious, or calls you a fool for having such incredible ideas that their little and useless brains simply cannot comprehend.

 Your Actions Define Your Existence

And if you make that differentiation and believe in yourself, trust me, there is nothing and nobody that could stop you.

You will become invincible, and those outside noises will soon become just noises in the background that you have gotten so used to that you have simply stopped giving a damn about them, for you know that what you know and what you believe about yourself and your ability far outshines what they regard as necessary or what they regard as suitable.

Your belief in your abilities far outshines their belief in your abilities. Your sense of yourself far outshines their sense of yourself. Your security about what you plan on doing with your life far surpasses what they try to project you about your life, with the mishappening of their lives and their insecurities. And once you can make yourself solid and ignorant of their opinions, nothing will stop you, and you will start to fly. At the same time, they would sit and sail on the waters they have no control, while you would be flying in a sky with winds you have no control over and yet would be able to reach great lengths, for you have better tools and are better equipped to handle even the strongest of winds, and that's where you become more prominent, better and more robust than them in every possible way, and that's what they hate, envy and be jealous about. For you have become what they could never become.

The Person of your dreams.

Your Parents aren't Gods

> *"To be in your children's memories tomorrow,*
> *you must be in their lives today."*
>
> **Barbara Johnson**

Whenever an outsider or somebody makes a sly comment or mocks us, we ignore them or try to give them back equally. But whenever a parent of either of our friends or an individual relatively senior to us mocks us, we generally ignore them and regard their comments as worthy and unimportant. We often say, "Ah, he is an old man; let him say whatever he wants and whatever the hell makes him happy". But whenever the same comment is made by either one of our parents, we lose our shit and declare war against them. We take things personally and try to pick up a fight or say things that might hurt them like their comments might have hurt us. But very rarely does it happen that we stay silent, as we feel entitled that we have every right to speak our mind to make sure that all our frustration against them is released and that they don't dare to say in the same way ever again. But situations rarely take such a good turn, and a fight usually breaks out. Or we are hurt again and again by them, and things get personal and nasty, especially if that parent of yours is a hideous creature. They will shift the entire blame upon you, and soon, you will feel like a criminal for even speaking up and standing up for yourselves. You will feel miserable for falling into the trap, and you will feel so disgusted with yourself, for that's the power they hold over you.

Even if your parent necessarily isn't a narcissist and treats you well, there is no reason for you to believe everything they say. As a child, it's understandable that you have no option. Everything they tell you to do and teach you has to be followed, for they give your life meaning and existence with their financial, physical and mental help. But once you have grown up, it becomes imperative that you start disagreeing with them over things you strictly believe and know aren't right. You have to start speaking up for what's right. They might not be evil, and they might not put you through trauma, and yet at the outset of any wrong decision or dirty little job they have asked you to do for them, it has to be questioned. It must be understood that and realised that they are humans like you. The moniker that parents are Gods is an insult to the Gods itself. For Gods, don't insult their children if they start getting overshadowed. Gods don't beat their partners to death. Gods don't mock their children for doing what they feel is right. At least, that's what we have read and learned about Gods. The Gods become Gods because of their ability to choose between right and wrong. It is that virtue of theirs that allows humans to follow "**Beings**" superior to them as Gods. But that doesn't mean all parents push their children to where they want them to be. Instead, many parents adore and push their children to great heights. They make sure that their children understand the true meaning of love and understand the necessity of acting responsibly and not simply acting as an immature adult who will do and say whatever they want to their children, all because they feel entitled to giving them the money for their education and bringing them up. Bringing the child into the world was their decision, so doing their best to provide them with what they can afford to the best of their abilities is their responsibility. Yet, we see children abandoned by their parents because they fall out of love with their wives/husbands. They realised they were unhappy with this relationship and wanted to try something new. As a result, the child is left alone with their single parent, and they can't simply find time for that child of theirs. So, they suffer unimaginably throughout their lives. And even when they have grown up, the trauma of abandonment keeps them tied to what happened during that childhood. So they end up becoming the same parent and make their child go through the same thing, although in many cases the new parent tries their best not to be the parent, their parents were to them and unfortunately in today's day and age that has become very rare and has become

   Your Actions Define Your Existence

a scarce thing. We live in a world where everybody wants to compete and do things they like, forgetting that bringing the child into this world wasn't the child's decision, and yet the suffering of the child becomes their decision. They are constantly mocked and made to feel like a burden rather than a blessing; none of that was what the child asked for.

Let me better explain this by sharing two real-life stories.

Let's call him Bryan.

So, Bryan is 30 years old alcoholic who I have known for over 10-15 years. Bryan was incredibly chubby and fun-loving in our childhood days. He was known by many for being the prank master and always turning up at my house way earlier than anybody else, as he wanted to stay out of his house as much as possible. We would play and chill with each other even when we weren't playing any particular sports. For I knew if I wanted to go out anywhere and ask anybody for anything, it had to be Bryan, for that much he always wanted to go outside his house and never spend any time over there.

During these times, I would often ask my mother why the hell Bryan wanted to stay out of his house so much and not chill with his family members, and my mother would tell me, "In time, you will know", and I didn't pay much attention to it. One fine day, I saw a massive gathering of people outside Bryan's house, as he used to stay barely 30 meters away from my house. And when I went closely to see what the gathering was about, it shocked me to the core of my soul. I saw Bryan's father beating Bryan and his mother to shreds, and everybody was witnessing it and not doing anything. In some moments in that particular evening, he even tried to kill her in front of the onlookers in front of everybody, until some brave individuals saved them. Seeing such horrific visuals destroyed my soul, and once all of this was over, Bryan called me up, asking me if I was willing to go for a walk. I said yes at first, and then Bryan honestly told me everything he had gone through his entire childhood.

Bryan's father came from an impoverished background. They barely had enough to eat one meal daily; such was their struggle. His grandfather was a labourer, and his grandmother was a housewife. There would be days his grandparents had to go and beg other people for food, and those people would shun them away from their sight. Then, once his father was born, he had to go from place to place to feed himself and do all sorts of things to afford even one meal a day. And then, somehow, Bryan's grandfather, through a stroke of luck, earned a considerable plot through a property dispute. After selling that, he got massive amounts of money, money his father's family could not even comprehend existed. And so, once his grandfather became wealthy, he lost all his nobility and started splashing all his money on alcohol, tobacco and women. Due to that, Bryan's father had to bear the brunt of all the insanities that his father started doing once they became rich.

Bryan's father and grandmother used to get beaten to shreds the same way Bryan and his mother get beaten today. His grandfather became notorious with women and became a sex addict and would marry whoever he wanted, as once he had that money, he could afford a lot of things that he couldn't do earlier. But soon, his grandfather passed away, and Bryan's grandmother and his father had to face a lot of obstacles to reach a particular position and do something worthwhile. It was then that Bryan's parents got married, and he tells me how in the beginning, during his childhood, his father was a role model for every Man out there, as he would love him and his mother to the core and in between tough days as well he would never compromise loving both of them. But soon things changed!

    Your Actions Define Your Existence

Bryan's father had started a business of his own, and by the time Bryan was about to end his schooling life, his father's business clicked, and he started to earn insane amounts of money. He bought his plot of land, built his own house and even bought his dream cars, which meant his father was now a self-made man who had earned an incredible amount of money all through his hard work and grit. And it is here that his father lost the plot, and history repeated itself.

Bryan's father started drinking daily and started harassing his mother almost every day for no good reason. He started becoming more and more arrogant and resentful. Soon, his father began having multiple affairs with multiple women; he even married one of them and started having an illegitimate family. Bryan's mother, by now, was beaten almost every day, and very soon, Bryan began to face these physical assaults as well. Bryan's father had now wholly taken the same path his grandfather had taken.

Soon, Bryan's father's rags-to-riches story became a rags-riches-rags-again story. He started selling all the land he had bought and naming it after his new love interests. His alcoholism increased, and soon, his mother became his father's punching bag. She spent half her day nursing the wounds that she had received from the beatings the night before.

Fast forward to today, Bryan's father has nothing after his name. He, Bryan, and his mother live in a rented property without cars. Bryan's father is unemployed and lives off the money he received from selling his company recently. He is bitter and physically abusive to them. Not an inch of what he does to Bryan and his mother is humane, and there is nothing both of them are doing to come out of such an abusive situation.

Fast forward to today, Bryan is an alcoholic, and as I had heard recently from my peers, he had recently assaulted his girlfriend and was jailed for a few days after she complained about it to the police.

This story of Bryan and his family is a stark reminder of how what our parents do, especially the negative things, can quickly spiral down generations. Bryan's grandfather was a good man but soon became an individual filled with malice who did things contrary to what a man with integrity would do.

Similarly, Bryan's father was a good man with honest and noble intentions, something I have seen first-hand. But like his father, he soon became filled with evil and destroyed his entire family.

Today, Bryan may not be as evil as his grandfather or father, but he is simply going down that path—a path that I am still trying to stop him from, but unfortunately, I have failed. But apart from these negative traits, do you know what is the one thing that's very common among these three men?

They all regard their Parents as Gods.

Bryan tells me that his father is not bad and does these things out of anger. He will always regard his mother and father as Gods, for that's how his father regards his grandfather.

When I heard this, I told Bryan, "Mate, I sympathise with you and feel sorry for what you and your mother are going through, but there is no way your father or grandfather are Gods. Based on what you have told me about your grandfather and what I have seen about your father to date, they are both evil, and they both should reside in hell"."

Bryan got up and told me I was wrong, that all parents are Gods, and that we should never blame them but always follow their example.

 Your Actions Define Your Existence

This is where Bryan or any other individual is simply undeserving of calling any parent a God. They could be good humans or imperfect humans. No parent is ever God, as that's beyond any human's reach in the current scenario. To be a God, you have to be an entity whose approach towards life goes beyond the understanding and comprehension of a normal human being. A Rolex watch nor an omega watch fluster a god; A god isn't willing to kill entire countries for a piece of land, and A god isn't lustful. At least, that's what a God is and what we consider it to be. And due to that, in today's hypocritical and materialistic day and age, nobody has the right to call any human a **GOD**, as that's simply an act of demeaning the Gods. And if somebody does so, that's what allows them to do all sorts of evil things, for that's what gives them misery as that particular individual has a flawed image of God in his mind, and that's no way to live our lives.

Let me explain the above lines referencing another true story.

Let's call my friend Leo.

Leo and I have known each other for almost 17 years. He is a 29-year-old individual who is doing incredible work in his life. He owns a small clothing workshop that he has opened for himself. Unfortunately, his father passed away during COVID-19, and his mother has been having severe illness and physical issues ever since taking the COVID-19 vaccinations, due to which he takes care of her in the best possible way. But his mother is one of the most gritty individuals I have ever met. She does all her work alone; even though the doctor advises against it. She has also taken up a teaching job in a nearby school for her mental sanity since she started her new job. She has become a different person. She laughs much more, is affectionate towards people and is always the first person to help when needed.

For Leo, he is one of the last rare few gems left on planet Earth for the Man he has become.

Of all the people I have ever met, Leo fits the true definition of the word "gentleman." His calm demeanour and incredible self-control in controlling his emotions make him one of the last few true gentlemen left in the world.

His approach towards his friends, women, and even people he had just met is all the same. He never judges anybody and never complains about any situation in his life. I remember during COVID-19 when we were all locked up in our houses and had nothing to do. We both had a lot of conversations over the phone, and that's when we got to know each other much more deeply and closely.

When his father passed away, I was the first person he called, and I didn't know what to say, as even during such an hour of crisis, he was able to control his emotions in such a way. He did cry, but even while crying, I was shocked to hear that he was handling the entire situation positively. He kept telling me how he wished he could have hugged his father one last time, but it was not meant to be. He told me how he would take care of his mother in every possible way, and by the looks of what I have seen, I don't think any son could have done more for their parents. So, then I asked him one day,

Me - Leo, can I ask you something?

Leo – Sure, brother.

Me - How the hell do you remain so calm in every situation? And what the hell makes you optimistic about every situation? What is the magic pill?

Leo takes a long pause and then tells me how his father played a pivotal role in making him the Man he is today.

 Your Actions Define Your Existence

His father, as he tells me, was a man who faced a lot of struggles in his life. His grandfather was a big-time alcoholic and a woman abuser. His grandmother had to face a lot of struggles throughout her entire life, and bringing up Leo's father was not easy.

On the other hand, Leo's father turned out to be a completely different individual, contrary to how his grandfather was. Once Leo became an adult, his father started standing up for his rights and speaking up against his father to protect his mother.

There were days when Leo's father was beaten by his grandfather, and his grandfather would often exclaim, "Parents are Gods; you dare not speak against them, or I shall show you what I am capable of"." These words, Leo tells me, used to echo in his father's mind until the day he last met him, until he got sick.

Leo's father would often tell him he was no God, and neither was his father, nor was any human before him, nor will any human after him.

Leo's father told him how God created such a marvellous and wonderful planet for his entire family (all living beings), yet all we have done is destroy everything it had ever built. We worship "Gods" out of fear because we are well aware of the fact that we have messed up the entire planet. We have created a society and a hierarchy where humans always suffer at the hands of a select few. His father told him how we destroy and kill each other to satisfy our egos.

God, who is almighty and all-powerful, creates when bestowed with power. But humans destroy when bestowed with power. God destroys as well, but God destroys only when Evil tries to create chaos and create an imbalance in God's creation.

But we humans destroy God's creations as if we are entitled to them. We kill people, we beat up our family members, abandon our children, destroy our partners, and when we realise we aren't Gods, instead imperfect human beings in flesh and blood, we bow down to the real God and seek mercy.

"No parent or no human could ever be God," was the line always stated by Leo's father.

We get arrogant even at the slightest of our accomplishments. While God has been tolerating us and creating new life for billions of years. To make yourself useful and do something good, consider yourself an ever-learning human being who has nothing to lose and nothing to gain in this short mortal lifespan. And if you could do that, wait and watch, you will do wonders.

His father told him that he would make many mistakes as a parent, and as his child, he would also make mistakes. But what matters is owning up to them and becoming a better person. For the sake of humanity, he must learn to exercise self-control and be an individual who knows when to use the sword and when to sheath it. This understanding of when to act and when to exercise restraint is not just a mark of strength but will also be a testament to his ability to protect his loved ones. He will become influential by mastering this, but he must remember he is not a 'God'. That power level is beyond him or any human and will always be.

These two stories serve as a stark testament to what happens when we consider our parents as God and when we consider them as good humans.

We have the choice to be Leos who consider their father a good man, take care of their family to the best of their abilities, and never find their parents' Gods.

The life lessons that his father gave him are worthy of him being called "Godly," yet his son refrains from them, and so does he. He knows the difference between bravery and foolishness and realises that being a God is too significant a burden for any human. Yet he has made Leo the best Man he could ever aspire to be, and that's something we could all learn from.

On the other hand, we had Bryan, who considered his father a God, and so did his father to his grandfather. And yet, all we see is three men always treading on the path of Evil. Their act of calling themselves Gods is a mask to show their fragilities and incompetency as humans. And any incompetent human to act simply as a human is too weak and too naïve to call himself a God. For their meaning of a God is too flawed, and that act of theirs is too cowardly to consider responsible. And so that's why they have three generations of weak, abusive, and mentally disabled individuals in their families. In the process of regarding themselves as Gods, they forgot to act like normal humans, and that's the reason they could not differentiate between evil and good.

The moment we stop acting like humans, we go down the path of evil, for being evil is always within our reach, but being a God isn't and never will be.

The choice is yours, to be a Bryan or a Leo!!

> *"What we do in Life echoes in eternity"*
> *Maximus Decimus Meridius*

TWO

Why We Choose to be in Denial

"People deny and blame other for their problems for the simple reason that it's easy and feels good, while solving problems is hard and often feels bad. Forms of blame and denial give us a quick high. They are a way to temporarily escape our problems, and that escape can provide us a quick rush that makes us feel better"

Mark Manson

"**Comfort**", well that's what most of us seek, right? We want our cars to be more comfortable, we want our clothes to be more comfortable, and we want the couch on which we can watch our sporting matches to be comfortable, but what is the one thing that gives comfort to most of us, well its easy, it's "**Denial**".

It's Denial that gives us comfort to never ever take any sort of responsibility for the things that we have done. No matter how cruel or vicious that particular thing might have been when we deny its very existence, we get the freedom to abstain from accountability. And as I had stated earlier, abstaining from taking accountability for our actions is a far easier task than taking responsibility for our actions. To take responsibility, we need to have an incredible amount of courage, to state,, "**Yes, I was wrong**" or "**Yes, I am responsible for that particular mess or for that particular fallout, and I am willing to take full responsibility for my actions**",

These responsible words can only come out of those people who might not be the biggest physical specimens or may not be the most powerful or richest individuals, but these individuals are far more courageous and have the hearts of steels to accept their failures and move ahead in life. These individuals are so big from the inside, that they are willing to lose anything to make sure nobody else suffers from their irresponsible actions. They make sure that if they are the reason for the incredibly negative outcomes then they should be the ones willing to be the fall guy, as that's what makes them far bigger and far richer than anything could ever count. Such individuals are getting so rare in today's day and age, that once we find somebody with such balls of steel, we are willing to go to any stretch to make sure such individuals don't rise again as the more we are going ahead in the race of technological development and human evolution, the more we are willing to put such people down as having such people in the realm of human dimension is simply too uncomfortable and is simply too scary. These folks give us a mirror of our incompetency and our cowardice in being unable to take responsibility for our actions, and that's why we are willing to go to any lengths to make sure such people never come up again, as having them around us is too uneasy and is too scary and who wants to be scared, for we all paint ourselves as strong, and tough. However, the reality is vastly different.

So, who are these people I am talking about as "Us" or "We" in these texts? Well, that's the large majority of us, that have inherited this planet and have been living here in the so-called name of noble nature of humanity. We are individuals who are always wearing the biggest necklaces, we are driving the biggest cars, flashing the biggest brands, living in the biggest mansions, and yet we are ones who are always running away from taking any sort of responsibility for anything. Why take responsibility for things that are not in our control? And then we would think, **"Who cares about society, it's me, it's always me, it should always be me". Why the hell should I go and complain to the police that the neighbour in the area is getting beaten by some intruders, Well that's not my job! As long as my house is secured and I am safe, I don't care!**

Why should I go and accept the mistakes I have made? Why should I ask my children or my friends whether they have been hurt by my verbal diarrhoea? Why the hell should I care if that old lady is being able to cross the road by herself or not? Why should I accept that I had beaten my daughter and smashed her head in the wall, well that never happened, my daughter is simply overreacting. Why should I ask for forgiveness from my wife, after I had slapped her last night, as I was so angry

at what my boss had told me? But simply because I was too scared of my boss, I used my wife as my punching bag! Why the hell would I ask my son if he is traumatized by what I did to him as a child? Why the hell will I apologize for the things that I have done in the past, I don't even remember any of it happening. And even if it did, it's no longer relevant!

Well, these are some of the questions and assumptions that often come into people's minds, when we are confronted with a very harsh reality about something we simply messed up. And guess what these individuals simply refused to acknowledge that any of this happened. Why? Because it's far more comfortable to let the narrative stay the same and the way it is, and why should they bother if people are terrified by their presence, at least it makes them feel strong and big.

But remember, these individuals who think this way and make these assumptions, may be holding some big seat in politics, business or any other world and might come across as such powerful and invincible individuals. Alas! In reality, these are some of the weakest, smallest, and most insecure people you will ever encounter! Why? Because these fools are simply too scared of owning up to their actions, what good will these individuals do the society? These individuals will shout and scream the most, and they will often boast about their achievements, which might have been incredible, but inside they are very timid and fragile individuals, who are so scared of their own selves, that they avoid confronting the truth, as that would make them uncomfortable and their entire grandeur would disappear into thin area, and that would expose their true timid selves, and so what do they do.

Well, they keep on avoiding self-reflection and accountability, as doing that would give them a mirror of their actions and

 Your Actions Define Your Existence

that's a sight they are too scared to witness, for that's how evil and malevolent their actions are. And reflecting on them would simply make them fear life and fear themselves. If that ever happens they may end up killing themselves, for the horrors of their actions are so dark that the very evil they often despise and hate, maybe reflecting upon them and that's a far too scary thing to witness even for them. And so, what do they do, they avoid, they never confront, and they continue on their path of evil and malevolence, as staying who they are and doing what they have been doing is far more comforting than changing and accepting their sins. Once they accept it, they have to realise that the very individuals whom they have been mocking and trying to remove from existence are a far more stronger and courageous species than them, and that's something they simply can't accept and witness. As that would mean their entire existence has been a lie, and their image has been nothing but a façade in order to hide their fragility. For once it has been exposed, they will be consumed by those very individuals who are now what they once were — "**avoidant**, **non-accepting** and **always in denial**. And they know when these monsters try to consume them, it won't be an easy death, rather the entire procedure of their death would be far darker and far more-tougher than death itself. And so, it's better to hunt rather than get hunted, no matter the cost, at least they will be in a position of comfort knowing who their next prey would be.

Let me share a real-life story about a man who destroyed his entire legacy all because of his fragile ego, fake grandeur, for lacking the courage to accept his sin and for staying in denial.

Let's call him, Mohit.

So, Mohit was a man I had known since my childhood days, as he used to stay barely 300 meters away from our house. He is aged around 70, and I have known his son named Dhruv since my childhood days, as we both used to play a lot of Cricket together (For all those wondering why all my stories start with playing cricket, well that's what I did my entire childhood and so did around 4-5 other guys, we just loved to play, play and play. It was like our bread and butter). And so, coming back to the story, Dhruv was a good friend of mine, and so he used to share a lot of things with me, but some of the things he shared were really traumatic and sad, and whenever he would tell me anything that was happening in the house, it used to break my heart and sometimes there would be times when I couldn't sleep imagining how somebody could do such evil and malevolent acts.

So, Mohit was once an affluent businessman known as one of the biggest contractors in our city. He had very good connections with a lot of politicians and you would often see him hanging out with some of the top individuals of the business world as well. He had started his business from scratch and so he used to boast about his achievements and his grandeur in a very loud way. His grandmother would often tell people how his son is often regarded as a God by people all around, something I witnessed firsthand whenever I visited the house to play with Dhurv. As soon as his grandmother used to say these words, which was quite often, a cloud of uneasiness used to surround the house as they used to get very uncomfortable seeing their evil father being compared to a God. And so, the readers might be wondering why I am calling him evil, well, let me tell you why.

Mohit is a man who has to be regarded as the most evil individual I have ever seen. I remember once me and Dhurv were playing Ludo on his terrace and suddenly Mohit came and smacked his elder daughter's head into the wall, I saw Mohit hide below the table. He then told me, that Neelu 'Run, run", and so I took the

 Your Actions Define Your Existence

backside exit and ran away from there. From a distance, I could see how his father was now beating his daughter with a bamboo stick and trust me his daughter was aged around 16 by then. Then he dragged his daughter to the terrace and smacked her head to the table below which Dhruv was hiding. And then as I was about to exit the main gate I saw a glimpse I will never ever forget, Dhruv got literally kicked in the face by his father, and that was the last I saw them for the next 1 week. A week later, I saw Dhruv and his right eye was absolutely swollen, he tried to tell me how he had fallen off his uncle's bike, but I told him I saw what had really happened, and within no time he hugged me and started crying. I tried to stay calm and I broke down as well. And then he narrated the entire story.

He told me the very reason his sister got beaten so badly was because she wanted to learn how to drive, and so she went to a nearby driving school and got herself admitted. The owner of the school who was good with her father, called him without any hidden intentions and told him that his daughter got herself admitted and that he is happy that his daughter has grown up and is now willing to be independent. This enraged Mohit and he couldn't tolerate people being outside the periphery of his control, so he went home and smacked his own children like animals, although I doubt whether any man with humane intentions would ever smack animals in the same way let alone his own children. But that's Mohit for you.

I guess that's a good enough reason to call him a bad person. But what if a person has been doing this to his family for the past 30 years?! Well, that would definitely categorize him as **"Pure Evil"** and that's why I termed him as evil.

Dhruv then told me how this is how their lives have been for the past 30 years (For him the past 10 years as he is 10 years younger than his sister) and this is the way he has grown up in a deeply bruised, battered and violated environment. Beatings like these had become too common for all of them especially his mother whose entire marriage for the past 34 years has been like this. And so, he tells me this is what their life is and this what their life will be if they don't leave this house.

Fast forward to today, Mohit has lost most of his property. He somehow is survived by his wife, his daughter lives in Delhi and his son is, in London. And whenever I talk to Dhruv, he tells me how even to date, his father is still the same, although he can no longer beat them around like he used to do but his behavioural instincts are still the same.

I asked him how so.

He then went on to tell him that he never ever accepts any of the brutal things that he has ever done to them. I asked him, what about the day I witnessed it first-hand?

He tells me, that his father told him, **"Neel is delusional and he is fabricating stories as in that way, he feels he could gain brownie points against me"**. Dhruv told me, hearing this he almost felt like punching his father in the face but resisted as he felt he was not worth his energy and time.

He also tells me how his father is often cribbing about how his entire family has abandoned him in old age, even though it was because of him that they got a good life. It was because of him that he had food on the table. He then tells them how they are such pathetic and miserable children always making up stories to demean him, as he feels he is the best father any child could ever get.

Dhruv tells me that hearing these lines almost makes his sister nauseous, as she can't comprehend how someone could have the

   Your Actions Define Your Existence

audacity to be in such denial. But that's what you should expect for a man of such low calibre. His father has never ever accepted even a single thing that he has done, and even if he does, he tells them had he not done those things, situations could have gotten a lot worse. And so, his actions were a measure to save them from disaster.

Hearing this I was like "What the hell is your father smoking". Is he a human! Or a monster?

And Dhruv tells me, "He is the King of Monsters". Hearing this really broke my heart as no son should ever speak in this way about his father, but what could he have done, his father's evil acts forced him to behave this way.

I mean like, just imagine, when we are young we are told to always look upon our father and our mother as our guardian angels. We are told that they are the ones who will always guide us on the right path, as for them having their children on the right path is of paramount importance.

But imagine being a child (imagine yourself) who has just gained the ability to hone his/her senses and the first thing he sees is violence. And that violence is his mother getting beaten to shreds by his own father. He is crying in his crib and then his father picks him up and puts him in a different room, then he continues beating his mother and then his sister who is handling him, is suddenly called into the room and now she starts getting beaten in the same way that her mother was getting beaten a few moments. Sometimes she is even sexually violated by her father, and that woman has no choice but to face her wrath, as she has considered that to be her present reality. Well, that's a house no individual would wish to be ever born into, for that's a house filled with malevolence and evil. God has left that house and only tyranny and evil reside there.

And then after facing all of those obstacles, you grow up and become a good man, a man who is aware of his actions. A man who is responsible and accountable for your actions, even though you could have gone the other way, especially because of the horrors you have faced, and that would have been far easier. For once you are in the company of malevolence it's easy to become evil for there is nothing new to learn. But the hard part is negating all of that, ignoring the easy things, and your choice to be quite contrary to the devil who once resided in your house in the form of a human.

You follow the path of Benevolence with its fare shares of ups and downs and you become a Man who is accepting of his mistakes, willing to take on responsibility, doesn't fantasize power but is the first one to answer when called up to it, well that's the man every individual should aspire to be.

But the one man who almost pushed you towards evil is now non-accepting of his actions and puts the entire blame on your own shoulders. And you might be asking, why, is that? How Can a man who has caused so much pain and misery in our lives, is unwilling to accept his actions? Why?

Well, it's because he is weak. He is too fragile to hone up to his actions. He is scared that once he owns up to it, he will be devoured by the very darkness he has accepted and unleashed upon you, he will have to embrace a darkness that is so dark and painful that it pushes the entire human spirit out of existence. And so, what does he do, to avoid that fate, he joins the evil on its rampage against good, rather than stand up to it and fight. And that's what Mohit did, and that's what men like Mohit do. They accept evil for that makes them who they are and exposes their true nature, but you are different, you choose to fight it, and you deny to be its disciple for that's what a "Real Man" does.

 Your Actions Define Your Existence

So, how do you live life when you have somebody like Mohit in your life, and how do you come out of such a negative shell and become a man who embraces responsibility and rejects denial?

Let's talk about it.

Understanding the truth – In order, to better acknowledge these situations you have to understand the simple fact that Men who show themselves as invincible and being really strong and agile are in reality one of the weakest and most fragile individuals you might have ever come across. Although that may not be the case at all times, most of the time that's the reality of these individuals. Always remember the fact that the strongest and the bravest men are often the calmest and quietest individuals.

These individuals are so secure in their own skin, that they don't need to show their might in order to put people down. Unfortunately, these kinds of men are very rare. Our political and business circles are mostly occupied in the category of people who shout and show themselves to be the strongest, and that's only possible because the general public isn't aware of their realities and is too scared to stand up to what's wrong. For that reason, we have only one Nelson Mandela and one Mahatma Gandhi. Without these folks, the entire civilisation may still have been under the rule of tyranny and suppression. But these men were different and they instilled a sense of belief and faith in the scared minds of people and that's the way they defeated the might of the British.

In a similar way, it is imperative upon us that we are able to remind ourselves and realize that until and unless we are on the wrong side of things, there is no reason for us to be scared of them. Their acts of intimidation, domination and suppression work only when we supplement them with our cowardice and frightened minds. Our weak and frail minds act like oxygen to their fake acts of superiority. The control is and will always be in our hands, how we decide to avail it is what matters.

What should always be remembered is the simple fact that these sorts of individuals lurk everywhere in our lives, they are in our homes, our offices, our gyms, everywhere goddamn place, and so it becomes crucial that we live upon what we believe in and remember that as the right course of action to deal with such individuals. For they are predators, and once they have sniffed their prey, they are very much well aware of who they could consume or who they could let go. And so, it is upon us, to truly differentiate between real courage and fake acts of courage, and once we can single that out, we become very powerful, and with that strength, we can reach heights and reach places, we could have never ever imagined. For it is fear that truly bides us to these weak monsters.

The reason I say weak monsters is because they pretend to wear horns like the devils we are often shown through various scriptures. The only difference is that today's monsters may lack visible horns. They use strength and a deceptive aura to instill fear in the masses, making themselves appear as powerful as the horned devils we've seen depicted for centuries. These invisible horns embolden them to act as they please, only to flee when it's time to take responsibility, returning the next day to continue their wrongdoings. Ultimately, it is entirely up to you how you choose to confront these weak and fragile individuals.

The choice is yours, either you ignore them and make them feel small and petty, or you fall prey to their false sense of strength. Either way, they will find enough individuals to prey upon, so why not act and live like there is nothing to lose, for the only thing that's there to gain by submitting from their false acts of strength, is misery, fear and suffering, and that's what you should envision for yourself.

   Your Actions Define Your Existence

Choose **the person you want to be** – Our society is filled with people whom you may be inspired by and may be willing to be like. Especially in today's social media day and age, our access to seeing different sorts of individuals doing different things in various aspects of their lives is absolutely incredible and quite refreshing. And so, the biggest question that you have to answer at some point in your life is, who do you want to become? Is it the footballers whose work ethic you were impressed by? Is it that businessman whose daily schedule has really motivated you?! Or is it that supermodel whose rags to riches story has motivated you to dream like her?

Well, if you leave it to me, your answer should be, I want to become that person who in 5 years time would be less bitter, less resentful and would be far more responsible for his/her actions than he/she is today.

And if this is your answer you are halfway down the path, as this path will for sure make you an individual who is anything like those with cowardly behaviours. Once you have these aspects as goals to become that person you are on that path, to truly choosing to become who you want to be. In this path, you will find that how being responsible and accountable for our actions is one of the hardest tasks you have ever faced, for it requires you to become a man who is unlike anybody in the crowd. For the most part of the time, you will look like an individual who often seeks to walk through the road less taken. You won't be easily tamed, and neither could you be easily dominated by those weak and unaccountable predators. Rather you would become a man who is willing to live and die by the rules that represent the true noble nature of humanity. And this will not go down well with those predators for anybody who can't be tamed is a threat to their very existence. Those who are tamed remain so out of fear, and because you carry yourself like a lion, your presence will intimidate and threaten them, bringing a significant amount of hardship into your life.

The suffering that you face by being yourself without fearing anybody, is far more rewarding than the suffering people have to endure in the name of fear.

When you become "one among a few" you will gain the attention of many who live among the "One among everybody" and once they decide to join you on that path, you will be able to change far more individuals. And, since it is people that give power to those weak predators, pulling more and more individuals away from them, will create fear in the minds of those predators and that would further weaken their authority and make people's lives less fearful and less bitter. Although these predators don't belong to any specific sex (Male & Female) if history is considered based on what we have experienced and seen, the former group (Males) have done far more destruction and annihilation to our society than the latter (Female), but that is no reason for you to consider one as less dangerous while other is more dangerous. Danger could come from any aspect of our lives, what matters is how well we are prepared to face it and tackle it with the greatest of our strengths, for that's where our real characters are formed.

Every time any of these predators try to harm you or submit you before them, remember you don't have to reciprocate to them and fall into their trap, rather it's your job to stay true to who you are and who you could be 5 years down the line, and if you do that you become completely unstoppable and you inspire more and more individuals to join you on this path, that is far more treacherous and challenging and yet is way more rewarding then anything ever could be.

     Your Actions Define Your Existence

Choose how you want to suffer – Why the hell should I confess to messing it up? Why the hell should I go and apologise for that? Why the hell should I fight, I am better off living no matter how bad it is!

I guess these are some of the questions that most of us often ask ourselves, or sometimes even ask others when I compel us to do something for which we are not prepared. At that time, we have to ask ourselves, **"How the hell am I going to be known for 5 years down the line"**?

A man who could never ever stand up to the abusive father who kept on beating his mother to shreds, A man who could never ever stand up to the senior who kept on beating his classmate, A man who could never ever stand up to that colleague who kept on disrespecting me in front of everyone, or a man who could stand up to all of them no matter what the cost.

Sometimes in life, you have to choose what you want to do and how you want to do it, and the costs are very significant, For, instance if your father always beats your mother and all this while you have to stay quiet because he is the only source of income. But now you have grown up and he still beats the shit out of your mother, you still have to ask yourself, is this the man I am going to be, am I going to stand up and not let my mother suffer or will I stay this way and let everything be as it is. Either way, you are going to suffer.

For if you stand up and defend your mother, your mother might hit you as well but there is a chance that you could save your mother as well. What if my father leaves and we get really messed up financially, these are some of the things that will often come to mind.

And at that time, you have to choose the suffering you want to face, while also remembering the man you want to be seen as 5 years down the line. And if you are truly someone who is now working on his own, earns your own money and yet chooses to let your mother suffer, then you definitely failed your mother and allowed your father to be the monster that he has become. But if you stand up, he will realise that his time is now up and a new alpha has emerged and it is his son, and he will not allow disrespect and toxicity to flow into his house, no matter who the hell that is. And at the present moment, your mother may scold you or your father may even slap you, but in hindsight, you have marked your territory and your father or any other man can no longer carry on with their actions, without any accountability.

They have to understand that as stated by Issac Newton,

"Every action has an equal and opposite reaction"

So, it is completely upon you, to choose the suffering you want to live your life with. For 5 years down the line, it is you will be answerable for the man that you have become. So, it becomes imperative that you choose the suffering for the days to come. Whatever that is, it will make you the person that you choose to be with your decision.

If you choose the suffering where you let people you know suffer knowing you could help, you will become a man who is vengeful and ashamed of himself.

If you choose the suffering where you stand up against that evil. You will suffer but 5 years down the line you would be glad you stood, for you became the man you always envisioned of becoming.

Remember, Suffering is everywhere, Weak predators who deny all their actions and choose to abstain from responsibility and

 Your Actions Define Your Existence

accountability are everywhere. All you have to do is make your decision, based on the person you want to become. For when you stand up, you create many enemies for nobody likes a strong man, and when you stay down you create one enemy. Both have costs and pain, choose what you want to do, and what you want to be known for 5 years down the line.

Mental Fortitude- As I have stated earlier, it does not matter how strong or how huge one is from the outside, if our inside isn't as strong as it should be, we all will be consumed by those predators. And so, it becomes imperative that the true purpose of our life is to help others to the best of our abilities and yet not losing our self. I have seen many individuals becoming someone else to accommodate the needs of these weak predators, and that absolutely destroys and traumatises them for a lifetime. For they are suffering the wrath of that weak monster and yet aren't able to live their lives on their terms. Sacrifices are a must if we want to make a change but that sacrifice shouldn't necessarily destroy to the extent that you are no longer capable of even completing that task, for that would bring more harm than good, and you are very much needed for the betterment of the world.

We have to understand that, we are all the purest of substances from our surroundings. The kind of people we live with, the individuals who share our lives, and those who influenced our childhood all contribute to shaping who we become as adults. To become individuals who own up to our actions, abstain from shirking responsibility, and avoid becoming like those who live in denial of their harmful actions, it is necessary to build our mental fortitude like armour and resolve that surpass our vices and desires.

As humans, it is natural to have vices; very few can entirely avoid them. For some, it is cigarettes; for others, alcohol; and for some, sex. These tendencies are often rooted in our upbringing. Among all vices, denial is the most insidious. Once denial becomes ingrained, it is challenging to overcome. In these moments, our mental resolve, shaped by our surroundings, becomes crucial. This strength allows us to rise above and become better than those who perpetuate harm and deny responsibility.

Acknowledging it is the first step towards overcoming them. It requires self-awareness and a willingness to confront uncomfortable truths about ourselves. By doing so, we break free from the cycle of denial and begin to take control of our actions. This process demands a lot of work on ourselves, as it is the continuous effort and introspection that would propel us towards becoming that individual. And once we reach there, we are rewarded with a life of integrity and accountability, a life where we are able to accept ourselves and grow as individuals, for we are so content with our own existence and feel good for the path we have taken. And all of these are only possible when our minds guide us towards a path we believe in, rather than the path we have been shown by those weak monsters.

Our surroundings and the people within them play a pivotal role in our development. But with Resolve we are able to achieve the needed determination to achieve a goal or overcome a challenge. The inner drive keeps us moving forward, even when things get tough. To develop such a resolve, we must have a clear purpose and a solid commitment to our values. We must be willing to put in the effort, stay focused, and remain persistent. Resolve helps us stay true to our principles and rise above our surroundings' negative influences. By fostering the resolve within us, we encourage responsibility and self-awareness within us and that allows us to support each other in rising above our habits of denying things that have occurred and that have had tremendous

   Your Actions Define Your Existence

repercussions. Through this collective effort, we build stronger, more resilient individuals who can confront their shortcomings and strive for personal growth. And truly lay down the path, where individuals are hesitant to cause someone harm, for they know they will be held accountable for their actions, and once that happens, denial and malevolence take a back seat.

Have faith in yourself - Sometimes you are stuck in that shitty relationship. Other times you are stuck with those toxic parents of yours and other times you are stuck in that toxic job of yours. Most of the time you are in denial of these realities as you feel accepting them would make your life so uncomfortable and scary that you rather stay where you are, and one day when you had enough and your parents are no more or your partner has left, or your company has fired you, you become like one of them and you choose to abstain from the responsibility that you have for yourself, for doing that is so much easier.

But what you don't know, is what's on the other side of the grass.

Yes, it's true, switching to the other side can bring a whole lot of different sorts of pain and struggle. And that might force you to think, **"What if I break up and end up becoming lonely? What if once I have started earning myself, I tell my parents how toxic they are and leave the house, I may get crushed by the outside world. What if I leave this job and remain unemployed and do not have good enough opportunities?**

Well, to be honest, all of these things could happen, in fact, worse things have happened to people, but better things have followed as well once that phase of their lives was over, but it was largely dependent on how they reacted to that particular situation of theirs.

When we decide how we choose to accept our realities and become better as individuals that's when we are able to accept the current realities of our lives and move away from our habits of denying things as they are.

As I have stated before, the reason people deny and stay where they are is because they feel it is comforting, no matter how particular the situation might have been, staying where they are gives them comfort and comfort that's addictive to most of us.

If you feel your father doesn't appreciate you due to his narcissistic tendencies and rather always pins the blame on you (similar to what Mohit did), well You have no option. You must accept that his behaviour and denials are not something you would ever want to embody. No matter what you do, say, or achieve, you will never be enough for him, as his denial of you is what brings him comfort. But chasing after his appreciation will only cause you discomfort.

And so, you have to accept the reality and start accepting the single fact that he will always be in denial of you and you have to take the primary responsibility for yourself.

Similarly, that toxic relationship that you are denying is true and is killing you. During such stages of your lives, take the path of solitude and jump the boat when it's only the two of you, for once you are married and have children, there will be added responsibility and jumping the wagon will get tougher and you will be perpetually locked in an area of permanent suffering, All because you choose to deny the realities and decided to live in a utopian world where your partner likes you and you are in happy relationship, which is most certainly not the case and never will be.

    Your Actions Define Your Existence

Denial is a disease that kills individuals from the inside, and we start to notice it only when those bruises start showing up outside as well, for our bodies had to wither and suffer its repercussions for so many years and now it has started to give up. And so it is important that you start having faith in yourself and start prioritising yourself way more than you have been doing until now, cause remember at the end of it all, **it is you**, who you will be answerable to, and when that day comes, if you keep on denying every goddamn thing that you could have done or the big step that you could have taken but didn't take, it is only You that you will be blaming, nobody else.

It is imperative that we conduct and live our lives in a way that we don't feel ashamed of ourselves 5 years down the line. The weak monsters and predators are lurking everywhere, and they will try to consume you, threaten you and even destroy you for reasons only they know. Sometimes it's jealousy, sometimes it's envy and sometimes it's out of habit. Whatever may be the reason they will always try to unsettle you in trying to do something that you aren't accustomed to, and at that point you have to ask yourself what you want to be known as a few years down the line. Either you become a man who didn't try things for fear of facing their wrath or didn't follow the path you wanted to follow as you were scared you may end up being labelled as something else by them. Whatever the reason, there will be endless things said by them, screamed and even entitled by them and that would give you enough reasons to not try and rather stay in your shell and become like one of them. But there is only one reason for you not to become like them, and that is the shame and regret you will have on your own self if you don't do things based on what you feel is right.

Becoming like one of them would feel and look easy, for that would mean less resentment and a life in which you would live without any pain or motives from the outside, but inside you will die new deaths every day. For the pain of regret is for more than the pain of suffering for your dreams.

When you ask yourself, **"Why the hell didn't I do that"**, or **"How bad could it have gotten had I tried"**! You will cry inside as you would feel so pained to have not given your best into doing things and becoming something, you could have become and that's a pain that would make your life way more miserable than you could have ever imagined.

But the pain that you would choose to follow your dreams and become the man that you wish every day you could become one day, well that pain is far more tolerable and far more rewarding than you could have ever imagined. Beyond this pain and suffering lies contentment, a life of accountability and responsibility—one truly worth living a thousand times over. And that's the reward you get by steering clear of somebody who embraced denial, denying to embrace it yourself, and accepting responsibility and accountability as your way of life, and that's what you truly make your life a life many envision but very few get to live.

So, take responsibility for your actions and reject Denial.

 Your Actions Define Your Existence

THREE

Identifying the Silent Sufferers

In a world where most of us are often striving to have something uncommon about us to feel that we are different from all of us, there is one thing that is pretty common among all of us, and that is "Suffering".

Suffering is something that is so well relatable to almost every individual who has walked on earth and those who will walk in the future. It's almost a given ever since the moment we are born. At first, as babies we struggle to walk due to which we often fall down and that creates suffering in our yet baby minds, then once we are admitted to school we suffer to stay there let alone study, then when we grow up, we have to suffer to get a job, and once we have done all of these things, suffering keeps on coming at us one way or the another, and we all get accustomed to it, for it becomes part and parcel of our lives.

Some people often whine and complain about how they are finding it difficult to cope with the expectations and pressures they are facing in the modern-day world. Some express their anger towards that particular way they are suffering. Some cry, some insult others to hide their suffering and their insecurities. And so, there are various ways, people from various aspects in different areas, react differently in the variety of ways they suffer.

But there is one species of individuals who suffer and yet nobody knows how deep their pain is, those are the individuals that I call the "Silent Sufferers'.

The "Silent sufferers" are a group of individuals that are incredibly prevalent in today's day and age. They have been present since former times as well, but in recent times these individuals and their struggles with suffering have started to come into the picture more often. The pain they feel is something some of us may not be able to relate to but most of us could, for that's what has happened to us as a whole. These individuals (could be many readers reading this book) are suffering pain and hurt from inside that has broken them to the extent that they no longer come out and even say what they are hurt about for that's how strongly they have been conquered by the pain. For some of them, it's a pain they have been vehemently consumed by and all they can see is darkness looming over their heads 24 x7. Pain has become such a constant in their life, that it no longer bothers them like the way it used in the beginning, for at that time they weren't really accustomed to it. But now numbness has taken over their entire soul, and unfortunately, they find no other way other than silence to keep their pain inside.

The damage they have gone through is so severe that some of them seek death in order to release themselves of this pain, some of them are already dead on the inside but simply lack the courage to kill themselves on the outside (which is good as death should never be celebrated) as it is that fear and lack of courage that has made them who they are. And for some, unfortunately, they gave up on their life and ended it without thinking about the consequences that could happen once they are gone. But what can you expect from individuals who are so down in their pursuit of giving up their hopes for a life that they have given up on life altogether (which is never the solution) as they wonder why stay and feel all of this loss in life, for there is so much and so many things that have already killed me from the inside and now through death I will finally relieve myself of all these things.

These individuals and their pain could be born out of a lot of things. A wife who has been domestically violated and physically assaulted by her husband for many years, a woman being raped by her family member, a son or daughter assaulted by her parents and then by their partners, a boss absolutely making life hell for one of their employees, a father suffering the pain of his children's exorbitant demands, parents whose entire savings are lost due to a bad investment but can't reveal it to anyone.

So, in a nutshell, suffering happens to individuals in so many different ways that we simply can't imagine and it breaks them apart into pieces. Some continue to live there, live in the same way and die with a bagful of regrets, some gain redemption, some give up and die, while some truly reverse their situations with their grit.

Let me share some really incredible real-life stories I have seen from close quarters in order to give you a better idea about what a silent sufferer looks like how they suffered, and how some got out while some remained where they are.

I will be using different names in order to keep their identities anonymous.

Story 1

There was a boy named David whom I have known ever since the age of 10. He was a very lively and incredibly chubby boy. Most of the time that I would meet him he would always greet me with a hug and smile on his face and that would instantly bring a smile on my face as well. He would often tell me how he regards me as his elder brother and that was very evident as he often came to me for advice on issues he felt I could give him solutions to. But then there was something really weird about some of his behaviours. There would be days when neither of his family members would come outside their house for days and it was only the father who would come and take all the required grocery things that he needed. Whenever I would bump into him, I would often ask him, "Hi uncle, how is David, it's been a while since I have seen him", his father would give me a death stare and never ever gave me an answer.

Then one fine day, there was a huge barrage of media outside their premises and it was then that I got to know that David's father had been arrested by the police for he had beaten his wife to shreds and had broken her neck, in such a circumstance, David ran away from his house and got hold of someone who informed the police and the media. It was then that everybody came and took his father away. And then David told me the entire story.

So, basically, his father has been beating his mother in this way for the past 30 years. Sometimes he even raped her. And whenever he did all these things, he kept David locked up in a room for several days and would only open the door to give him food. David told me how sometimes while being raped he could hear his mother's cry for help, but he was simply helpless. And sometimes his father would not even give them food if he felt they didn't deserve it. Due to such instances, he explained to me why he would disappear for weeks sometimes. I asked him, "Why the hell didn't you lodge an official complaint"? He tells me how his father has many friends in the police department and they were well aware of the things that were happening and yet didn't do anything.

Once I heard this, I felt like punching those demons, as that's what they are. And then I asked him, how the hell do you keep on a smile on your face.

He said, "What else can I do, I am hopeful one day this suffering will end and we will come out of this crisis".

And guess what, it's been almost 12 years since that incident happened and today David and his mom no longer live with his father. As David has bought his own 2BHK apartment and is now working in one of the top firms in Mumbai, along with that he is giving his mother a life which may not be the most luxurious, but certainly seems like heaven for where she was once. And I feel so happy and proud of him. For we do meet occasionally whenever I travel to Mumbai and have a few drinks and talk about how far we have come, sometimes we both tear up regarding our own pasts, but the night always ends with a hug and a big nice dinner.

The basis of this story was to make us understand how often individuals are stuck in situations they feel they can't do anything about. Imagine had David not run out of that house that day, his life would have been so much different, but he did and it changed his life for the better. Also, the fact that he always smiled even though he was literally living in a hellish house gives us an example of how "Silent Suffering" happens, has been happening and will keep on happening. His mother went through one of the worst ordeals of her life during those 20 years and nobody knew about it, and even those who did didn't care to fight for her.

 Your Actions Define Your Existence

The moral of the story is sometimes when there is nobody to fight for us, we have to fight for ourselves or else, we will forever live our lives being a "Silent Sufferer" and that's a life not worth living, for death is so much better than that.

The only way we could come out of such a situation is to have that particular courage at that moment to do the things that we have been enabled to do, for if we don't do it at that moment, the next moment may never come. For when that moment comes, we should grab it with both hands and change our lives for the better and truly get ourselves out from such hellish and toxic lives that no human should ever be made to witness, especially when your intentions are benevolent.

Story 2

There was a boy named Jacky who once lived near our house. His existence was something very few people were actually aware of, for he barely came out of his house and played with any of us. His mother was extremely strict with him and wouldn't let her son come out and play with any of us. Her mother once beat him for almost 2 hours as he had broken his father's bike's rearview mirror and that was the last time, I had seen him play. Even his younger sister was turned into an extremely weird girl by her mother, as she wasn't allowed to go out and interact with anybody. Their father was like an absentee landlord and would be out on his work duties most of the time, and whenever he came home, he would drink from morning till night and sleep the next day. Well, that was basically his schedule for whatever duration he used to stay at home until he went away again for work.

For Jacky whether his father was at home or not, whether his mother was sick or whether his younger sister had been heckled by some stranger (it happened quite a few times), none of that mattered. Sometimes, I wondered whether he was confused about his own existence or what was the way in which he lived his life, and that's how he went about his life and all the other aspects related to it.

He always seemed so detached from any sort of human emotions or sentimentality and I always wondered whether that's really the case. Then one day I saw him smoking just outside the periphery of our house, and I told him "What the hell brother, my mother will think I have been smoking", he ignored what I said and kept on smoking and then once I got angry he left but not before giving me a death stare, and by this time we were only 14 years old, and from where I am from, 14 year old's don't smoke. During this time, I had heard that his mother had even caught

 Your Actions Define Your Existence

him talking to a girl over the phone and she left outside the house for the whole night (which was way too extreme). Due to all of these restrictions, he ended up becoming an individual who literally had no friends. And I was the only one with whom he used to be on the "Hi" and "Hello" terms. Until one day I finally learned the truth about him.

One day, He was in an absolutely intoxicated state as he was barely able to stand. And then he told me, "Neel, I need your help or I am going to die". My friends and I quickly paid the food bill and somehow controlled him from falling down and took him to a nearby place which was owned by my friend's father. There he opened up about everything.

He told us how his mother is mother is often bringing different sorts of men to the house and has sex with them in his room, as she can't do that in her room for her husband will get to know about that. Then she always threatens them that if they tell anybody or their father she will throw them out of the house (Trust me she was very capable of that). Then he told us that the reason his father only drinks when he is home, is because he himself has countless affairs and once even molested his own daughter, until he saved her. There have been times his mother even asked her daughter not to say no to her father (By this time I was shocked and couldn't believe what he was saying). I told him, I didn't believe him. He then showed some very obscene pictures of both his mom and dad doing sexual acts with their partners.

Hearing all of this kept me awake the whole night, something which even surprised my mother, for I was known for my amazing sleep during my childhood days, I still sleep well but not out of habit, but out of necessity and for a good health.

Jacky's story is a prime example of an individual who was a "**silent sufferer**" along with his sister. Countless individuals go through such situations in life and have no idea how to get out. Their suffering is so intense and cruel that you would wonder how you would react if that ever happened to you. Such cruelty by our parents breaks us down and makes us individuals who have no soul left in our bodies, for they themselves have forgotten about their human nature, and all they are doing is causing harm and pain with their dirty and inhuman character and malevolent intentions. Such selfish individuals don't deserve to be parents but unfortunately, they are and they ruin lives along the way and make people suffer for no fault of their own. They make people go through such trauma that individuals no longer feel any sort of emotion and are simply surviving for reasons unknown even to them and some individuals end up killing themselves due to this. It's like taking out the souls of individuals and crushing them to suit your needs and making sure they fail miserably, and when they do make sure you take no fault of theirs and pinpoint the entire blame on them, for you are too scared to take responsibility for your inhuman actions.

Fast forward to today, I had heard that Jacky married a girl he fell in love with (something that I had doubted at first for forgetting about a girl, I haven't even seen him talk to a boy), and then he threw both his mother and father out of the house. I literally asked the individual telling me this story, "What are you saying"! he said yes Neel that's the truth, within no time I felt like going absolutely numb and speechless and I didn't utter a single word for almost 30 seconds. When my friend asked me what happened and why I didn't go so quiet. I told him, why.

No parent should ever face this faith of being thrown out of their own house by their children for that's a fate I don't wish upon even by biggest of enemies (we all have some, in my case it's an old man who hates me from every strain of his body). For

     Your Actions Define Your Existence

nobody wants their enemies to face such a situation where the once mighty individual (at least portrayed themselves as) has now been shown the door by their own kids. But in this case, Jacky's parents asked for it, for the amount of suffering they have made him and his sister go through was way too traumatic and intense and so they paid the price for their actions.

In regards to his sister, he made sure she passed out of college and she also completed her graduation, which showed how Jacky became so much more than what his parents could ever be. He took such great responsibility for his sister and did the least he could so that tomorrow she could go out and be her own woman, and that's what she did as she recently secured a government job. His father still drinks and spends his days alone in his rented house, for his mother well she married someone else.

What this story signifies is how there is so much evil and hate residing within each of us. We are capable of such deplorable acts that even the demon would be ashamed and ask us, whether he is the demon or us. And that's what Jacky's parents did, and so many individuals do to different sorts of individuals in different sort of ways. What Jacky did is by no means right if we look at it from a human perspective, but when we look at it from Jacky's perspective it forces us to accept the truth and believe in Karma. Also, what he did for his sister is really commendable for he could have gone the other way, but he didn't, rather he showed what being a responsible man is and how being helpful and being kind is the least we could do to anybody, especially our loved ones. This doesn't mean that Jacky doesn't have any issues, for he still struggles sometimes with alcohol related issues, but he is far better than the man his father was and a far better human than his mother was. This shows how Jacky may have lost many battles in life, but as of today he has won the war, and is in charge of his life and has been able to stay away from the path of causing suffering to others, for he knows that what he does today will one day come back to haunt him, and if he makes other a casualty of a silent sufferer today, tomorrow he may become one himself and face the faith his parents faced and so that would make him aware and be cautious of his actions and at the same make him understand why being a good person and being a parent with good and noble intentions (along with the occasional vice and imperfections) is an absolute necessity to make sure we play our part in creating a world where there are far less individuals suffering in loneliness and despair and without a voice, for he knows how that feels and how traumatic and killable those moments are, and that has helped him to create a path for others.

And that is something we all could learn from him in order to make sure we play our part in creating a world with far less desperation, resentment and anxiousness. Humans are capable of doing extraordinary things, so why waste it away in pursuit of creating hell for our own species, for that's an experience of disheartening and soul crushing and none of us should aspire to do that.

Story 3

While I was studying in my school, there was a girl named Jenny, who in many ways was my first ever female friend, as until then I had not been so close with any girl in my life. We both used to talk a lot and during those days there would even be times when she would come to our house and really have some nice and incredible times (we were around 7-8 years old) and her parents being good with mine really helped and that's the reason we shared some really incredible and amazing times.

But as time passed, she underwent a significant transformation. In the summer of 2015, during my college break, I came home for about 30 days. Though the vacation was longer, a month felt sufficient to spend time with my family, especially since I was also playing professional cricket at the time.

One night, while returning home with a friend after an amazing evening at one of the city's best pubs, I noticed a girl walking alone on the street around midnight. Initially, I thought of ignoring it, but as we got closer, I realized it was Jenny. It surprised me, given that she now lived far from my house. The moment she saw me, her eyes widened in shock, and before I could say anything, she grabbed my arm tightly, as if trying to ground herself in that moment. Then, out of nowhere, tears welled up in her eyes. My friend and I exchanged awkward glances, unsure of how to react—after all, who bursts into tears after seeing someone after so long? But Jenny did. She then asked us to come with her (not for what readers might assume). She explained that both her parents were away for work, leaving her alone with her brother. After some deliberation, we decided to go. Once we reached her place, she pulled out a bottle of Jack Daniel's Honey and, with a weary sigh, began to open up about everything she had been through.

Jenny went on to tell us how life has become so miserable for her of late. She was dating a boy whom she met around 3 years back. In the beginning, he was an incredible boy, but with time his behaviour changed and he turned into a completely different man. She then told us how she often catches him talking to some other girls and even going out with them, but could never question him for that for she liked him so much, but what happened recently really messed up her mind. During a house party when she had gone to buy some food from the nearby restaurant she came back and found that her boyfriend was nowhere to be seen, and when she went to look around for her, she found out that he had been having sex with one of her closest friends, and when her boyfriend found out that she had seen that, he simply smirked and told her to go away. This absolutely broke her, and there have been times when she even contemplated suicide, something she is still doing but hasn't mustered enough courage to do that (For which I am happy). Then she told us how when she often tries to get close to her mother by telling her these things, in order to get some mental help, her mother often shifts the blame on her and really insults her badly and tells her that she has no time to listen to any of her issues. But whenever her mother had any issues she would come and tell her and she would always take it upon her to solve it, but she never got it reciprocated from her mother. She told us how her father has different affairs almost every month (something I have witnessed myself many times) and so he never pays any attention to his family, and simply gives them money, for he believes money is the answer to everything (most rich people think). These are nothing but signs of a highly toxic relationship that turned Jenny into a **"silent sufferer"**, all because nobody around her was willing to help her, for sometimes all we need is a hand of faith in order to support us during times when we seem all is lost. Something she later on told me, was

    Your Actions Define Your Existence

how she was so grateful that we met and she could share all of these things, and then at around 5 am, we left for our house, completely emotionally shattered after hearing her story but at the same really happy that we were able to give her that support and be there for her and listen to her issues if not anything else. But I felt and I knew I could do more.

As humans, none of us are ever perfect and never will be, for that's simply unattainable. But what we can do is give our best and help those around us, even though we are fighting our battles.

Me and Jenny during this time started talking a lot with each other. During this time we even got into a casual relationship as that was something both of us had not expected, but the fact that we were traumatised similarly with our family issues, unintentionally attracted us towards each other. We stayed with each other for almost 1 year and during this time we really saw each other grow on a different level. Jenny during this time was in Guwahati and she really started becoming more grateful for her life by working more on herself. Even for me, I had gained a lot of weight during this time and had scored poorly in my semester exams, then with Jenny, I decided that I could make myself better as well.

And so, we both went on a transformation journey and soon we both reversed our situations. For Jenny, these situations affected her way more than anybody, because in my case my mother and my sister were always affectionate and supportive towards me, but for Jenny, she was literally waging a lone war and today she is an established journalist in one of India's top organisations and recently got married as well.

Through this story, we can all understand how we as individuals have so much power within ourselves and change somebody's life for the better if our intentions are in the right place. Someone like me who was going through some really turbulent times in my own personal life, decided to reach out to her and give it a shot to help her. Neither of us had met since ages and yet when we met, we met absolutely at the right time which shows how if we don't give up things happen when they are meant to happen. And that night Jenny was bound to meet me and change her decision of giving up her life, for she no longer had any faith or trust in anything or anybody.

There was a very high probability that when Jenny was telling me all about her life story, I could have interrupted her so many times and cried about my own sob story, for I had every right to share my feelings, but I didn't! Why? Because there is a right place and a right time for everything and sometimes listening is the best thing we can do, especially for an individual who is having worse than you. But she doesn't need solutions, she simply needs someone who could listen to her and then connect with her and guide her through a path she feels she could go, and the fact that we both decided to go on this path together meant a lot to me and those are the moments I will cherish forever.

She often tells me that had I not met her that night, it may have been the last night of her life for she had every intention of giving up on her life, and the fact that she met such a familiar face at a time and place she had not expected, really made the occasion even better. It was really upon me what I did with her, for the first few months it was really an emotional and wretched experience to even discuss anything with her as she was hesitant and wanted to stay in the crib of desperation and misery for that's what gave her comfort. But with time things got better and she really changed.

For her, it was an incredible experience as she was hell bent and overly dependent on her boyfriend and was in the middle of such a toxic relationship, knowing the fact that it was killing her, but

   Your Actions Define Your Existence

how can you expect someone to come out of their own misery if those around them keeps on pounding negative and toxic energies one after the other. Even the best motivational speakers would succumb to pressure for that's what evil is capable of, and for her it was her Boyfriend, mother and father who appeared in the form of evil, fighting for him in making sure she gave up on her existence itself and whatever soul she had left was sucked so deep into misery that there is no light. But me simply being there for that night made all the difference as she told me how for the first she could tell something to someone without fearing judgement or being interrupted or without being labelled.

She saw how I was going through my own issues and was fighting my own monsters (something we all do our whole life) and yet was willing to help her, for that made an even bigger thing for her, for she knew how exhausting and tiring it was for me. That's something we can all do—offering a hand to someone in need won't cost us much, especially when we know that, even if our boat is damaged, it can still carry one more. And sometimes, that extra space can mean the difference between survival and drowning for someone barely holding on. And that is something we could all do, and should always be willing to do, for who else will help these "Silent Sufferers", for their suffering is so mute and so silent that none of us could hear if we keep on staying oblivion to our own needs, for that's way easy as helping someone else requires courage and patience, and only those with the willingness to make a difference can do that, and that's within all of us but unfortunately very few trust themselves to make such a change, for they know how difficult and painful it is to change, and yet those who have changed know how rewarding it is, once we have endured those difficulties and suffered the pain that comes in the process, as in the process it makes us better, stronger and more responsible human beings. And when we become that we have far more faith in humanity and we become so much more powerful and increase our own self-worth, for we have not realised how powerful it is being human and yet we choose to live our lives on our own selfish endeavours, knowing that there is so much space in our boat and yet we choose to ignore the people that are drowning, without realising how we could be one of those drowning one day, for life is weird and storms are lurking everywhere and our boats are nothing in comparison to the power or those monsters. But when we have help and we have company, there is a higher probability for us to reach the shores way before the storms could hit us, and that is something we should all strive for, for that is what makes us humans and that's what enables individuals to have more faith in the beauty of this world and have faith in themselves, for there is so much beauty to be enjoyed, if only we had the will to see and help others to see it, for that would make all of us so much more grateful and less bitter, and that's a world we would all love to live in.

   Your Actions Define Your Existence

Story 4

A woman, by the name of Emily (her real name is different), was once one of my family's closest friends, as she was close to both Mom and Dad and our extended family as well, as her parents were close with our grandparents. And so, growing up, I always saw her flashing all of her riches in an absolutely insane and incredible way for she was known to be a spendthrift. Her husband had an incredible transportation business and apart from that they also had a pretty decent clothing shop, which meant they had multiple sources of income in different ways and all of those sources of money were giving them a really good and amazing flow of money into their lives. They would visit 3-4 countries every year, which was quite fascinating for me, for I myself may not have heard of the number of countries they had visited, as I was a kid back then and plus during those days information wasn't as easily abundant in today's day and age. Anyways, and so her family's life was something so many people envied, for that was the power of their incredible lifestyle. Her daughter was studying in the most expensive school in the city and the cars they would use to drop their daughter to the school was something that would grab everybody's attention, for that's how incredible and extravagant those cars were. And so, in a nutshell, they were really an incredibly wealthy family (at least looked so) and the things they did back then around 2004-05 are some of the things nobody in the family has ever done. I remember once I had gone with their family to a nearby resort and over there her younger brother was also there, and he had been an extravagant fitness freak back then. And so, he saw the gym equipment and asked the manager why such incredible equipment was not being maintained properly. The gym manager told him (in front of me) that barely anybody uses the gym, for people come to here and to have drinks and rest and that's why I have been looking for somebody to buy these products. And so, the brother asked the manager how much, he said around 10 lakhs Rupees (12,000 US dollars), as soon as he heard the price he went to his sister and I could hear him telling her that he could use these products in his new gym that is planning to set-up and told her how it would be a bargain for he is giving them at discounted rates. And guess what, within barely 5 mins of the conversation Emily had with her brother, she used her and her husband's credit card and bought that equipment, and I just couldn't believe what I had seen, for it was absolutely ludicrous to even think that somebody would make such a huge transaction in 5 mins, that too 17-18 years back. And then while coming back I didn't say a single word in the car for I couldn't believe what I had seen, as I had heard about big millionaires spending like this, and I literally felt like being inside a movie for that's how surreal and incredible the event was.

But then about a year later, her husband passed away due to alcoholism and Emily's life changed.

Emily had never ever been involved with her husband's business in any stretch for she was known as the one spending all of her husband's hard earned money (that was literally how she was known everywhere), but there was a side very few people had seen of hers. She was an extremely helpful and non-diplomatic individual. She was somebody who would lend you money at the first instance, especially if she ever knew that you were in some sort of trouble. I have seen her help so many incredible people in so many incredible ways, something which very few people knew about her. And the reason I appreciate her is because, no doubt the money she helps with is her husband's, but what we do with the money really matters. She wasn't one of those snobbish and rude rich women, rather she was so helpful and simply lived life

    Your Actions Define Your Existence

on her own terms and always carried her heart on her sleeve, for she often told me how she doesn't care what people think about her. I used to often tell her why she keeps this part of her hidden, she then told me how it's not hidden, it's just that even if people know about this side of her they choose to ignore it for it gives them comfort and they don't have to change their opinions about her, and that's why they choose to deny it, while at the same time at the first onset of any trouble they would come to her, take her help (mostly financially) and then gossip negative things about her behind the back (something she was aware of). Which I guess is general human nature, for we always put far more emphasis on things that don't make sense and make little out of things that make sense, as that's what makes most humans such insufficient and bitter creatures, who always look at how bad their lives are rather than doing something about it. And so that was Emily for you.

With her husband's death, her managers started cheating her on huge amounts of money, something she had never expected, as a few managers literally fled with huge sums of money they had been given access to by her husband for they were such loyal to him, but with this death, they turned their back on his wife when she needed it the most. Within 1 year after his death, Emily had to sell all the businesses that were owned by her husband and the worst part was that nobody ever came back to help her, which further killed her, for she has always been there for people when they needed it, but when it came to her, she couldn't find anybody. There were times when she would go back to those people to whom she had lent money when they needed money and guess what the very people who once treated her like a Goddess, would now shun her away from their homes. Why? Because she was no longer as rich as she used to be before and she no longer had her husband's finances to back her up in life, and once everybody realised that they took more and more advantage of her. She suffered another tragedy in the form of her dog, as she had to shift her dog to NGO for a few months until she had sorted it all out and guess what, the Dog died within 1 month as he had stopped eating anything for he had gotten heavily depressed and due to that she got broken even further, as that Dog was her support in ways very few people would understand, and now with his death, things really took a turn for worse and she was staring at a life with nobody there for her. And then an even bigger disaster struck.

Her husband who had taken some loans for his business had overdue EMI's left, for she had sold her business and now she was no longer able to pay the EMI's, and due to that, the government kept on coming to her house every day. Then one day what I saw really broke me.

I saw Emily going around in different properties to ask for a place to stay for rent, and when I asked her who is she looking for, she told me for her. I asked her, But WHY? She then told me how the banks had taken over her house because she was unable to pay back a huge loan her husband had taken from the banks. And so, the banks gave her 7 days-time to pay back the entire loan or leave the house, and when she realised she couldn't pay the loan she had to leave the house.

Hearing all of these absolutely crushed me, and taught me how cruel life can get when we least expect it. the woman who was once a queen was now turned into a commoner in no time, and she had to expect the fate, but it was a really brutal period.

But the worst part in all of this was her family's response to all of it. Nobody like literally not a single family member came forward to help her, while she was going through literally the worst crisis of her life. Even her brother for whom she had done so much had

  Your Actions Define Your Existence

abandoned her and had refused to give her a place to stay as now he was married but yet he should have stood up for his sister, for she has always stood up for him and has given him way more than any sister could have ever given for. He completely cut her from her life and literally told her not to bother him anymore as he was a husband and he could no longer look out for her, something which I once got to know from several individuals made me lose all the respect, I ever had for him, for as a man he should have gone and taken control of himself and helped his sister in whatever ways he could have, for that's what a man does.

We often prioritise our own selfish needs in comparison to somebody's lives and that's the reason humanity has collapsed in the ways it has and if it continues things will continue to get worse. Our willingness to satisfy our own luxurious and self-centered needs often creates far more chaos and panic than being content with things. At the same time, I truly understand that when an individual is facing so many obstacles in their lives, going and saving somebody else is overkill, but what about those who are in the position to help others and yet decide to choose themselves rather than making a difference? Why is it that Jenny's brother who had 4 storied buildings all for himself and his wife couldn't find a single room for his sister, the same sister who never ever said no to any of his demands and yet this is what she got in return.

But guess what, When I told these to Jenny, her response was-"Neel I cannot go and force people to help me, if they do it will be incredible and I will regard them as my saviour and if they don't what can I do". And once she finished saying these words, I saw how she broke down in the middle of the road and left. And that's a suffering that she was battling all alone, and the decision of her family members and her dear ones, to not help her and rather let her stay in misery and suffer alone, made her a "Silent Suffer". People who once greeted her with a wide smile and called her 'Mam"were now suddenly treating her as a nobody for she no longer lacked the financial prowess she once had and that led to her feeling one of the lowest in her life, due to which she often contemplated giving up her life, for she no longer had any faith left in humanity and was now drowning in alcohol and cigarettes, for that would enable her to never come back in sense of all the misfortune she had to endure in the last 15 months, and if possible it would also push her towards an existence where she is no longer present and that would mean that people would no longer hurt her, for she no longer exists anymore and that's not something any of us had ever imagined would happen to her. But that's the reality of life, and that's when life really tests us and breaks us in ways we could have never imagined, and that's when a helping hand makes all the difference.

And that's exactly what happened.

Jenny During this time met a man through social media. How did I know? Well once while taking a walk across a nearby hill area I saw a familiar face of a woman sitting with a man, at first, I couldn't recognise her but then she called out my name and then introduced me to him. I told her how I was genuinely happy that she had finally decided to come out of her house, to which she told she had left the house after 3 months, I asked her what about food, and she said she ate whatever was there and in case she needs anything she tells the grocery delivery man to give her a bit of something (no online apps back then) but bring some good bottles of whisky, for which she paid extra to that man for his own alcohol, and that's how she has been surviving. She tells me she drinks a bottle every-day and eats food like Maggi or maybe some junk to survive and sometimes she has gone even 2 days

    Your Actions Define Your Existence

without food and only drinks and smokes, as she felt there was no point in living any more, for every moment she was awake and was in her senses, it only brought her more and more pain.

Hearing all this shocked me. Then while coming back I realised how Jenny may be one of the cases somebody I know. As similarly so many other individuals in different parts of the world, may be going through similar or even worse struggles in their lives and with nobody to help them. And these are the individuals who when falling into the wrong company of individuals end up becoming the next mass shooter, rapist, or criminal, for they no longer have any sympathy for humans and want others to feel their dread and pain, with no fault of theirs, and that's how innocent lives are impacted. But for Jenny, she was lucky to have met that man and turns out as she told me, that today was the first time she had not drunk or smoked a single cigarette in 3 months as the man she is with, who I would call Marcus, had not allowed her to do it, and that's when I felt she has found somebody who is pulling her out of this misery she is in, although I still had doubts for we should not trust somebody at our first meet, but you can make a lot with somebody's eyes and body language (something I learned during my trip to Azerbaijan where a local guy who took me around explained to me how to read people for he once was in the police department) and Markus looked like somebody with good intentions and the things that followed proved me right.

Markus was a low-ranking government officer, who didn't have much wealth or property to lure Jenny towards her but what he had was a heart of Gold something he shared with Jenny, for she was also a woman with a Golden heart. He started meeting her more frequently for he himself was divorced and even after knowing how everybody asked him to stay away from her, for they had told him incredibly fabricated stories about her, he didn't budge for he felt a sense of connection with her. As he had himself gone through a similar phase during his own divorce (he told me) and so he knew how it feels to be so helpless and so hopeless about our own existence, that we give up on life altogether. But what that experience helped him was that it made him understand the crucial value of support during this time. And that's what he decided to be for Jenny and support her during this tough time. He started by making Jenny drink alcohol only 4 times a week as before it was 7 days a week. In the meantime, I started seeing Jenny on morning walks with Markus, something which was incredibly rare and yet great to see. Then within a few months, Jenny was drinking only once a week and going to the gym thrice a week, and within a year, she completely left alcohol and ran an incredible 7 KM marathon, which was impossible for her if we compare it to her situation a few months back. She smokes once in a while, but she told me how she is no longer dependent on those things but rather consumes them whenever she feels like it, as those vices have become very rare and she told me how it was all because of Markus that she has become who she has become, and she regards him as sent by God to save her life. But his gestures didn't stop there, as he was hellbent on making her turn her life around.

Soon after putting her life back on track and making her move away from her vices, Markus realised it was time for Jenny to get back in the game, and soon he opened her a new clothing shop, for clothes were her love affair as she owned quite a few shops of it. Although the ones Markus opened weren't as grand or big as the previous ones Jenny owned, they were an incredible thing for Jenny for she was back in working in a business. And guess what happened, the day the clothing shop opened, Markus proposed to Jenny, and they both got married that day, and since then there has been no stopping her. Today she owns a total of 5 clothing

     Your Actions Define Your Existence

shops in the city, while her husband is now among the biggest officials in the entire city for, he really worked hard for himself and his new family. Jenny now has a daughter with Markus and they both have really turned things around. They even bought a few plots of land to start their own agriculture business and recently bought an apartment to permanently shift over there, and they both now really support and love each other and ensure that they grow together. Their daughter has grown up to be an absolute beast, as she is so independent and self-sufficient in her own ways, any guy would get intimidated (something she has learnt from her mom), but at the same time she is compassionate and helpful to anybody who comes to her for help and makes sure that she does what she can do in her power, and that's what makes the difference. Her brother's business has gone all downhill, but Jenny has learned from her past mistakes and left her brother to fend for himself, unfortunately, he has failed miserably at it, as he had to sell his bungalow and is now living in a rented space, divorced from his wife and financially dead. This shows how "what goes around often comes around" and that's what he is suffering from.

What this story teaches us is how when we break the shackles that have bound us for so long it often takes us to places, we had never expected to go. Jenny was stuck in a place where she felt death and giving up on life altogether was the only option to rid herself of the pain she had been feeling after being stabbed, bruised and betrayed by the people she once considered her own. There were days when she felt unworthy of being alive and so secluded and lonely as if the devil had himself come to reside in her house and be the shadow in her life, for that's what she was going through. Her house had been taken away, her business shut, her money lost, and her dog's death, she literally had nothing to live for and maybe in a few days we would have heard the news of her death (which would have been devastating for me), but it was then that I have to believe that Destiny sent Markus into her life and he completely changed everything. At first, she was skeptical to meet him for he may turn out to be another one of those strangers who traps her, but she took that leap of faith and met him and that completely changed our life. At the same time, Markus has to be credited for being the man that he is and for doing what he did. For his actions define what humanity is about, and he showed how even though we may not be living the best of our lives and we ourselves may be broken but we should help people who are facing it worse than us, for most of the time it makes us twice the person that we could ever be and that's a life that we should all strive for. For what else is our short mortal existence on our planet about if not to do what we can and help others, especially the ones who are about to accept death and reject life?

It's a reminder for us that sometimes we have incredible power within ourselves that can do things we have never thought we are capable of, for that's what makes us human. We must understand that we don't have to be a higher dimensional being or a superhuman to help others, rather we should emphasise the fact that being human is super in itself and when we learn how to use that power, we can make incredible impact in people's lives, and that impact can help people come out of incredible amount of misery and hell, and that's what we should all strive for.

Markus's acts were simply out of a well-intentioned nature to help someone who had deviated from the path, and that's the least we could do to help individuals suffering in silence and whose suffering has crushed their souls. The fact that he negated people's opinions about Jenny and their pathetic fabricated stories about her, tells how he is ten times the man that Jenny's brother could ever be and that's what being Man is about. Being

     Your Actions Define Your Existence

a Man is about being responsible and accountable for our actions and helping people to the best of our capabilities while negating general opinions and yet being careful, for when we are able to do these things, we become the person of our dreams, and there is nothing better than growing together and doing things that we always imagined, and if a small act of help, initiates a process where there is one less "Silent sufferer" than the world would be a much more happier place and have far fewer people who have embraced misery and have lost their faith in live itself, as that's not the world we would want to live in, and that's the society we should strive to have, for that's a very bleak and dark way of life. Especially on such a bright and beautiful planet of ours, that's a waste of potential and the incredible ability that comes along with being human and having the capacity to change the world for the better.

Learnings

These stories simplify and detail the fact that how it takes only one small thing to change somebody who is suffering in silence and has fallen into the category of a "Silent Sufferer", and that small act is having the courage to lend out our hand and asking the other person to come on our boat as we know our boat (our lives) is strong enough to hold another person, especially if that person is drowning and is starring at death head on. Suffering comes in different forms, some are its victims of war, some because of domestic abuse, some due to bad parenting, and some due to sexual assaults, I Mean it can come in such shapes and sizes that we simply can't fathom ever being prepared for it, no matter how strong we are, but what matters is how we react to it.

It's important that as humans we open our eyes to the limitless potential that we have within ourselves, truly trust our gut and are willing to be there for people who are in need. The one we should always keep in mind is the fact that helping somebody in need might make us lose a bit of ourselves in the form of time, finances or sanity as it's tough pulling someone out who is 3 feet away from hell, but in the future it makes us twice the person we could ever be. For when we enable another individual in their process of growth we grow along with them, and in that process, we are made to face up with situations and moments in life we had never thought we would face, and that makes us way tougher than we had ever imagined. And in that process, we also rid the world of individual suffering in silence, for our hand has propelled them towards the path of growth and that makes life way more worthwhile than we could have ever imagined.

It is upon us how we are willing to live our lives on this planet, either we choose to be involved and be pre-occupied in our own selfish indulgences or we are willing to step outside our own selves and be of use to the world as a whole. And choosing the former gives us internal conflict for we choose to be involved in our own desires and realise how being delusional in our own needs doesn't give much meaning to our existence. But when we choose the latter option, we are able to make our lives so much more than what we have learned about ourselves. We become individuals who are willing to be answerable for somebody who has given up on their life, and when that somebody sees you stand up for them, it motivates them to stand them for themselves, and when that happens, they are halfway down their road to their recovery and that makes their lives so much more than bitterness, despair and anxiousness, and that's a life they always dreamt off, but simply lacked the courage and the willpower to go for it. But once you offered your hand to them, you once again make them believe in that dream of theirs and that makes them far more powerful than they had ever imagined, and that's something we should always aim for.

   Your Actions Define Your Existence

We must understand the simple fact that from the time we are born and until we are dead, troubles, setbacks and issues will be there. There is a very high probability that some of you may always be on tenterhooks and may always be in a state of risking everything either for good or bad. But ask yourself, am I capable of handling myself in the most basic of ways, and if that's a yes you can for certain help someone climb out of their misery for the least that is needed to help them is your willingness to be there for them and complementing and reminding them that their lives mean to you, and you don't care about the number of people for whom their lives does not matter, for that's beyond your control. And so, once you put that faith in those individuals it enables them to get up and fight for themselves and that's what all of these individuals did in all four of these stories.

All of them at one point of time in their lives, felt it was all over and that misery and desperation were their only form of existence. But once they were given a vision of what the other side holds and what they could be if they said "yes" to these courageous individuals who have come to help them negate their own self, these same depressed and bitter individuals become somebody they had never imagined and that has given a new meaning to their lives. And once they have tasted the other side of what it could be, they are motivated and encouraged to help those who are in that broken and butchered state they once were and that creates a chain effect of individuals helping each other and pushing themselves out of misery. And when we do that, we start realising that the Devil is now being pushed out of all those places he once considered home, and when he tries to fight back the resentment is far more than he could have ever imagined, and step by step we are able to eradicate Devil ourselves, for that's where the hope on "God" or "universe" begins with, for God is always within us, it only matters whether we are willing to listen to it and fight our battles ourselves with its help. And once we choose to fight, we become what we could have never imagined and that makes the surroundings and the people around less resentful and less bitter than we could have ever imagined, and that's a world we would all love to wake up to.

 Your Actions Define Your Existence

FOUR

The True Cost of Being Yourself

"There is a price for everything", well that's what the old timers used to say and there is a truth to it as well, especially in today's capitalist modern day and age. But do you know what's most expensive thing in today's day and age? It's not those expensive watches, neither those expensive cars, those first-class flight tickets or those incredible sneakers that you had seen your favourite celebrity wear but simply can't afford.

The most expensive thing, the thing that would cost you the most and that would take away everything from you in order for you to achieve that goal of yours, **is your decision to be "You"**. Your decision to be yourself and become who you are and accept with no qualms will always be the toughest thing that you could ever want to buy. Being yourself comes at a price which only keeps on increasing with time. Unfortunately there are never any flash sales or discounts, and that's the reason a very minuscule number of individuals are able to afford it. For to afford it, you don't need to have a million dollars in your bank account for that's rarely the case, rather what we need is the courage to say "NO" and "Yes" when needed. And that comes only when we are willing to take responsibility and accountability for ourselves and that's something very few people are willing to do.

.In Today's, day and age, it has become really hard for people to be themselves and be authentic and upfront about who they are. For social media often enforces the identities we are able to witness on the various platforms it has. And due to that individuals are having more and more problems in truly knowing themselves for everybody wants to fit in.

There is a great quote by renowned Youtuber **Chris Williamson** who runs his podcast **Modern Wisdom** with around **2.5 million followers** where he gives this famous quote-

> "If you want to be exceptional you are going to be different from everyone else for that's what makes you exceptional. You can't fit in and also be exceptional both have discomfort.
>
> When you fit in you have internal conflict because you are not being 100% you, when you are exceptional you have external conflict, because everyone sees you as different.
>
> Pick one!
>
> When your friends start to say you have changed, remember it's because they don't know how to say you have grown"

This quote very much sums up the fact that being ourselves comes with a lot of price tags and one of the biggest price tags is that we are going to be shamed, judged and battered by the various different judgements of different people from various aspects of our lives. These events make it an extremely difficult and arduous task for us to do things that we feel or judged to be right, for there will always be opinions and different perspectives on the same thing at the same time, and it is at those moments that we are truly tested and we have to truly believe in what we have set for, as all of them who disagreed with us are anticipating our failure to complete that task and that's why it becomes such a difficult thing to implement and do things based on what we feel like doing and what we truly believe in.

Doing things in our own ways sets the two types of people apart. The ones who lead and the ones who follow, and to lead we have to be willing to embarrass ourselves to an extent we may have never imagined for those who lead oftentimes have to take up tasks that have not yet been tried due to its herculean natures or may have either be abandoned due to the repeated failure in completing those tasks and that's why very few are willing to lead.

For the latter half, it's all about doing what the leader has asked them to do, for there are very few risks and many question marks in implementing the tasks given out to them as the tasks and their difficulties have already been tested out by their leader. But most of the time, the ones following the leader give up or leave the journey midway due to unfulfillment or due to the rise of their ambitions, for they are tired of being somebody else and allowing somebody else to make a profit out of their hard work, but sadly very few can do that, as doing that makes our life unpredictable and invites criticism while following the crowd gives us company and gives us the feeling of doing what we can, while in reality we are capable of achieving incredible things as humans.

Yet, the most common question many individuals ask is why being ourselves is such a big deal. What's wrong with falling in line?

Well, there is nothing wrong in falling in line and not being ourselves, for who wants to be shamed and questioned for every goddamn thing they do, as not doing them is much easier than doing them. But ask yourself this question, am I content with who I am? Am I doing things based on what I feel like doing? Am I doing things that fulfill me? If the answer is Yes, I guess you are doing incredible, but if the answer is No, it's about time you start being true to yourself. And doing that will cause a lot of pain and suffering in your mind. As you reflect on your actions and choices to date, and when you come to realise that you have been living a life and being somebody you aren't proud of, you are pushing yourself to a life filled with regret and resentment. And with time both of these factors would be made more and more miserable, as your life is no longer an extension of your needs and choices, rather it's an extension of the choices and needs you have been forced upon by the ones who surround the vicinity of

    Your Actions Define Your Existence

your life. These individuals with their own burden of regrets and their own lack of courage to accept their true self is pushing you towards becoming an individual who laughed at you when you decided to introspect by looking at the mirror and being honest with yourself. And the reason it laughed at you, was because it was sad that you weren't even trying to do your part in achieving that version of you that is less bitter and less resentful and is far more content with the life than you are living right now.

But the larger question is, if it will make us less bitter and less resentful of ourselves, why isn't everybody doing it, for that would make a world far more peaceful and content to live in?

Because taking that path of retrospection, by reflecting on those actions of ours is a path that's filled with shame and regret over our past actions. For who wants to accept the cowardly path they took out of fear of retaliation, as it is a peace that we all want, and yet we are at war with our minds most of the time. We are fighting several battles with ourselves each and every day all because we want peace on the outside. But was it really worth it? Was it worth to spend such a short mortal lifespan of ours imitating and becoming someone we are ashamed of?.

The answer is, it's easier said than done.

For example- **In an article published by Forbes magazine, they found out while interviewing around 100 participants regarding their biggest regrets. An astonishing 72% of them regretted not becoming their ideal self, or becoming that version of themselves they could have, by trying things they should have.**

This data very much points out how individuals don't regret buying that watch or that car they once loved. Rather the fact that couldn't muster the courage and ask themselves

whether they would like to go on the path that would make them capable enough to afford themselves, is what kills them. The reason they didn't ask that big question is because of one thing, FEAR.

Fear is something that paralyses us, for it is fear that dictators use to rule over people, it is used by narcissistic parents to dominate their kids and it is used by the winners to dominate the losers. Most of the time it's our simple minds that allow us to stay where we are for everything that we once wanted to do, and did, was first conceptualised in our minds and only then were we able to apply it in the material world. And it is the mind that wars and battles are won or lost, and it is the mind that allows a human to dominate others and make them subservient to them.

Some might think, well I am not afraid, I am willing to go out there and achieve the things I can achieve, but it is responsibilities that are tying me down. Well, the bad news is, from the time of our birth and until our death we will be burdened with responsibilities. .Men will have different sort of responsibilities while the women a different sort of them. Both genders will have to make their own chunk of sacrifices in order to live even the most basic of lives as without sacrifices we make our lives the most miserable any human could ever witness, but in many cases, our sacrifices account for our families and their overall personal goals and there are far too many people who become bitter and resentful that they had to give up on their goals for their family. And that's the truth, if you are a responsible man you have a lot to worry about for people will count on you, and you have to deliver for them, or else you will be regarded as an individual with pathetic potential. And so, you work late hours, avoid the gym, leave your hobbies, and stop attending your favourite events all because you want your dear ones to be happy, and yet when you come home you

  Your Actions Define Your Existence

are greeted into a hostile and unwelcoming atmosphere either by your parents or by your partner or maybe even by your immature kids, and you feel sad and you get depressed. And you ask why only me? I did so much for them and this is how they treated me, well I guess I should give up on my life altogether, for that might make them happy.

Honestly, this is the life story of many individuals in today's world. Some completely give up, while others appear alive on the outside but feel dead inside. So, how do you navigate such a situation?

In order to avoid such a scenario and make yourself less bitter than you are, you have to accept where you are who you are. And once you do that you are better prepared to tackle such challenges. You have to accept the universal truth that, no matter how hard you work and no matter how much you sacrifice, you or your actions will never be enough, even for your dear ones, for only you can see it through your eyes, while most people see it through their own and that gives them a different point of view. And then my question comes, since now you are aware that even your best will disappoint them, so why not shift some energy towards your own selves, and towards your own ambitions and aspirations, as they had been buried under the burden of responsibilities. But now you are aware of the fact that these responsibilities will remain and you can't do anything about it, but rather than doing it to make them happy, why not do something to make yourself more content and that might lead to you a path of happiness you always dreamt of and that's a path very few are willing to take.

Becoming aware of our capabilities as humans is like being reborn. It's as if we took a dive inside a deep tunnel and on the other side was a life where we are far more becoming of ourselves. Although the road that goes through that tunnel is one that is filled with incredible amounts of obstacles and setbacks, it is upon us to make ourselves aware that what lies on the other side will make us far stronger and way more competent in handling these obstacles and setbacks. And that would mean we are halfway on the journey to becoming the true version of ourselves. Along the journey, we gather various brownie points that make such a tough and arduous journey worth our energy and time.

Let's explore the incredible ways our lives improve and become much more fulfilling once we choose to align our life decisions with our true selves.

Earning back self-esteem

Earlier when you were living your lives and fulfilling the day-to-day responsibilities with time and with focus like you are used to, it creates a sense of monotonous habits and choices in both you and your dear one's lives. And one of the biggest things that happen is that your family members (parents, partner, children) start taking you for granted for they are well aware of the fact that no matter what happens, you will always fulfill your responsibilities and you will always be there for them and you will always do the needful no matter what happens. They could ask you for things even when you are not prepared, or things you simply could not afford and yet you will deliver it to them sooner or later, for you realise that's your responsibility. But the change happens when you take back control of your lives.

For example- earlier you would come home from work and do all the chores that your kids had not done and your wife may have ignored you as she was busy with her own passionate work, but now you simply refuse to budge. You stand up and tell them, **"Everybody listen"** I love you all, and I know I have been doing everything all along, but some of the things need to be divided as I have decided to join the gym to lose some weight and take

    Your Actions Define Your Existence

health in my own hands, or maybe join this singing class to help with your mental health.

The moment you say these things, your family will rebel as they are simply not used to you standing for yourself and putting time aside for yourself in such a focused way, for some time in your lives there will be disharmony, there will be opposition as your partner (could be wife/husband as change could take place for both sexes), partners and even your children might tell you that you are simply too old to either hit the gym or start music classes all over again as that's your past and you are more suitable with your job and your household chores. It is that time you will be inclined to go back to your own self and stay on this new path of yours and be resilient and be hell-bent on achieving your newfound goals regarding either your physical or mental health. And once you muster up the courage to no longer fall back into the trap, you will have to take that leap of faith and make that jump, and that's something that will put you on a path of becoming an individual you could have never imagined.

While taking this path, the beginning won't be as incredible or as insane as you had imagined for you would be inclined to quit either your gym classes or your singing classes but trust me once you get past that barrier you will simply be unstoppable. You will become someone you could have never ever imagined and in the process, you will start respecting yourself and your decisions and choices far more than you could have ever imagined and that's when the real change would happen.

Your family or your peers would start noticing that you have changed as a person, it could either be a fitter or happier you, could be both and once they realise that they would start to accept that you can no longer be taken for a ride or taken for granted. People will start treating you with much more courtesy and respect, and will think twice before crossing your boundaries for they know now, how much you value yourself and how hard you have worked on yourself and when that happens they will be cautioned (in a positive way) and that would make your self-esteem become so much better than you could have ever imagined and that would further propel you into the path of becoming the best version of yourself, while at the same time staying true to your responsibilities. The only difference you made was you made some extra room for yourself in your own life and yet kept on shouldering the burdens needed for your dear one's well-being. Once you do that, your life improves significantly, as you not only take pride in handling responsibilities but also in investing in your personal growth. And when that happens the people around you start regarding you much higher in esteem aspect and that makes you feel powerful and far less bitter and less resentful and that's something we should all aim for.

It's not rocket science or anything complicated, it was simply an act in which an individual made some time for himself in the hope that he would be less resentful and that's what exactly happened. And that is what we need to do. We don't need to negate our responsibilities or be cruel or harsh towards our dear ones for giving us so much responsibility, as that's a given. But what we can do is set some time aside for ourselves and make ourselves less of the complaining and bickering individual we are at the moment. Once we start doing things based on our intuition and for our own betterment, we become more confident and can fulfil our responsibilities with less bitterness, as now we have something to look forward to in our lives, and doing that really pushes us towards a life that is incredibly better than the unfulfilled and unhappy life we are living for our entire lives. Taking up this initiative won't guarantee you a happily ever after life, for that's a fantasy and nobody gets to witness that, but

    Your Actions Define Your Existence

what you can witness is a life in which you wake up from bed knowing you will get to do that thing you love. And that means even if 80 percentage of your day is gone doing things you don't like, 20 percentage of is now spent doing something you like. And if you continue to persevere and stay consistent, with time that 80 percentage will go down to 60 and even further, while that 20 percentage will go up to 40 and even further, based on your grit, willpower and dedication towards having a far more fulfiled and less bitter life. And once these changes happen, even your surroundings change and that would mean a life where your family, peers and dear ones, no longer look down upon your choices, but rather admire them and look upon and that's something you should always strive for.

Makes you accept failures and wins gracefully

Has it ever happened to you that you were made to do something that you were completely critical of? You were absolutely against it and yet your boss, colleague or maybe even someone from your family made you do it for their own self-interest! And then that particular thing absolutely failed and you were gutted and you were made the scapegoat for not implementing it well enough and the pain that you felt for failing that particular task killed you, but what killed you even more was that you were made to do something you had not even wanted to do, and now you are being forced to face the brunt of its failures because the plan failed, although in a contrasting way had the plan worked and had it succeeded than you would not have been given any credit for it, rather the ones who made the plan would get all the credit, then why should you take the blame for their failures?

Well, unfortunately this is what individuals have to go through their lives all the time. They are made to do things that would have made no positive impact on their lives and now they are being made to face the brunt of all the things that have happened for no fault of theirs. This is what happens when we do things that we neither believe in nor feel inclined to do and once we are made to feel the repercussions of that decision, we feel even worse about ourselves and most of the time we end up blaming others in order to negate responsibility. And this does not happen once or twice such things will keep on happening as long as we continue to live our lives in the same pattern that we have been living for the many years we have been alive, for how can we expect the situation and the outcome to get better when we are doing the same thing and have been living the same way. For if we keep on doing what we have been doing, we are going to keep on getting what we are getting. And so, in order to change the situation and tilt things towards our way, we have to take a step, and that step is going to ensure what or how things pan out in the future.

For example, picture yourself working on a project you designed, running a company you founded, or taking on a challenge entirely at your own risk. And you fail at them. Either the project you had undertaken has failed miserably, either your company has deviated from the path you wanted it to take, as you made some really bad decisions, or you got injured while working out in the gym. Now all of these things could happen, in fact, they have happened to an incredible number of individuals in their lives, but you know what, there will be a huge difference in the way you will react to them. For, in the previous situation, you had complained about how this situation had been warned by many and yet they decided to go through, but in the latter situation you won't complain rather at first you will get angry or sad, and you will be frustrated or scared for a little while, and after that, you will get down to fix the issues that led to such a negative outcome, and that's the biggest difference that would happen.

    Your Actions Define Your Existence

The reason you would start fixing the issue rather than staying in a perpetual state of bickering and bad mouthing those who compelled you to do it, is because this time you were the reason it failed, your decisions led to that particular mishappening, but you know what, you take full responsibility for it, why? Because it was your choice to do it and nobody else's. Somebody else or maybe your employees may have assisted, but if you are true you will take responsibility for yourself, rather than blaming it on your employees (something your crooked boss had done), and when you take responsibility, you realise the feeling that comes along with failure and when that happens it motivates you to make sure it does not happen again. And the only reason you are willing to do all of it is because you are in charge of yourself and you failed to do something you believed in, and that makes all the difference in how we approach and do things.

When we fail after doing something that we either loved or had to do as the onus was upon us, it creates growth rather than resentment. As we no longer feel frustrated about where we are or who we are. Rather we take it in our stride and move ahead with what has happened and make sure we do things in a much better and more efficient way. Although that may not guarantee success, what it will do is that it will create a process in which you are willing to take more risks but in a much more calculated manner and that will create the path for a much for favourable success. But the biggest thing that would happen in this process is that you will embrace failure and have a smile at it, and due to that when you succeed you will be much more content and graceful as you will know how failure can happen in an instant and when these changes would happen, it would make the twice the person you could have ever dreamt off, and all of this was only possible because you decided to make that change and do something you wanted to do for yourself.

Now, some of you might be saying well I cannot quit my job in an instant or I cannot take up something new as I am already overburdened with so many new things. Well, that's true, and if that's the case then you better stop complaining or cribbing about your situation for it was you who decided to take action or take a new step to change your life. As I had stated before, **"If you do what you have been doing you will get what you are getting"**.

And so, if you want your lives to change and your current situation to get better, then you have to take that step. Now that does not mean you have to necessarily quit your job, for that would be foolishness especially if your family depends on it. But you could start by starting a side business on something that you are interested in and you could work on that after your office timings, and that would mean, certain sleepless nights, investing some money on something that could fail badly, as these are risks that could backfire your decisions. But at the same time, these decisions are what will guide and define who you will become in the next 5 years and what will be your situation. And if you such risky and bold steps, chances are 5 years down the line you could be doing something you love, and winning and failing at something you love would make you far less resentful and far less bitter. When you win your company and you along with its employees and while you lose you will lose, but this time you will be doing all of these doing something you believe in and that makes a world of difference.

Making impulsive decisions and maybe arguing and fighting with your narcissistic boss and blaming your situation is far easier, as in this case you don't have any responsibility and could shift the entire blame on him for treating you this way. Tomorrow when you wake up you will be back again doing something and become

     Your Actions Define Your Existence

somebody you absolutely despise. But if you take that step and have that faith in yourself you will do all of those things, but you will be doing it by being in charge of something you absolutely believe in and that would make you a much more contend man for you will be able to take responsibility for your actions and that would push you towards becoming the best version of yourself.

So, choose how you would want to take wins and losses or embrace success and failure. As all of them are guaranteed in this short mortal lifespan of ours. The decision you have is whether you want to embrace them by being somebody and doing somebody you despise or doing something and becoming who you embrace. Whatever you do will decide the future course of your life. It's all upon what and who you choose to be, the only thing that is required is the courage, grit and willpower to believe in those decisions and the faith and work ethic to persevere towards them, for they will make you uncomfortable but the rewards will make you contend for life and that would make your existence far less miserable and would actually propel you towards living life becoming the "You", you yourself know about and the "You" you are able to respect, for you endured so many things to become this version of yourself. For in the end, it's all worth it, so why don't all of you try it out at once, for how bad could happen in all your already miserable lives?

Take the step and make the decision to embrace success and failures by doing something you believe in.

You start appreciating everyday

Our minds have been conditioned in a way. We are made to think that, Monday, Tuesday, Wednesday and Thursday are made to live out in the most unhappy manners, cribbing almost every minute of our existence within these days, sulking over the fact that why isn't the clock moving faster so that you could go home and be yourself and also being unhappy and angry with yourself that you have to live your lives in a way where most of the week is spent doing things and being somebody you hate.

Then comes Friday, Saturday and Sunday, these three days are like your guilty pleasure, similar to having an incredibly delicious dessert after the end of your main course, for that's what exactly these days are as they are the end of the week. You party, meet your friends, travel and really have a great time until the dreaded Sunday evening hits and you realise that tomorrow morning will once again be a struggle and you will find it really hard to get out of bed as you hate the coming few days.

But, ask yourself this question, **who asked us to live this way**? Who told you that this is the way of life and this is how it's going to be?! Who made the rule that it is only on weekends that you are entitled to feel happy and the next few days are meant for your suffering? Does death come on weekdays for it wants you to enjoy your weekends? No right.

Then why the hell do you choose to live your life and be happy only on weekends?

At that moment, we must choose how we want to live within the brief time we have.

Now, let's get one thing straight, if you are a competent individual then your job is going to stay for that's what is earning you and your family the livelihood, Mondays will keep on coming and your boss will keep on hitting at you, either for your mistakes or if he is a narcissistic and coward prick he will keep on picking you out in order to hide his incompetence. So, what do you do in such an instance, well why not add something on your Mondays?

Why not start writing something you have been planning for quite a while? Why not start planning something with your friend

 Your Actions Define Your Existence

or whoever you were planning with! Why not go for that run you thought would make you look forward to Monday! Why not go for the gym session before the office, in order to set yourself up for the day?

There are tons and tons of things that could be done by people and yet we avoid it. During my stay in Mumbai, I once met an individual who used to travel 3 hours up and down and yet attend the office, do her yoga classes and get back home. And I used to admire that women so much. And I used to often ask her, how the hell do you do it? She gave me a simple answer, "Because I want to". I asked her, "But how do you manage time?" She replied, "By avoiding the obvious", and I was like what was that, She said "Avoiding useless office gossip, cutting down the time on my phone usage". She even told me that no matter how much she tries to gel in she will always be judged for who she is and how she is, and it gives her comfort to know the fact that no matter what she does and how much good she does they will never ever accept her for who she is, and that gives her peace and that allows us the willpower to push through her day, by being someone who doesn't complaint but is rather willing to utilise the short amount of time that she gets in a span of 24 hours. Today she has founded her own small bakery and it's an incredible success. She started her own café and is now planning to start her own yoga centre while all those gossiping about her are still in that office discussing things about her, but she is long gone. But what is to be pointed out is that everything was the same to her. The boss was as rude and cocky towards her as he was towards everyone, he was as demanding towards her as towards others, her in-laws were as judgmental towards her as others, and all she had to do was choose how to react, and that's where she won.

She was really able to negate all of it and do things that she knew would one day change her future. She negated her in-laws' demands for a child and their shaming for a woman being ambitious and yet today nobody is prouder of her than her in-laws. During covid, her husband lost his job and it was then that she asked him to join her business ever since then they both have been working together and that's the reason they are going from strength to strength and are now contending for who they have become and what she has created. But at the same time, she had her setback, for some time she would doubt and ask me whether this would work and I would often tell her what was there to lose, and she would smile and tell me thank you. There would be times (especially covid) when she felt that what all of them said was true and now her business was going to flunk due to her ambitious nature, but guess what she faced and endured all of it. And today she does feel it's all worth it and every day there is a new challenge, but guess what she looks forward to those challenges as she knows how the outcome is largely on her and her husbands and that makes them look forward to tomorrow and the many Monday's and Tuesday's that would come.

Similarly, through this story, I don't intend to force people to start their own businesses for if everybody owned a business, who they would work for them. But the least we could all do is find a bit of clarity in our lives, what we want to do and where we want to be 5 years down the line. And along the way we will disappoint a lot of people, we will be judged by a lot of people, we will be shamed, taunted and embarrassed many times even by our own parents or partners, but what we have to realise is that maybe they don't see the visions we see and that they are right in their own way and you are right in your own way. And that would give you much more comfort rather than fighting a battle you know where there would be no clear winner. Rather than

 Your Actions Define Your Existence

hating the Monday, why not start implementing something after your office hours, and will it allow your lives to be the same, of course not, you might get sleepless nights. For instance, it's 2 am right now as I am writing these lines as I couldn't sleep tonight, I was in the zone to finish these words, especially for someone like me who regards sleep as one of the most important pillars of life and due to fitness freak nature, due to which for the last 8 years I have been sleeping by 9 PM and waking by 4:30 AM. And yet here I am writing at 2 am, and will it feel good, of course not. As I have work tomorrow, and I will have a bad headache tomorrow and will feel really lethargic, but I can't have it both ways, as I know once this book is completed, I will be able to get back in my old time zone, and even tomorrow If I have no ideas I could sleep really well, but I cannot waste this phase of mine as the **"writer's block"** might once again happen.

That's why it's important that we are willing to do what matters by thinking about who we want to be 5 years down the line, and rather than having 20 years of pain choose 5 years of it, as that would ensure the rest of your life would pass by without you expecting for weekends, rather you would be excited and hyped up for every single day that every day would be the same for you, and that's where you will start appreciating every single day of your lives and not just the weekends, and that is only possible if you are willing to do what is needed to become the best version of yourself, and that is only possible if you start making time for things that matter rather than cribbing about what you have.

Think as if you don't start it today you will regret it tomorrow. There are two types of pain, one that comes from suffering while choosing to become you and one that comes with regret. And the former would fulfil you while the latter would drain you and would make every day of your life as miserable and as bitter as it could and that's the reason you need to do things that make yourself who you know you could be but are simply scared to implement for its uncharted territory. But remember it is in the unknown that we stumble upon things that define our lives for the future. And you should aim for a future where you are an individual who appreciates every single day of your life, as you are living it by becoming who are meant to become and who you could become, and that's a life very few people are able to live and that would make you one of the many and that would also encourage you to truly appreciate every single thing that life gives you every day. And that is only possible if you start moving away from the hatred, resentment and cloudiness by the bitterness of your life, and that's a life where you would hate every single day and that would make you much more miserable and bitter than you may have ever imagined.

So, start the action and do things that would encourage you to appreciate life for its blessings rather than focusing on its bitterness. And remember everybody's actions and plan are different, all you have to do is find yours, for that's where you will find your true purpose in life and that's when you will start cherishing life for what it is, rather than being angry for what it could be.

And remember there are versions of you that even you aren't aware of, for that would be unleashed only when you decide to step out of the comfort zone of being unhappy and staying bitter with people similar to those intentions, and that could only happen when you decide to take a step and start doing things that would make you appreciate and look forward to each and every day rather than hating them. There is so much wisdom and learnings to be gained from each and every day that we simply can't fathom and yet we are so bound and restricted by somebody

   Your Actions Define Your Existence

else's opinions and judgements and that keeps us in a perpetual state of misery and that is something none of us should ever choose to become or choose to do, for life is a blessing, use it and make it worth it, while you are alive, for once you are dead your statues would be ignored and your glories would be forgotten sooner than you could imagine and that should give you the motivation to live life as it comes, rather than wait for it happen, for that rarely happens.

Every day of every week, every week of every month, every month of every year and every year of every decade, is upon you to determine how your future will look like, and based on those initiatives and actions you will be able to either make your days filled with a lot more content or either filled with frustrations or helplessness.

So, get up and make sure you make your days count and do something every day even for a brief moment, for with time those brief moments will soon become lengthy moments, and if you stay consistent those moments will transform into incredible every day, and that's what your goal should be.

Your detractors become your admirers

In life whenever we plan on taking a new step to nourish our lives and become somebody we could become if we push ourselves, we are bound to come upon obstacles and face situations that would push us away from taking on that task and do something worthwhile with our lives. And most of these obstacles come from our fellow humans. They could be our work colleagues, they could be our college mates (aspirations have no age), and in some cases, they could be our guides who may tell us to back down and ease out our lives as doing that might be risky, and in many cases, it could be our family (parents, siblings, partners), for they may be scared that what if what you are planning to undertake might fail horribly and that really scares them. And most of the time these doubters and their reasons are very much valid, for they are simply not used to you taking up such tasks and becoming somebody who is so accountable and responsible for his/her actions and so in the beginning, protests or any sort of turmoil will be quite evident, and if they are not either your goals are too damn small or you could have an amazing company of people around you, which to be honest is very rare in today's day and age. For most of the time, there are reactions to make sure you stay where you are, and it's no fault of theirs for seeing you there has been constant and they are used to it and that gives them comfort. But the bigger decision lies in your hands, whether to keep on doing things that give others comfort and make you uncomfortable today and tomorrow, or do something that would make them uncomfortable today but would make you comfortable today and tomorrow. And when you choose the former you will continue to live your lives the way you have been living, while choosing the latter would make you twice the man you could have ever dreamt of.

The thing that often happens in life is that in order to grow and become something extraordinary we have to integrate some things in our lives that propel us towards a life that we would feel happy and fulfilled with. For instance, as children, we are very curious and often stumble upon things and do them as we are naïve to understand what fear or shame is, but by the time we become adults we end up restricting ourselves in such incredible ways that we start limiting ourselves. What happens during such times is that we go to school and start learning the ways of society. With time, the ways of our general society start getting more and more ingrained into our minds and hearts. And when that happens, we end up becoming individuals who are easily able to fit in with the larger share of the masses and

     Your Actions Define Your Existence

forget who we really are. What it basically does, is it creates a sense of ourselves where we feel we are happy and okay being where we are, for we have such incredible and amazing company surrounding us all the time. We want to grab a beer after work, and we will get many individuals coming along. The sole purpose of that drinking session would be to relieve ourselves of the daily frustration that we had at our unsatisfying workplace, and unfortunately, that satisfaction and the drinks and their effects only last for that particular night, for once we are awake we have to once again go back to our old ways and that cycle keeps on repeating again and again. Similarly, in other aspects of life, if you want to do things that neither elevate you nor neither help you in your growth, you will find an incredible amount of company along, for doing those tasks would give you comfort and would make you feel less miserable for the timing, but in reality most of the times you feel miserable and pathetic about yourselves, and the fact that even those around you end up doing the same things creates an environment where there is no growth and where you keep on repetitively doing the same things and the conditions surrounding you and your environment isn't conducive enough to do things other than what everyone is doing, and that is where we end up losing a sense of ourselves.

But what if you decided to make a change! What if you chose to do something different? What if you decided that you love these folks and these colleagues or friends of yours, but at the same time you do not feel like you are doing everything you could in order to live a life where you could be doing so much more than rubbing shoulders with them, for if they truly are who they often exclaim to be (friends, best friends, lovers) than they will support you in this new path that you are willing to take for your own betterment, and that's where change happens.

Change happens in different ways and at different times. For instance, rather than waking up late and somehow rushing to do the basics before you leave for the job, why not start waking up early so that you can get some things done? It could be either doing your household chores, reading a book, could be hitting the gym or going for a run or could be implementing something on the new business you were planning about. In the same way, you could be reducing the amount of time you were wasting away after office by either indulging in useless and never-ending gossip or going for that out, rather you could be doing all those things in that particular moment that I have stated could be done in the morning. Engaging in these activities will set you on a path where you pursue things you genuinely enjoy. As a result, you'll gain control over certain aspects of your life, leading to continuous growth and improvement over time. In those moments, you'll feel significantly better, experiencing a deep sense of contentment and fulfilment.

But what about the fallout of me now doing things with such a self-centred approach?

Well, to be honest, there would be fallouts. Some would be big while some would be limited to basic reactions. For instance, your colleagues might taunt you, as the very guy who once used to initiate those after office plans is now going on a different path, and once they see those results in you, they will start to ignore you, doubt you and even call out. They will try to push you out of it, they will try to tell you how it's not worth the risk, in fact, there would be moments when they even entitle you and call you things, but one day when you make it and do these things that starts impacting your lives in an incredibly positive way, they would start admiring you for in many ways you are basically living the life they always wanted to live and when that

    Your Actions Define Your Existence

happens it's upon you to take them forward and create a group of individuals who love their existence, rather than despising every moment of it. And when you take them together along with you, they will start admiring you for they stayed the same while changing your entire life around, and that's when they turn into admirers from detractors, and that's something we should aim for. For what is life worth if we are not able to pull somebody else along with us in the journey of growth, for the happiness of growing together far outweighs the happiness of lonely growth, but at the same time, you should also prepare for solo/lonely growth, as not everybody appreciates a helping hand, for some might regard it as demeaning to take the help of somebody who was once their colleague, and individuals with such an attitude towards life, are bound to get jealous and envy you, for they refuse to see the world beyond the lens they feel familiar with. And the very fact that the unknown scares them, makes them stay in that lane of bitterness and resentment.

But when we look at it from another perspective, we can't really blame them, for it is the conditioning of our minds that forces us to stay and contend where we are and become individuals we had never imagined. And so having a bit of jealousy, envy and even hatred is valid towards somebody, especially somebody we know. But the decision to stay there or get up from it makes the difference in our lives, and where we go with it. For either we choose to stay in the same situation and continue calling them out. Or we could join them in this journey of self-discovery along with them, and most often as it happens, doing the latter creates individuals who are far more content with their lives, rather than joining the former. So, it's important that you ask yourself the basic question of whether you want to stay that guy who has hatred and envy towards somebody filled in his heart or you want to be known as somebody who changed his life around by taking that leap.

For the one who made it, Kudos to you, but remember you only have crossed the halfway line, for now, you have to inspire and make the effort to grow collectively and only then will you be regarded as somebody they could look upon. Helping others escape the reality imposed upon us is like being

Demi-God to them, as most of the time, people are so strangled in their basic day to day lives and duties that they forget who they truly are. And if you could do it, even they could, depends upon how they look towards those things and grow together. And once they do that, you would have an armada of admirers who want you to succeed even further, for you have helped so many escape the trap of their hellish existence, and made them appreciate life much more than what they could have ever imagined, and that makes them feel powerful and makes them look towards life with eyes and vision they had long abandoned for they got trapped in the ruins of life, until you pulled them out of it.

This is what existence is about and this is what life should be. Sometimes there isn't much that is needed to do to change our circumstances, all that is needed is the courage to take that leap, or if somebody you know has already taken that step, you should seek their assistance and grow together and if they don't do it, take it upon you to make that change, for that's what life is about.

Make your detractors your admirers, and if they can't admire you, they will hate, either way, you will win, for hatred towards success comes only when you have outwitted them, and that's a win anybody would take any day (at least I would).

Become Stronger than your social media platforms

In modern times we live in a world where the moment we open our phones we are instantly bombarded with an incredible amount of information that we may have never believed could be witnessed in such a short span of time. We are bombarded with information regarding sports, politics, sex, models, fitness, world affairs, and personal information, I mean we are literally bombarded with so many incredible amounts of information that our brains simply can't process at one go.

Jordan Peterson who I consider to be one of my idols, once stated that modern men in today's day and age are able to witness more beautiful men in a day than an emperor might have done during his entire lifetime in the ancient times.

And that statement of his very much defines how individuals in today's day and age can witness so many things daily that it becomes extremely difficult to figure out what's good and what's bad for them. And it is at these moments that we often see how individuals with incredible talent and potential get wasted in the realm of unlimited options, for they start wasting their time doing things that are simply wasting their valuable time. And the worst part is that even your circle is doing the same thing, and due to such things happening, what often happens is that individuals get lost in the plethora of options and are unable to find who they really are, what they really like and what they could become. Choose a path of self-discovery when there's so much to discover in the world around you, and that's where the cardinal sin is committed.

What we have to understand is the simple fact that discovering ourselves isn't just what we should do, rather it's a necessity in order to live a life of contention and a life where we stay true to ourselves and who we are. And what the constant scrolling, liking and commenting does is, it create an illusion in our minds, whereas we end up thinking that all those incredible pictures that people have posted of themselves having a great time are the truth. And that makes us feel sad about ourselves and our own life conditions. It makes us feel as if we are the worst and living the worst of our lives. Whereas the reality is very different.

The reason is that the reality that is shown to us through the various social media platforms, is in truth a lie that is being sold to us by everybody who is on that particular platform. And even if they do tell the truth, it's showcasing the truth of a very small amount of time in an individual's life and yet once somebody uploads a picture of them enjoying and having a blast, we end up thinking that, that's how their lives look like all year round and that's what leads to the rise of insecurity in our minds.

In order to truly become somebody who is content and less bitter with themselves, the first thing we need to do is make ourselves stronger than the incredible number of social media platforms that are prevalent in today's day and age. It's also true that these platforms are often times backed by billions of dollars, and all of them are vying for one thing and one thing only, our time. And when we end up falling into the traps, we make sure that our miserable existence continues to fall into that trap, while individuals continue to make money and get richer in our name. During these moments we have to understand the most simple and basic fact is that nothing is better for us than a secure and truly content version of ourselves, For when we are that person we become an individual who is out there being our own selves without complaining, whereas what social media does it enforces such images and ideas on our minds that we continue to feel miserable and feel bad our own situation, even though we are doing anything that bad, and it is at that moment that we should understand one things, "**Comparison is the thief of joy**".

And once we understand this basic and yet simple fact in our lives, our lives truly become so much better than we could have ever understood.

 Your Actions Define Your Existence

What I mean is that we have to understand that every individual has a different life story and different paths in their lives, and most of us were never ever meant to see what each of us doing for that is our personal prerogative, and it is only in recent times that we have been forced to compare each and see each other and witness each other lives from such close-ups and with time it will only increase and keep on creating individuals who are getting more and more unhappy and getting more distant from reality and from their true selves and that is where we end up destroying such a beautiful thing known as life, for very few individuals get to witness it in a way we have been doing it in recent times and yet we tend to throw it away in our own ways that simply should not have been the case. It's important to understand that we are all born with our own gifts and blessings and they could either come from God or from a higher divine purpose depending on what we believe, but it's important that we understand that not everything is under our control and never will be, but what is under our control is our actions and how we react to it, and unfortunately we often end up reacting in a negative manner towards our own lives while appreciating somebody else's lives, not knowing what current condition they may be in, as that's what allows us to feel miserable and sometimes allows us to feel comfortable and that's where we mess it up badly. As the very reason, I say we feel comfort in misery, is because we feel gaining sympathy from someone either through any social media or any other platform would make our lives better, but what we are doing through that is we are reliving ourselves of the power to heal and get stronger, as we are concentrating on outside validation to make ourselves feel better and that's where we make the big mistake.

Social media is an absolutely incredible and wonderful tool and it is something that has allowed us to leverage so many incredible things in various aspects of our lives, it has allowed us to increase our brands, it has allowed us to take several careers, it has allowed us to get access to an incredible amount of information from an incredible number of sources, but what it hasn't done and will never do, is define who we want to be, what we want to be or who we could be, for that is and will always remain in our hands to decide the path we want to take. And sometimes while following a path of our selection we stumble upon and are forced to take a different path in our lives. When that happens we have to trust that it is that defining force which has started working for us, all because we decided to take things under control, and that force is now pushing us towards a path that we were always destined to go. But in order to reach or travel through that path we have to first take action and be responsible towards our own selves and only then do miracles happen. And trust me, you can go and look at any celebrity or any individual who has done or is doing incredible things in their lives, and they will all say, "Miracles do happen", but in order to make them happen we have to make that step to come out a from the self-centred and virtual world of social media which is mostly killing our true selves, and when that happens we continue to live lives that we felt could have been avoided and yet we aren't able to avoid as the social media and its powers have trapped us in this palms and isn't willing to let us go as it now has control over the most important things humans often find hard to control, "Time" and "Our Mind", these two things are two of the strongest things known to happen. While the former (time) can never be controlled, the latter could be controlled, but for that, our minds have to be a lot more willing, capable and less fickle than what they are right now. And that could only happen if we are willing to look at the outside world through the lens of our own eyes and not through the eyes of these social media platforms. And once we are able to do that, we are able to become that version of us, that either we never imagined to be or either we found extremely difficult to attain. And that's what makes them so extraordinary and so valuable. For that's what makes ourselves so special and so blessed by the

    Your Actions Define Your Existence

incredible capability we have as humans and that's what makes us the person we were always destined to become.

Our ancestors faced different sorts of obstacles that we prevented them from living a fulfilled life, the ancient ones faced many natural calamities and tribe wars, then the historic ones faced invasions and fierce battles, then the colonial ones faced colonial rule and its impacts on their lives, and that's what allowed them to become fierce warriors and incredibly ruthless individuals, for those obstacles were preventing them from living lives in their own terms. But in the modern day and age, wars have reduced and peace has been way more than it could have imagined (although occasional wars keep on happening as that's what the ruling elites want, for war is hugely profitable for them and other stakeholders) and yet all of us fighting battles that are mostly mental and that are mostly messing up with our psychology, with making us get of our houses and shed blood, and that's where things get trickier as our previous enemies were fierce and yet visible, but the modern enemy (social media) is invisible and comes in beautiful colours and great tools and yet kills us from the inside and break our souls. We have no weapons to fight with it, except one, **"our minds"**. And if we are able to guard our minds and make them far more resilient and stronger than those distractions, we will truly be able to reach our potential and in many cases, even surpass it, for that's what we are capable of doing, and that's what we are meant to do, for nobody is in charge of our lives more than us. Not even those gurus and motivators who motivate you without knowing your real circumstances. Those individuals could guide and help you, but at the end of the day you have to help yourself, and if you aren't willing to do that you will never find your true self. If you manage to stay true to your intentions and manage to do that, you could simply become the person you always wished you could become, for even the worst of villains wished if he could do something good, for nobody wants to be abused after death, for we often put such a huge price tag on our lives, even the creators might feel shy about. But that's what we do with ourselves, we seem to make ourselves so important and precious, and yet hurt us every day (without witnessing) through those pony and simple virtual social media tools, and that's why we have created generations of individuals who are simply seeking answers to questions that don't even exist, and yet have been made to think they exist by the virtual world, and that's what we need to stop. For there isn't and will never be a world and place better for you than your own self, and once you realise that, **you will feel so loved and comforted by our own presence.** And when that happens, everybody around you would feel the same way, and that's when you would make social media weak and powerless in front of your mere existence, and that's something we are all capable of. What we need to do is simply believe in it and move forward, for that's what we all could do, and that's all we should do, and that's what makes our lives special and makes us who we are.

And who I am, what I am doing, and what I could be doing are far more important questions than what he/she is doing. And if you could ask these questions to yourself every day, you would become the person you were always meant to be, and that's someone who is himself/herself, who is responsible and accountable towards their actions, who knows how incredibly capable they are and who knows how everything is meant for everyone, depending on how you look towards the things around you and that's what makes you truly contend and gives you sleep at night and makes you appreciate your life. And that's something you should all strive for.

   Your Actions Define Your Existence

FIVE

"Validation": The Silent Killer

> *"The Only permission, the only validation, and the only opinion that matters in our quest for greatness is our own."*
>
> **Dr. Steve Maraboli**

Life, as we know it, is quite treacherous, filled with incredible obstacles and troubles throughout. But it can get even more challenging and nastier if we seek validation from others. Now, what is validation?

The Oxford Dictionary defines 'validation' as "recognition or affirmation that a person or their feelings or opinions are valid or worthwhile."

This definition encapsulates a significant concept: it highlights how the opinions of others about us hold substantial importance in our lives. We often empower these opinions, granting them the capacity to elevate our mood and make our day exceptional or diminish our spirits and dismal our day. Far from being a passive act, validation is a powerful force that can inspire hope, motivate us to persevere, and strive to become the best versions of ourselves. It transcends merely uttering pleasant words to impress someone or saying something so kind that it leaves the other person flattered. Instead, validation should be regarded as a multifaceted interaction that can manifest through various means in our lives. It can occur through actions that acknowledge and affirm the positive contributions of others, reinforcing their sense of worth and accomplishment. It also involves acts that inspire hope, encouraging individuals to persevere and continuously strive towards becoming the best versions of themselves. In essence, validation not only transfers a significant amount of influence to those whose opinions we value but also opens up opportunities for growth and self-improvement. Whenever you seek validation, you inadvertently place yourself in a position of vulnerability, allowing others to wield considerable power over your emotional state. However, this vulnerability can also be a source of hope, as it signifies the potential for growth and change.

 Your Actions Define Your Existence

Validation can manifest in different forms and contexts. For example, receiving acknowledgement from colleagues or superiors can enhance your confidence and drive in professional settings. Conversely, the absence of validation in the workplace can make you feel devalued and inefficient, directly affecting your work.

In personal relationships, validation is crucial in fostering intimacy and trust. Feeling understood and appreciated by your loved ones, strengthens the emotional bond and promotes a sense of security. Acts of validation in relationships can range from verbal affirmations to supportive actions that demonstrate care and concern. On the other hand, a lack of validation can create emotional distance and undermine the foundation of the relationship.

Social media, a prevalent aspect of modern life, is a significant arena for seeking validation. The number of likes, comments, and shares can serve as metrics of social approval, influencing your self-esteem and sense of worth. However, this pursuit of online validation can be a double-edged sword. While positive interactions can boost our mood, negative or insufficient responses can lead to feelings of rejection and self-doubt. The transient nature of social media approval underscores the importance of not placing excessive value on these virtual affirmations.

The desire for validation is a natural human inclination rooted in our need for social connection and acceptance. From an evolutionary perspective, being valued by others enhances your chances of survival and reproduction. Humans have relied on social bonds for mutual support and cooperation throughout history. This intrinsic need for validation is ingrained in your psychology and influences your behaviour and interactions. However, the pursuit of validation can become problematic when it becomes the primary source of your self-worth. When we rely on it heavily, we risk losing touch with our intrinsic values and goals. Your actions may become driven by the desire to meet others' expectations rather than aligning with our true selves. This can lead to a cycle of seeking validation, experiencing temporary satisfaction, and craving more validation to fill the void. So, it becomes imperative that we understand that to cultivate a healthier relationship with validation, it is essential to develop self-awareness and self-compassion.

Recognising your intrinsic transcendence of external opinions allows you to navigate the complexities of validation with greater resilience. Practising self-compassion involves acknowledging your imperfections and treating yourself with kindness and understanding. By fostering a strong sense of self, we can engage in validation from a place of authenticity and not dependency.

Another critical validation aspect is understanding constructive feedback and validation-seeking behaviour. Constructive feedback can be a valuable form of validation when given to help us grow and improve. It provides us with insights and guidance to enhance our skills and performance. On the other hand, validation-seeking behaviour is characterized by constant characterised approval and reassurance, often at the expense of our authenticity. Striking a balance between accepting constructive feedback and not becoming overly reliant on external validation is crucial for personal development.

Furthermore, the role of cultural and societal influences in validation must be considered. Different cultures and societies have varying norms and expectations regarding validation. Understanding these cultural dynamics can provide insights into how validation is perceived and sought in other contexts.

In many ways, it encompasses the recognition and affirmation of our worth, feelings, and opinions by others. While validation can

 Your Actions Define Your Existence

inspire hope, motivate us, and strengthen relationships, it also carries the risk of dependency and vulnerability. Understanding the complexities of validation and its impact on our self-perception and emotional well-being is essential for leading a balanced and fulfilling life. Through this lens, validation becomes a dynamic exchange in which the recognition and appreciation we offer to others can have profound implications. It can motivate individuals, giving them a sense of purpose and direction. However, it also underscores the delicate balance of power in interpersonal relationships, where the seeker of validation may find themselves at the mercy of others' opinions and judgments. This interplay of influence highlights the profound impact external validation can have on our self-perception and emotional well-being. Therefore, it becomes necessary to understand the multiple natures of validation and talk about it in detail.

Let's dwelve deep into the various ways validation often weakens us, and learn how to shield ourselves from them.

Validation through Social Media

Validation is neither an individual's birthright nor something that individuals should expect from others. Instead, it is up to us as individuals to choose how we use that power that we have in us and that human civilisation often bestows upon us.

For instance in today's day and age, whenever you accomplish any specific feat in our respective lives, your first instance is to announce it to the outside world. You may have bought your first car, your first house, You may be travelling in a beautiful country, or you may have recently gotten engaged to oyur loved ones. At that moment, your first action is to upload those feats on your perspective social media platforms, as that puts that out to the outside world that **"Guess what? I have recently accomplished this feat, and I would love for you to take notice of something so wonderful and incredible done by me"**. None of us would expect that we would put it out there for people to see. Instead, you would often say that we are simply doing it for our own selves, but that's pure bullshit because had you done it for ourselves, you would have stayed quiet and not informed anyone about it, for those who really matter to us, they might have already known.

But that's human nature, for who would accept and say, **"Hey Guys, I am simply doing this to show off and tell you guys how I have recently accomplished this feat."** Well, if we start being so honest with our intentions, the world would be a much less complicated place. People would not have done, described or said things within a filter. Still, alas, that's how the world works in today's day and age. And so when such announcements come, what do we do? How do we react? What do we comment on it? These are some ways people validate others on social media.

     Your Actions Define Your Existence

Social media in today's age is a validation factory. People often upload their photos and achievements to garner attention and responses from people they know, don't, or might never know. If you are famous enough, it gets even trickier as people who are strangers to you would be following you in huge numbers. Those individuals would have complete control over what they want to say and what they would like to do. At that time, be prepared for some really contrasting forms of validation. As people would abuse you left, right and centre. They would make you feel so horrible about yourselves that you would start doubting whether the accomplishment you are so proud of was really an accomplishment. You will begin to feel a loss of energy as you will no longer feel like you have accomplished something; instead, all your mind will be on those hateful comments, emojis and reactions that people might have given you when you uploaded that particular picture of yours. And so your achievement, which you were so proud of and were flying so high for, suddenly makes you feel like a complete loser. Those comments will hit you in ways you could have never thought about. But do you know what's the surprising part? Hardly 10 % of those comments might have been hateful, as 90% of those may have motivated you for your incredible achievement, and that's where the psychology of human minds comes into play. Our willingness to go always gives more attention to the negative rather than the positive things; this phenomenon is known as the negative bias. So what is negative bias,

In an article published by Kendra Cherry, a renowned psychologist, she stated:

Negativity bias is our tendency to register negative stimuli readily and dwell on these events. **Also known as positive-negative asymmetry, this negativity bias means that we feel**

the sting of a rebuke more powerfully than the joy of praise. This psychological phenomenon explains why wrong first impressions can be challenging to overcome, and why past traumas can have such long-term effects. In almost any interaction, we are more likely to notice negative things and remember them more vividly.

So, Kendra Cherry very precisely states how negative bias often enables us to look at different negative things at first and how paying more attention to those negative things usually creates a mental imbalance. That's the actual cost of opting to get validation from social media.

In earlier times, we had to think twice before saying what we felt like saying as we were well aware of how it could backfire and cause tremendous pain and tension between the recipient and the one saying those things. However, social media has made it easier for people to avoid accountability. Through this platform, I can collect and like any individual's picture at any point unless they are not on that particular platform. And so it becomes so much easier for us to insult, break or really demean someone we might not even know or have not met.

Validation through social media is like fighting an opponent with one hand tied to her back. When we are our absolute best, and everything is going in the right direction, it is the best place to be. As we are liked, loved, and adored by millions of people. Those millions share our achievements, which sometimes make us an overnight sensation. We start becoming the person we had always hoped to become in our dreams. Everybody wants to be like us and be seen with us, and that's the power of social media. Opening any social media application feels like being on

  Your Actions Define Your Existence

cloud 9 during those times. The love, respect and adoration are so incredible and infectious that you almost feel like the biggest and best in your field.

And then, within no time, it all goes downhill.

One small or big mistake can make you feel like the worst person the world has ever seen. Suddenly, you feel like someone no longer loved, respected, or adored by anyone. One single picture you posted suddenly invites a barrage of abuses. You start becoming a hot topic for jokes all over the internet. Your photos and videos are cropped and referenced, turning you into an absolute joke in no time. And suddenly, from feeling like you are on cloud nine, you feel like you are a few steps away from misery.

The troll's hate comments and all the negativity surrounding you can suddenly turn your entire life around disastrously. This sudden shift, often unexpected, can be overwhelming. Many celebrities and influential figures once celebrated and loved on various platforms suddenly feel like they are the most hated and despised individuals the world has ever seen. They often have no other option but to leave these platforms and live their lives in a much more secluded and private way.

As a general rule of life, accountability for our actions differentiates us between uncivilised and civilised. s Social media holds nobody accountable; it turns every individual into an opinionated monster, which none of us are ever fully prepared for. The anonymity and detachment of online interactions often embolden people to say things they would never dare to express in person, leading to a toxic environment. During such times, It is crucial to maintain a balanced perspective and not let the opinions of faceless strangers dictate our self-worth. This requires a conscious effort to separate our online persona from our true self, recognising that the value recognition on social media is fleeting and superficial. Developing a healthy sense of independence from online validation is essential for our mental and emotional well-being. This involves building solid and real-life relationships, pursuing meaningful activities, and cultivating self-compassion and resilience.

By focusing on these aspects, we can create a solid foundation of self-worth that is not easily shaken by social media's ups and downs. We can learn to appreciate positive feedback without becoming dependent on it and to handle criticism without letting it destroy our confidence. This balanced approach allows us to engage with social media more healthily, enjoying its benefits without falling prey to its potential harms. Ultimately, the key to navigating the double-edged sword of social media validation lies in understanding its limitations and maintaining a robust and independent sense of self. By doing so, we can protect ourselves from the emotional rollercoaster that social media often brings and lead more fulfilling, balanced online and offline lives.

So, next time you complain or are bitter about those negative or hateful comments that have ruined your day, remember the power with you, whether you let those strangers into your life or not, whether to share that personal or intimate moment with others because it's not them asking about your details; instead, you giving them access to your life. You make yourself vulnerable when you keep the door open at night because you feel nobody will enter the house. This metaphor extends to our online presence. We invite the world into our private lives by sharing personal information, thoughts, and moments on social media. It's crucial to think twice before doing so because humans are capable of incredibly evil things.

The anonymity and detachment of online interactions often encourage people to say and do things they would never dare

     Your Actions Define Your Existence

to do in person. Seeking validation through social media is akin to asking the devil to act on your wishes. You may hope for positive reinforcement and affirmation, but you are also opening yourself up to the darker side of human nature. And when you understand that, you become capable enough to take control of your online presence.

As individuals, you must learn to be mindful of what you share and with whom. Remember that you have the power to control your narrative. You can engage with social media on your terms without letting it dictate your self-esteem or happiness. Maintaining a healthy relationship with social media involves recognising its potential and taking proactive steps to mitigate that risk. By being selective about what you share and valuing real-life connections over online validation, you can safeguard your mental health and ensure that your sense of self remains intact. This emphasis on real-life connections makes you feel valued and connected, reminding you that proper validation comes from within, not from social media's fleeting and often fickle world.

Ultimately, the transient nature of online validation is a stark reality. While momentarily uplifting, the likes and comments on our social media posts hold little lasting significance. The individuals who extend their virtual accolades often forget about us soon after as they become preoccupied with their lives. This reality underscores the need to stop using social media as a barometer of success or a measure of self-worth. Regardless of our status, wealth, or follower count, what truly matters are the genuine relationships we cultivate. Our closest loved ones who would mourn our death the most are the ones who scarcely engage with our online content, as that's how a real relationship works, for they don't have to comment that they like you; it is through their actions that they would prove how much they adore and care for you in their lives.

Therefore, viewing social media as a tool rather than the focal point of our existence is essential. When we prioritise social media platforms , we inevitably invite misery into our lives. This misplaced emphasis causes us to lose touch with the natural world and leads to detachment from authentic experiences and relationships. Social media's virtual facade can distort our perception of reality, making us forget the true essence of life.

To live meaningfully, we must leverage social media's positive aspects to complement our lives rather than the centrepiece. By doing so, we can maintain a balanced perspective, ensuring that fleeting online interactions do not dictate our self-worth and happiness. Instead, we should focus on real-life connections and activities that bring genuine joy and fulfilment.

Remember, social media was invented to enhance our lives, not as the sole determinant of our worth. When you understand that, you will learn to prioritise authentic real-world experiences, as that's where growth happens. Taking that approach can help us avoid the pitfalls of seeking validation in the digital realm. Embracing this balanced approach will allow us to lead lives filled with far more solitude and gratitude, primarily rooted in genuine connections and meaningful activities, as that's what life should be about.

    Your Actions Define Your Existence

Validation from Parents

In the earlier topics, I wrote and talked about how life becomes easier when we start considering our parents as humans and not Gods. Similarly, to make our lives much more accessible, self-loving, and secure in our skin, we should start doing one thing that would make our lives unbelievably easier: "**Stop expecting Validation from our dear parents.**"

It's an action that, when taken correctly, will save you a lot of pain and make you a much happier individual. But that in no way allows us or anybody in the world to start disrespecting our parents, rebelling against them, or always disagreeing with them for the sake of disagreement. Instead, it's for our own selves that we start accepting whatever way our parents choose to react based on our actions and whether they choose to respond or not. Our job is not to expect them to react, as that's our only job. But unfortunately, it's easier said than done. Some of you may be reading this and asking yourself, "Why the Hell am I not allowed to expect anything from my parents?" or Suppose you are doing remarkably well in your life. You might often ask, "Why won't my parents appreciate me for doing something so incredible"? or you may be taking care of your parents in an absolutely fantastic way. Yet, they may never appreciate you for the things that you have done. Maybe Your brother is wasting his entire life while you are taking care of the whole family. Yet, nobody ever appreciates the work that you are putting in.

Instead, they keep on pampering your younger brother. So you fall into a mild state of anxiousness about never being enough or worthy enough to earn their respect, which inevitably kills you from the inside. It starts making you bitter and starts making you wonder whether all the work that you are putting in for your family is actually worth anything. You begin imagining scenarios of you not deserving love from anybody. You start neglecting the compliments that various people give you, all because your parents never compliment you.

Such a situation creates a very toxic environment in the family, where the one doing all the work is largely ignored while the one doing nothing is given all the attention. Such a place creates disharmony among the family members and makes the perfect recipe for a hostile situation. It produces individuals with unhealed trauma of non-satisfaction and non-appreciation. During such times, our minds begin to descend into a dark abyss. This abyss is a place where we find ourselves isolated and overwhelmed by a myriad of negative emotions such as frustration, loneliness, depression, anxiety, and self-doubt. These overwhelming feelings contribute to an increasing sense of resentment towards ourselves and our behaviour. We start questioning our self-worth, wondering if we are ever enough or capable of being loved by anyone. Despite the reality that we are often loved and appreciated by many people around us, excluding our parents, we tend to fixate all our energy on those two individuals. This undue focus on the negative aspects of our lives frequently stems from the traumas we have experienced.

These traumas can arise from various sources such as narcissistic parenting, where parents are excessively self-centred; selfish parenting, where parents prioritise their needs over their children's; inattentive parenting, where parents fail to provide adequate attention and care; and non-appreciative parenting, where parents do not acknowledge or appreciate their children's efforts and achievements. At the same time, the child's stubbornness and adamant attitude can also contribute to these issues. These factors collectively lead individuals down a path of misery, particularly when they have parents who subject them

    Your Actions Define Your Existence

to these detrimental behaviours. Moreover, some children never genuinely understand their parents or what is expected from them, which further exacerbates their struggles.

When our minds begin to plunge into this abyss, we feel as though we are trapped in a void devoid of light and hope. The feelings of frustration stem from repeated failures or unmet expectations, both from ourselves and from others. This frustration often spirals into loneliness as we believe that no one can truly understand or empathise with our plight, which then paves the way for depression, and soon anxiety joins the fray as well, manifesting as a constant worry about the future and our place within it. This toxic cocktail of emotions culminates in a deep-seated self-doubt, where we constantly question our worth and abilities.

In these moments, we must understand that the resentment we often feel towards ourselves during such times is destructive. It makes us harshly criticise our actions and criticise ourselves, leading to a cycle of self-loathing and guilt. We dissect our behaviours under a microscope, scrutinising every flaw as scrutinising. This hyper-focus on our imperfections often closes our eyes to our strengths and achievements, making us feel unworthy of love and affection. Even though we are surrounded by people who care for us, their support often goes unnoticed because we are too engrossed in our negative narrative.

To better explain this phenomenon, Let me share a real-life story about an individual whose life I had closely followed for 27 years until we broke apart for our own reasons. We were best friends for quite some time, but soon, things turned wrong, and she became the monster she always despised.

Let's call her Carmen.

So, Carmen and I both grew up together. We often played with each other from age 4, as she lived near my house. She was incredible and would usually look after me, as I, being my usual self, would always get involved in the naughtiest things. But she was actually 1 year older than me, so she would often use that to her advantage and behave as if she was 10 years older than me, always acting like my elder sister. But I never regarded her as one, for when nobody was there, she would do things twice as funny and naughty as I could. But the moment somebody walked in, she knew how to put on a mature face, and she would start acting responsibly and maturely. We both shared some incredible and unique moments throughout our lives.

Even though my parents sent me to a boarding school at the age of 10, we always stayed in contact. We really valued and trusted each other in ways that very few people could fathom. But something pains me even to this day, and that was the environment that Carmen had at her house.

Carmen's home consisted of her younger brother, mother, and father. Her younger brother was notorious and often barely passed marks in his exams, while Carmen, on the other hand, would usually rank among the Top 3 in her class. Her brother wasn't even half as talented as her, and yet he would always get appreciated by his mother and father. While his sister would often get appreciated by every random stranger, but never received any appreciation from her parents.

As time went by, it was found out that her brother had now started taking his life in a much more profound way, while she was already twice as good as him. Her brother changed his life and became better. It started earning him appreciation from several corners, which Carmen was used to but never her brother. Slowly and steadily, her brother started getting better

     Your Actions Define Your Existence

grades than her, and soon, he moved out of his hometown and started making his own reputation. In contrast, Carmen, who was out of her hometown, continued to prosper. And so, with her brother doing so well, he was now the biggest in his entire neighbourhood and hometown, and his parents would often be proud of his accomplishments.

During these times, I started seeing differences in Carmen's behaviour. By now, we both were doing our masters at Mumbai University and the Carmen that I Had always known to be had started to change. She started getting irritated at the most minor things; she started going off the radar and was no longer the bubbly and lively person she used to be. As friends, we often got into arguments. During earlier times, whenever we both would fight or argue over something, we would soon settle it out and forget it within no time. But now Carmen was different. Whenever we would argue, she would keep on saying certain specific lines, and those were,

"Nobody loves me! I am not worth it! My parents hate me! No wonder they always love my brother! I would be better off dead!'

These are some words I had never thought I would hear Carmen say, as she was one of the most mature, secure, and responsible people I had ever met.

From that time, it so happened that whenever we would meet, her topics of discussion would be only about trauma, parental assaults, insults and sibling rivalry. Contrastingly, a few years back, we used to have incredible discussions about world politics, the national economy, new movies we had been watching and our future and life goals. Alas, those times were gone by. Unfortunately, seeing Carmen and talking to her even for an hour or so started making me feel horrible about myself, as that's how negative and resentful she had become. But being who I am, I simply could not let her go down the path.

Soon, I started taking her on small 1-2 day trips; we often hung out and went to some incredible places. I started taking her to the gym as well with me. Also, whenever I would order a book for me, I requested a copy for her. I did these things for almost 28 months, as I felt it was my duty towards a friend who has always adored and supported me. The same goes for me, as she had always been there for me whenever I needed her. But alas, everything stayed the same!

Carmen kept on going down the abyss and started being more and more miserable, due to which I got her hooked up to a therapist, and even that didn't help. One day, while I was going out with somebody to play a bit of cricket, she got so angry that she shouted at me for not receiving the call. I told her I was playing cricket downstairs, but she wouldn't budge. She even said some very nasty and personal things to me on that day, and ever since then, I haven't been in contact with her. Lately, I had heard of her from her brother, who told me how she had become so bitter. She keeps on fighting with her mother all the time. Her father and she also get into fights regularly, and she and her brother even get into physical battles once. He told me she would push that person away whenever somebody tried to help her. He told me everybody appreciated her and that she was doing so well, yet she had decided to throw it away. She gets angry at her brother when he takes his mother on vacations, as she often tells her mother how she does not deserve these good things as they make her life miserable. She usually says nasty things to her mother and brother, and because she is scared of fighting with her father, she has blocked him on all platforms. She barely has any friends and lives alone in one of India's biggest cities. And the

 Your Actions Define Your Existence

only thing and messages she keeps on sharing with her brother are about trauma and anxiety. Just like me, he tried to set her up with a therapist, and unfortunately, she fought with him as well. The situation has become so dire that she is always looking to find people to fight with, and due to that, she has pushed everyone away and is now living her life without any support from anyone. All of our friends are now on our own paths; some are married, some have started their own ventures, some are employed in certain firms, and some even have kids, but nothing has changed in terms of Carmen. Whenever my other friends ask me about her, I have no answers. They often tell me she is simply not doing well based on what they have heard.

So, the existential question that has come up is, how did a woman such as Carmen, who was so well loved by everybody and was so responsible and mature, end up becoming the depressed, resentful, and bitter woman she became, and who is at fault here? Let's start from the beginning.

From the start, Carmen's parents were so engrossed in their own lives that they failed to acknowledge the remarkable person their daughter was. This lack of recognition and appreciation profoundly affected Carmen's mental well-being. Although, in present times, her parents have realized their negligence and role in pushing Carmen down this path, many believe it's too late to repair the damage. However, there is still a glimmer of hope, as hope is what gives meaning to our lives.

Carmen harboured a deep-seated longing to be accepted and appreciated by her parents. This yearning gradually took a toll on her mental health. The situation worsened when her brother began to excel and received more appreciation from their parents. This added pressure made Carmen feel increasingly insecure. She found it difficult to cope with the overwhelming feelings of inadequacy and anger that developed within. Her frustration with her parents, particularly her father, led her to often lash out at her mother, who unfairly bore the brunt of Carmen's emotional turmoil. Despite her father being equally guilty, she was the one who faced the most immediate consequences of Carmen's anger.

As time went on, the world around them continued to move forward. Friends and acquaintances became busy with their own lives. During this challenging period, I was the only one who remained steadfastly by Carmen's side. Despite my loyalty and support, Carmen chose to push me away. It also showed how, during such times, we often cannot recognise and receive support from others regarding our life situation and the conditions we have put ourselves into. She fixated solely on her parents' actions and neglect, ignoring the good wishes and efforts of others to help her. This behaviour exemplifies the concept of "Negative Bias" I mentioned earlier, where one's focus on negative experiences and emotions can have incredibly destructive effects on one's mental health and turn them into highly bitter and resentful creatures. Something people barely realise they do themselves, for who else can we hurt more than ourselves?

These situations turn Carmen into someone she would have despised a few years back, yet she has become the monster she dearly hated. And so it brings us to question and realise that going through such an ordeal all because you were never validated by your parents is an overkill. We have to understand that our lives are too precious to be wasted because of the lack of appreciation we receive from our parents.

Let's discuss in detail what happens when we start demanding validation from our parents and how to escape a situation like Carmen's.

- **Putting parents on a pedestal**- One of the primary things that happens when we seek excessive validation from our parents is our willingness to put them on a pedestal. In such a situation, we bestow them so much power that they indirectly control our lives. We start seeking their approval for everything or any noble act we might have done without asking ourselves some of the fundamental questions regarding them. Such as-

- **What if my parents weren't appreciated by my grandparents?**

- **What if my parents are too traumatised or traumatised to me?**

- **What if I accept too much from individuals who barely have the courage and willingness to appreciate someone?**

- **What if I ask them to love and respect me the way I want to be received rather than accept it the way they want to give it to me?**

These are some of the many questions we should ask ourselves before seeking or demanding validation from our partners. We could only understand these issues by increasing our awareness of them. And how do we do it? I learned more through books, articles, and podcasts and then applied them in real life. Once we start learning these things, we automatically increase our awareness and become much stronger individuals while dealing with the urge to seek validation from our parents. Now, making ourselves more aware, learning more about this phenomenon or even asking these questions won't necessarily solve these issues and won't take us towards a happily ever after life. Still, it will undoubtedly make us much less miserable, which we should strive for and live by.

- **Compromise of our well-being-** The following issue when we start seeking validation from our parents is our willingness to compromise our well-being and put it in someone else's hands. I witnessed how Carmen, once the epitome of a responsible and talented adult, became one of the most miserable people I know, solely because she placed too much emphasis on her parents' reactions to her actions. This is no way to live our lives, for our time on this planet is so short and futile that once we begin treading the wrong path, it becomes challenging to return to the path of solitude.

We must start focusing on what we can do rather than spending so much effort trying to make others do what we want. This task is incredibly challenging because humans are built differently. If you try to convince your parents, who have recently appreciated you, to change, you will likely face disappointment. This is simply how some individuals are, and blaming yourself for trying to convince them will only make you more miserable and resentful of your efforts, regardless of how well you might have been doing.

- **Neglecting Our Own Needs-** When we seek to attend to our parents' needs and do things to make them proud or appreciate what we have done, we often start doing things based on what they deem good or essential, neglecting our needs. For instance, one of my close associates skipped his wife's birthday because his mother wanted them to stay home and celebrate. His mother had always hated her son's wife, and the son, fearing his mother's disapproval, chose to compromise his own needs and his wife's happiness.

This decision led to his wife losing respect for him, eventually destroying their marriage. After their divorce, his mother criticised her, and he realised he could not even maintain his marriage.

 Your Actions Define Your Existence

This additional blow made him even more miserable because the person he always wanted to make happy and gain approval from was now disappointed in him. This disappointment pushed him into a spiral of depression and pain.

In his effort to stay in his mother's good books, he ended up being in the bad books of both his wife and mother. The root of this problem was his desire to show his mother that he loved and appreciated her. However, he could never effectively convey this due to his perceived inadequacies as a man. This tragic scenario highlights the detrimental effects of neglecting our own needs and seeking validation solely from our parents. It shows that compromising our well-being for the approval of others can lead to severe consequences, including strained relationships, personal unhappiness, and a deep sense of unfulfillment.

- **Accepting Our Parents' Imperfections** - To truly live a life where we can breathe easier, it is crucial to recognise our parents and have their own imperfections. This realisation first realises a peaceful and fulfilling life. For instance, some parents may never apologise; the apology might become overly emotional when confronted with such issues, making it difficult to have constructive conversations. Some parents might consistently show favouritism towards a sibling, leaving the other one feeling undervalued and overlooked. These behaviours are common among many parents, and consequently, many suffer. The key to alleviating this suffering lies in acceptance. Accepting our parents for who they are, with all their flaws and shortcomings, is essential. This does not mean condoning negative behaviour or allowing ourselves to be mistreated. Instead, it means understanding that our parents are human beings with their own set of imperfections, challenges and limitations. Once we can accept this, we can make our lives way better than we could have imagined, bringing relief as we no longer carry the burden of unrealistic expectations.

By accepting our parents' imperfections, we begin to free ourselves from the constant need for their approval and the unrealistic expectation that they will change. This acceptance can lead to a more compassionate view of our parents, fostering a better relationship with them and reducing the emotional burden on ourselves. Moreover, such acceptance paves the way for us to focus on our growth and well-being.

These measures allow us to set healthy boundaries, prioritise our needs and learn to prioritise fulfilment outside our parents' validation. This shift in perspective will enable us to take control of our lives, making choices that align with our values and aspirations. Taking this first step of acceptance can be challenging, but it is profoundly liberating. Once we accept our parents for who they are, we stop wasting energy trying to change them or win their approval. This newfound freedom liberates us, enabling us to live more authentically and pursue our desired life. Doing so creates a healthier dynamic with our parents and fosters a sense of peace within ourselves.

- **Take Accountability**- To truly reach our maximum potential, it is imperative to trust our instincts and put more belief in our convictions. For instance, you might be contemplating taking up "Humanities" as your field of study, but since your parents want you to take up "Science," you reject your own choice and opt for "Science" instead. A year down the line, you find yourself scoring horribly and performing terribly in all your classes. At that point, you start blaming your parents, claiming their preference led you to choose this

 Your Actions Define Your Existence

field, but in reality, your wish to be validated by them led you to make that particular decision. Their response to your rant was, **"We simply suggested our preference; we didn't force you to become a doctor or an engineer."** Hearing this leaves you shattered, and you end up blaming them, but in reality, it was you who should have stood firm in what you believed was the right choice for you.

The truth is, you chose not to be responsible for your actions and instead blamed your parents, saying, "I wanted to make you happy, and now you've left me out to dry." This harsh truth highlights a crucial lesson regarding making your life less miserable; you must be brave enough to own up to your actions. If you want to reach the pinnacle of misery, continue blaming your parents. But remember, this is not the end. It's an opportunity to learn and grow. Taking responsibility for your decisions can turn past mistakes into valuable lessons, paving the way for genuine success and fulfilment.

So next time you prioritise your parents' needs over your own, you should remember that when you fail, you will fail alone. However, if you succeed, they will grow together with you. Unfortunately, failure is often the destination when individuals decide solely to gain validation from non-validating parents. Taking accountability means recognising our decisions and their outcomes and recognising possibilities. It means understanding that while our parents' suggestions and preferences may influence us, the final choice and its consequences lie with us. By standing by our beliefs and making choices aligned with our true desires, no matter how difficult those circumstances are, we pave the way for genuine success and fulfilment. This is not a burden but a liberation. It frees us from the burden of misplaced blame and allows us to live independently on our own terms. And that's a life many dreams of living, filled with less security but more fulfilment.

- **Forgetting our purpose-** We often need to find our true purpose to meet parental expectations and adhere to societal norms. This struggle to please others can overshadow the essence of why we do things in the first place. To lead a fulfilling life, it is crucial to remain true to ourselves. We must remember that in our short time on this planet, each individual's journey is unique, as some might succeed at 19 while others may come at 49. What truly matters is how we treat ourselves and cultivate patience, as personal fulfilment is paramount. The fundamental objective of our existence is to be as authentic as possible. By staying true to ourselves, we allow destiny to take its course. Our actions should stem from genuine intentions and personal happiness, which is a trustworthy source of validation. When we prioritise well-being and pursue our passions, we achieve a sense of validation. This self-validation, in turn, satisfies our parents without the need for deliberate efforts to please them.

Living authentically means aligning our actions with our true desires and values. This approach not only brings personal contentment but also makes our parents proud. Their pride is a reflection of our genuine accomplishments. Therefore, rather than focusing solely on making our parents happy, we should concentrate on what fulfils us. When we do this, we create a positive ripple effect, leading to mutual happiness and pride. The joy that comes from living authentically is genuinely inspiring, as the key to a purposeful life lies in self-authenticity. By embracing our true selves and being patient, we can navigate our unique paths to success. This journey, driven by our passions and values, not only brings personal joy but also earns the heartfelt pride of

    Your Actions Define Your Existence

our parents. This authentic approach to life ensures that we live meaningfully and leave a lasting impact.

Through these topics, we can quickly evaluate how seeking validation and forced appreciation, even from our parents, often harms an individual's mind and body. Every individual in this world, at some point in time, might have wanted to be appreciated by his parents but may have never gotten it. And for them, it is essential to remember that it's not you who should be suffering. Instead, it's them who should be responsible for your actions. You did what you could best, and what happens later is not in your hands. We can only control our own actions, not others. The result of our actions is never in our hands, and once we become content with that by becoming more aware, we start becoming a happier version of ourselves. Although happiness isn't a lifetime attainment, disappointments, sadness, resentment and defeat are part and parcel of human existence. What makes us different is how we choose to react to it.

Having our parents' support behind our backs is genuinely encouraging and makes us propel even further and faster, but what can we do when we don't have it? It's upon us to choose what we decide to do with our lives. Sulking and being disappointed at them would soon make us disappointed in ourselves, which is something none of us should aspire for, for life is too short to seek someone's love and validation. Instead, we should let those things flow through our deeds. And when that happens, you start being more gracious about your lives and truly become a person who is willing to face any obstacles in life, for that's what life should be about. We start becoming more accepting of our parents. When that happens, the toxicity fades away, and so does the need for appreciation and validation. And that's the person we should all aspire to be. For that's the life we should all aspire to live.

Validation through friends

*"You will never gain anyone's approval by begging for it.
When you stand confident in your own respect follows."*

Mandy Hale

In my previous book, "**Why We Become Who We Become**," I stated that friends are those individuals who fall in the category between "**Family**" and "**Acquaintance**." These individuals with whom we don't have any connection through blood yet share a deep and incredible bond that sometimes lasts a lifetime.

This truth became evident during my years in boarding school, starting at the tender age of 10. The transition from the comfort of home to the unfamiliarity of a boarding school was overwhelming, and truth be said, it was a frightening experience. As I was suddenly placed in an environment where I knew no one, and straight from the comforts of my family (especially Mom's love and pamper), I was put with absolute and ruthless strangers, and trust me, the initial days were tough. But slowly and steadily, I learned the way of life over there, and those initial setbacks gave way to some of the best years of my life. Individuals that were once strangers turned into friends, and friends turned into brothers. Even today, the bond we share is unbreakable. And the moment we meet each other, it's literally like the best moment of our lives, and time flies faster than ever. Through these experiences, the thing that I learned most about is that friendships give us space to be ourselves without the fear of any sort of judgment. It allows us to reveal a side of ourselves that very few people see, making these bonds invaluable and those times forever cherishing.

In many ways, friendship is a sanctuary where we can let our guard down and be our most authentic selves. The bonds formed through friendship lead to some of the most cherished memories of our lives. We spend our entire lives reminiscing about the fantastic times we've shared with friends, and these moments become a part of our very identity. The value of these shared experiences is immeasurable, as they shape our understanding of the world and our place in it. Some friendships formed during our formative years grow stronger over time. However, not all friendships follow this ideal trajectory. Changing life circumstances often lead to shifts in behaviour and personality that end up straining these once incredible bonds.

Because as life progresses, we sometimes find that friends who once felt like siblings start to change. They become so absorbed in their lives that they forget the bond they once cherished. Sometimes, some individuals truly achieve the rags-to-riches journey, which changes them. And unfortunately, as time passes, these friendships no longer remain as they were. This change affects both parties, leading to a mutual understanding and acceptance. This acceptance is crucial in navigating the changes in a friendship, as it allows both parties to acknowledge and respect each other's growth. However, the real challenge arises when one friend changes while the other remains the same. This can lead to false expectations and unfulfilled hopes. The friend who progresses and improves may begin to feel unappreciated by the one who stays behind, leading to envy and jealousy.

These differences in opinions and lifestyles start creating severe friction in the relationship, as it is often the case that the very success we all have wanted for so long starts creating a rift between individuals. The one who has excelled starts facing resentment from the one who remained stagnant. This resentment transforms a once supportive and nurturing friendship into a toxic relationship. Arguments replace appreciation, and the willingness to learn from each other disappears. Validation becomes a constant need, and authenticity fades away. When one friend feels overshadowed by the other's achievements, the foundation of the friendship begins to crumble. What was once a source of joy and support becomes a battleground of egos and unmet expectations.

To better explain this, let me share a story about an individual with whom one of my cousins had been friends for almost 22 years. I used to know that guy quite well, but over time, things went downhill, and now we hardly stay in touch.

Let's call my cousin James and his friend Charlie.

So, Charlie and James were literally the best of friends since childhood. They were often given several nicknames by people all around, as they were literally the biggest troublemakers in the vicinity of our entire area. Some days, James would go to Charlie's house and wake him at 5 am so that they could play the game of cricket, and on some days, Charlie would go to James' house and do the same thing of waking him up to play. They were such fanatics and were so close to each other that even during winters when mornings were so cold and foggy, they would start playing cricket at around 6 am and disturb all of us during our sleep. That's how much they loved to play. And guess what? My mom would make lemonade drinks, and we would all drink that and continue to play till 2 pm. I loved to play with them, as that's how much we loved to play. Things became so extreme that Charlie's father had to bring a stick to take him back home, as we barely cared about what we ate or drank. All we wanted to do was play and really enjoy our lives.

Sometimes, the matches would get so intense and exciting that we would start shouting so much that the neighbours had to call my dad. We would further ruin the situation by breaking glasses everywhere, as that was the intensity with which we played. And

   Your Actions Define Your Existence

then, due to me becoming such a nuisance, along with them. I was sent to a boarding school, but we would start playing the same way again whenever I came home during vacations. My father had to give me tuition to make sure that I stopped playing and did something resourceful with my life. When we grew up, we replaced playing with chilling. We would hang out with each other almost every evening, often going out to eat and having some nice chai at some good tea stalls.

Once James grew up, he left for Delhi to complete his studies for his graduation. But even then, he and Charlie stayed as close to each other as they could, something I witnessed as I saw how often they called each other up and had some adorable and funny conversations. And Charlie, unlike James, came from a significantly lower middle-class background. They never had any issues with him because James's father kept him on the lowest possible budget. He wasn't allowed to use any of his cars and had no debit card until college. Due to this, he always travelled by public transport and lived with whatever money his father gave him. Sometimes, it made him angry as everybody knew his father was an established businessman. Everyone wondered why he travelled on public transport with a substandard T-shirt and shorts and literally without money. They would often think he was a cheapskate, but only Charlie and I knew his reality, and that's the reason they both never ever had any issues.

And then, once Covid hit, James had to abandon his plans to go to London and study and had instead come back to Guwahati as there was no option. His master's final semester exams were also on hold, so after I convinced him to join his family business, he decided to join it and learn some things from his father. In the beginning, everything was going well, but then things changed. James's father was a very hard taskmaster, and to test his son, he started taking him around on his site visits. Due to that, he barely had any free time and sometimes appeared on various media platforms. During these times, I had noticed how Charlie start bitching me about James in a very negative way, and I would always talk to him with a very susceptible voice. I could understand why he felt that way, as suddenly James was driving his father's cars while he was doing his same job, but everything was still the same, and he was one of my closest friends. And James, even to date, has mostly stayed the same. Instead, he has become calm, composed and appreciative of other people's actions. At the same time, Charlie takes an entirely different route, becoming very hateful, envious, and bitter towards his friend for something he has not done but is simply doing his role.

And then, one day, Charlie asked me and James whether he should start a business, and we both told him, bloody hell, go for it. He asked me for some money, and I gave it to him. When he asked James, He gave him 3 times more than I had given, which showed how James still adored and cared for Charlie as a friend, even though Charlie had started changing. And trust me, James never ever does any sort of financial dealings with his close ones, as relationships often get ruined when money comes into the picture, but with Charlie, he was secure enough and knew he was the last person to change.

Then, within 2 years, his business started to grow, and he was earning equivalent to what James was earning and sometimes even more. It was then that I saw how he began treating James. He used to brag in front of his friends , infront of me as wel. He said that everything he did was by himself while James was simply enjoying his father's money. I would laugh at it and ignore it. James's mother got ill during this time, and he seriously needed some money. So, when he went to Charlie along with me

   Your Actions Define Your Existence

to ask if he could return him some of the money he had given 2 years back, as he is in urgent need of it, he gave him a mouthful of words and told him how he should be ashamed of asking him for money. He told him that he was a self-made man and that James's money meant nothing to him, even though it was through my and James' money and some of his family members' money that he could start his business. Still, since he had become self-sufficient, he told him he was no longer needed. At that time, I interrupted and told Charlie, "Brother, chill down" If you don't want to pay, it's okay, but don't disrespect my brother. He still regards you as his only best friend, but Charlie was adamant. He asks us to go, as he feels we are wasting his time.

When he asked me to go, it really hurt me. I told him he didn't have to become someone he was not, and he was still the same person inside. He then called up another mutual friend of ours and absolutely berated us.

And unfortunately, that was the last time I met him. I could have punched him and tested my Boxing skills, as nobody dared disrespect my brother, but I realised it was not worth it. But really I should gave given me an elbow and an uppercut, but something within me told me it was not worth it, especially to a narcissitic retared like Charlie. I told James to forget about it and learn from such a mistake of being financially involved with a dear friend and never ever let someone else disrespect him, but had it been someone else instead of him, things would have turned quite ugly, but in this case, I decided to exercise restraint, as I know some things are better not said.

And guess what? Since that day, James has really changed as a person. He realized that people can often change in an instant. He realized money had wholly changed his friend, but he was happy that it had not changed him. But noticing from a third person's perspective, I knew something like this was bound to happen due to the chain of events leading up to this tussle.

No matter how close James and Charlie were, there were always things that I noticed. My cousin James grew up in a very non-appreciative environment where nobody ever appreciated him, while Charlie was the only one always there for him. Charlie, on the other hand, came from a very appreciative family and a family that had always put him on a pedestal, and due to that, he had various narcissistic tendencies as well. During our playing time, I often noticed that Charlie never agreed with James about most things and that James would always comply for fear of losing their friendship. James always took advice from me and Charlie, but when he messed it up, Charlie would often scold him.

But on the other hand, Charlie, no matter how badly he messed it up, never took James's advice, and if either I or James ever told him that he shouldn't have done that particular thing, he would go absolutely mad over us. There would be times when Charlie would even taunt James for our dysfunctional family and use very personal information against him, something that I have witnessed first-hand. "He constantly criticized James for using something he deeply trusted and believed in, never expecting to be mocked for it someday. James had always been the one to overshare, hoping it would encourage Charlie to do the same. However, Charlie, who always felt the need to outshine him, never shared anything. This dynamic had existed since childhood, but things worsened when James started working in his family business—and escalated even further when Charlie found success.

Whenever Charlie did anything good in his work or something incredible, I would be the first to appreciate him along with James. But as soon as James started striding, Charlie stopped his

    Your Actions Define Your Existence

appreciation and often underwhelmed James with sly remarks like "What's the big deal, deal? Anybody would have done it". At first, James ignored it, but later on, it started killing him from the inside as these things started happening more and more. But whenever Charlie would do anything even noteworthy, James would often compliment him, and Charlie would reply, "I know I can do anything".

But maybe that's what Charlie knew; he knew he always had the upper hand over James, and that's why he could take him over for a ride. Had I been in James's place, trust me, the other person would have really regretted it as I am calm when needed, but the moment someone disrespected I knew what to do, and that was enough. But James was a typical nice guy, and his validation cravings from his best friend had really messed up his mind for a long duration. Had I not been there, things could have gone even worse. There would be days when I would tell James that he was fine, but he would ask me, "Brother, why is Charlie hating me? Am I that Bad? Am I doing something wrong? And I would tell him how it's not you, but it's Charlie. And he shouldn't be fussed so much about Charlie's validation as the fact that he is simply doing good and still staying humble is for good for his own self, while the arrogance that has crept inside Charlie is short-lived. I told him that even if his friend mistreated or ignored him, I should just let him go.

I told him a line I had once seen in an Instagram reel,

"Sometimes in life when you love people so much, you have to do anything to protect them or, in your case, protect yourself, even if it meant letting them go."

"James tapped my shoulder after I said this, and from that moment, he transformed into an entirely different person. He walked away from his family business, realizing he no longer

needed his toxic and narcissistic father controlling him. To put it bluntly, his father was pure evil. Now, with a business that generates seven-figure revenue annually, he is in a loving relationship with an incredible woman and is one of the most self-assured men I have ever known.

Now and then, when we have a drink, we reminisce and laugh at how much he had lost himself—all because a friend failed to appreciate him. He admits that he was deeply insecure at the time. When I mentioned that Charlie's business wasn't doing so well, he responded without hesitation, 'He will handle it and come out with flying colours.' Hearing that, I felt a lump in my throat. How could he remain so kind, so noble, and harbour no resentment toward someone who had hurt him so deeply? But that's just who James is.

Today, he has become the kind of man many aspire to be. His past need for validation nearly destroyed him, but by staying true to his work and being honest with his loved ones, he has built strong, meaningful friendships. These new friends appreciate his successes and hold him accountable when he falters—exactly what true companionship should be. The most remarkable thing? James no longer expects people to do this for him. Yet, they do it anyway because he focuses only on what he can control: 'his actions and his emotions.' After all, nothing else—whether it's a family friend or a lifelong companion—is ever truly within our control."

This real-life story can teach us several things, allowing us to make our friendships less toxic, and help us become less dependent on even the best of our friends for appreciation.

Let's talk about them step by step.

  Your Actions Define Your Existence

Avoid oversharing – To keep our friendships genuine and authentic, we should always share our thoughts and feelings to let the person know that we trust them enough to share these particular things. But at the same time, it is our responsibility and job to make sure that we keep a part of ourselves within ourselves and do not end up sharing every little detail about our lives with even the best of friends. And even if we do, it shouldn't be to gain compassion or sympathy. Rather, it should be through a genuine urge to share and let the other person know that we trust them, and if they ever use these things against you, it would be largely disappointing. And trust me, there would be a lot of Charlie's out there, as we have all had friends that genuinely felt like the best in the world, but somewhere down the line, we lost touch with them, and now we have barely maybe 1-2 people left with whom we can share most of what is happening in our lives. This is something most people who are in their late 20s might relate to a bit, and those in their 30s and 40s would definitely relate to as that's when we end up losing most of our friends and manage to retain only a select few, for that's what life is about. Life isn't what we hoped for, and that's okay. But we can only guard ourselves today by realising who we can share things with and who we can't. For that, we need to increase our awareness, as awareness enables us to single out and discover the red flags within our friendships and prepares us to discover what could happen and what could be avoided. And we can do that when we make ourselves aware of who is least likely to use the information against us one day.

I have seen people say terrible things to individuals they once considered their best friends. In some cases, I have seen people maintain their friend's trust till old age, as that's what friendship is about. But remember, we attract the people we are. The only way to attract the right people is by being ourselves, but that doesn't mean everything will be perfect after then, as there is every chance of you being in James's place, but at least it will allow you to make yourself the best and the most authentic individual you could be. And that individual never ever seeks validation or appreciation; he works and does what he can and what he must, for that's all we can do, and that's all we must do.

Avoid discussing with people who don't listen – In life, we often find a variety of individuals throughout our entire lives. Whether it's someone among our friends, someone among our family or maybe someone among our working peers. We are bound to find different sorts of individuals throughout our lives. In between those, one species that annoys us the most are the **non-listeners**. These individuals regard what they say and what they know as the only truth and the only way the world works, so dealing with these individuals is very tiring and toxic.

There might be moments when you might be discussing some really incredible points On some fantastic issues, but you will never be able to get your point across when you are with these individuals. So what do you do when you are not being listened to, or you see the things that you are saying are getting completely ignored? "**Well, you stop talking**", as simple as that.

"You must understand that the words you speak hold meaning for you and carry a certain value. When you encounter individuals who refuse to listen, ensure you don't allow such situations to repeat. The only way to do this is by carefully choosing your words and timing while recognizing that these individuals don't instinctively know they should listen.

The truth is, it's not your fault—it's their narcissistic tendencies that prevent them from accepting different perspectives. That's precisely why they remain stuck in their ways. Each time you attempt to engage in a meaningful conversation with them, you risk diminishing your self-worth.

 Your Actions Define Your Existence

Always remember—no one is more valuable than you. You are the architect of your own identity, and your actions largely dictate how others treat you. You owe nothing to anyone, and your respect and pride rest solely in your hands."

Avoid being insulted – Your respect and self-worth are entirely in your hands. And there is and will always be a skinny line between jokes and insults. Jokes are made to lighten up and to make sure that there is always a friendly banter and fun atmosphere around your friends. But insults are done mainly to demean or be shown to you by them. Guess what? That's who you are. At the moment, you have two choices: either you ignore them thinking that if you defend yourself or say something they will get offended!, Or you tell them these simple lines, **"Hey mate, I know you meant it as a joke but I didn't find it funny, rather felt a bit awkward and humiliated by it"** and once you say these lines, it automatically creates a line of defence around you and your friend. At that moment, your friend might get offended by how you hit him back, but the probability of it happening again will lessen considerably in the long run.

By saying that simple line, you created a space for yourself that your friend would dare not cross again, and that makes a tone of respect and caution as well. And once you do that to that one friend, you could do it to anybody. And it also makes you someone who is now known as a person who does not take shit from people, no matter how close they are. And when you know people feel like that around you, you feel far more powerful than you could have ever felt, and that makes you someone who appreciates yourself more and is confident of your own worth. And that individual no longer seeks the validation or appreciation of anybody, not even his goddamn best friends. In this process, you will lose many friends, but the best part is you can keep the ones who genuinely respect and appreciate you without your longing. And that creates a far more healthier environment than there ever was. That makes life much more fun, and less resentment and anxiousness no longer runs through your veins. Now, you are with individuals who regard you as their equal and regard you as a person who is up for fun and incredible things but will never ever accept insult or disrespect. Your mantra in life towards even your best friends should be simple.

"If you can't make me laugh, you have no right to make me cry."

Once you live your life based on this ideology, you will start being around friends who know what genuine self-respect and self-worth are and who are themselves cautious of letting somebody else invade their safe space. So, why do they do that to yours? And even if they do, you know what to do, for only you are responsible for your actions, nobody else.

Avoid expecting compassion—When we talk about compassion, I guess who doesn't want to feel compassion, who doesn't want to feel loved, who doesn't want to feel sympathy? Compassion is a basic human need and desire. And it is something we all wish we received from our dear friends, for that's what friendship is all about. But that is where we are taking things in the wrong direction.

In life, there are moments when we are feeling at our lowest, our mind isn't going in the right direction, one of our loved ones might be going through a significant health issue, or facing something that has completely overwhelmed us. At that time, we felt incredible and assertive when we had a friend who shared our pain and was willing to stand by our side through thick and thin, as I certainly had 1-2 such mates who were always by my side during such times. But I have also seen people who had

 Your Actions Define Your Existence

to face some absolutely harrowing obstacles in their lives, and unfortunately, they had to face it alone as nobody was there to give them a hand and tell them, **"Hey Buddy, we are in this together"**.

And it's such a cruel and heartbreaking thing to face for who "would want to suffer alone". It is these individuals who end up getting traumatised which leads to an unbelievable amount of trauma for years ahead. But in these moments, we all must exercise restraint and solitude within ourselves.

"We all carry traumas in some form, often beyond our control. As we grow and become more aware of mental health, we start recognizing the subtle experiences that shaped our pain. What we *can* control, however, is the extent to which we allow that suffering to dictate our lives. When we find contentment within ourselves and our own space, we cultivate an atmosphere free of desperation and neediness. In doing so, we naturally attract people who feel safe enough to share their struggles with us and, in turn, stand by us during our difficult times. After all, who wouldn't want to be around someone so at ease with themselves and their surroundings—someone whose inner security inspires others to offer their support?

As this transformation takes place, you no longer cry out in frustration or feel abandoned when left to navigate challenges alone. Instead, your self-sufficiency and confidence make you magnetic. People offer their help willingly—not because you demand it, but because you create an environment where kindness flows both ways.As more people gravitate toward you, they come to realize a fundamental truth: when we stop seeking validation from others to prove our worth, we develop a love for ourselves so deep that admiration from others becomes a natural byproduct. We become the very person we once aspired to be—

the person others now look up to. In an era where social media is often a tool for seeking sympathy, you become a rarity. You appreciate help when it comes, as it makes life easier, but you are also prepared to move forward alone when needed. That's the strength of a secure individual—one who does not expect unwavering support yet remains grateful for those who choose to stand by them.

When we learn to rely on ourselves, we become the kind of person people want to be around and want to emulate. And that is a far better existence than one spent in false expectations and helpless longing for things beyond our control.

So take ownership of your life. Let go of expectations, even from your closest friends. The person you truly aspire to be is not bitter or desperate, but someone who understands that human potential goes far beyond what we can imagine."

Stop treating their opinions as perfect – "Opinions", well, that's what we are the recipient of most of our lives. In life, we often have a variety of people that we are grateful to call our friends; we meet some of them in our early childhood days, we meet some in our senior school days, we meet some in our college days, and so we end up meeting a lot of people in different time of our lives. But very few remain with us for the remainder of the journey as that's how life is, for with time, everybody's priorities change, and everybody moves on with their lives. And so very few are left with us. At this point, we grow up and become individuals we were forced to be due to parental or peer pressure, as very few of us can grow up without keeping people's opinions in our life perspective. And so those individuals who grow without keeping people's opinions in their life perspective end up two ways- either they reach incredible heights of human excellence or incredible heights of human failure. The only difference is that the one

    Your Actions Define Your Existence

who excelled always dreamt big and followed their dreams while ignoring everybody else's opinions. At the same time, the one who failed miserably followed his own opinions. The only problem was that he had no goals or aspirations. He was either pampered to the core or is a spoiled brat and is so opinionated that he regards his opinions as the one and only, and that's the reason for his failures.

But there is also the 3rd type of being; I call them the "**opinion seeker**" ones.

These individuals are capable of doing incredible things in their lives and even think about pursuing them or going after them, but they simply fail to do so. WHY? Because they care too much about what people have to say or give too much power to people and their opinions, and this is where they mess themselves up.

You see, in life, you will find various kinds of people with different upbringings and personalities as they grow up. Due to such contrasting and different upbringings, they all will grow up with other ideas, emotions and philosophies. And so, it is your responsibility to put much more faith and far more trust in your ideas, whatever that may be. For instance- when planning to start a new business, write a new book, start an online hustle or maybe even plan on hiking to the top of the mountain, you must absolutely believe that you can do it, and you must do it. But to do that, you must put far more faith and trust into your ideas and self than somebody else's. Because at the end of the day, it's your instinct that is guiding you towards that goal of yours, and you have to believe that what you are doing is being done to make you a better, stronger and much more competent person and no matter what the price, you should be willing to pay it, without causing harm to anybody.

You will always find an individual who thinks your ideas are crazy, you will always find individuals who believe your ideas are too far-fetched, you will always find individuals who think you are too obsessed with your goals, you will always find individuals who think you are too monotonous, but the only individual who thinks this idea might work is "You", nobody else. "You" can transform them into reality and make yourself the person you have always dreamt of. And if you are lucky, you will find a friend or two who believes in you (Certainly yes, in my case), but for most of us, it's not going to happen. They will first doubt you, and then they will laugh at you. They will envy you, and then they will admire you, and the only way you could do that is if you pay far more attention to your benevolent (As that's necessary for malevolence is painful) ideas and goals. Once you have done that, you could aim for those things you so dearly feel you could achieve. Your true loved ones will always validate you when you reach your goal, although you don't expect it. The ones who don't appreciate you will wish for your downfall, for that's how incredibly they have conquered failure and hope the same upon others, and that's the person you should ever dream of becoming.

And the only way you could stop paying attention to their opinions is when you accept that in pursuit of your goals, you could either succeed or fail miserably. But suppose you start paying far more attention to what they say than you do. In that case, failure is automatically guaranteed as that's the lowest you will reach, for that's where these individuals with your cruel opinions and evil motives reside, and you are better than that.

Lord Krishan's quote in the Bhagavad Gita perfectly surmises how to live our lives.

 Your Actions Define Your Existence

"Fight for the sake of duty, treating alike happiness and distress, loss and gain, Victory and defeat. Fulfilling your responsibility in this way, you will never incur sin."

This quote is an indicator through which we could understand how we could never ever achieve what we want to achieve if we start paying more attention to the outcomes and what people have to say. Doing what we can to the best of our abilities is our responsibility, ignoring those opinions is our responsibility, and not considering what they say about us as the truth is our responsibility. At the same time, defeat or Victory isn't our responsibility; it's our destiny, and once we consider this the true motive of our life, everything else follows.

SIX

Nobody Cares

> *"No one cares about you, No one cares.*
> *You will die and be forgotten."*
>
> **Frederick Lenz**

Has it ever happened to you that you were going through a really terrible day or maybe facing really troubled waters, both in your personal and professional lives, and yet your boss asked you, '**Hey did you finish that task I had given you**?' Or maybe someone dear to you (wife, husband, partner, parents) asked you, '**Hey why didn't you do that, I had told you again and again to get it done!**' After hearing those words, all you could do was think how pathetic they are, for even after knowing how messed up your current situation is, they simply don't care, and you may have reacted to those statements in different ways. Some might get into an argument for no compassion, some of you might rage inside, some of you might cry and some of you storm out of the situation. And so, all of you could react in different ways, to a similar question or statement, but the common thing among all of you is that you have realised the most basic and unknown truth about human life, and that is the fact that "**Nobody Cares**".

What this realisation has done is that it has made you understand how everything that you once felt or had thought matters, does not matter at all. If you are not able to deliver upon their expectations and meet the demands they have regarding you, you are as good as dead. I mean literally, "dead", for it is the contribution that gives meaning to human life, and if you are not able to contribute today, the Glories of your past will soon be forgotten and you will soon be termed as a finished product, maybe an incompetent employee or even a bad husband, son, father, daughter, mother, sister or brother. You could be seen as any of these things simply by failing to meet their demands, and everything you once believed would define your legacy turns out to be nothing more than a self-created illusion. All the times you didn't do something as you felt they were watching you or judging you, was nothing about a self-grandiose image you had built about yourself, thinking the world revolves around you and

   Your Actions Define Your Existence

your actions. But in reality, you are nothing in their eyes, and that is something that you should understand.

But how is it that should you react once you come to this harsh and yet basic realization?

Well you should bloody hell do what you always wanted to do and absolutely smash your goals and propel yourself towards a path you once thought wasn't worth going towards for you feared judgement or being shamed, or being termed as something or somebody you didn't like, but in reality you will always be termed as somebody you are not by somebody else, and that is what has been keeping you under permanent constraints, but now that you have come to the realisation, it is about time that you give yourself a slap in your face and move the bloody hell ahead, for either you are dead or alive it won't make a difference. Although maybe for a few days, your family members might mourn you, soon your very existence and its achievement would disappear from this earth, and you won't be remembered by anybody, and that's something once you know, should make you feel powerful in the most incredible of ways. For now, you have realised that you are not going to get out of this alive, this thing known as "Life", so why the hell should you not do and aim for the things that you once felt would liberate you from your miserable and bleak existence? Now you are longer held by the shackles of fear, judgement and disappointment, for you have come to the most basic of realisations that your life is in your hands, and you are the biggest creator of your actions and the most qualified judge of it, and nobody can take it away from you, but for that you have to brave enough to confront the truth regarding your existence, and its mere non-essentials to other human beings. And that could happen to you no matter who you are. You might be the Prime Minister of this country or the governor of your state, but once you are out of office, your existence is nowhere to be found, and that's what should enable you to aim higher, for you have realised that a life where we hold back ourselves by fearing things what people might make of it, were all a lie. And that lie has held you back and kept you from becoming somebody you were always wanting to become, but could never become and now you have the chance to prove it and make it count for yourself.

Khabib Nurmagomedov who is one of the most successful and popular MMA (mixed martial arts) fighters to have ever graced the game due to his impeccable unbeaten record once stated a famous line- **"Nobody cares, you might be tired or maybe having personal problems or maybe going through some sort of an emotional issue, nobody cares as it is not their business. They have come here to watch you fight as they have paid for those tickets with their hard-earned money (mostly hard earned) of theirs, and so all they care about is how you fight and how you can entertain them. And if you can't do it, then don't fight, Go home, Bye Bye."**

These words from Khabib would give you a better understanding of what exactly I am talking about.

We have to come to the very basic realisation that the world as we see it, banks on only one thing for our overall well-being and our overall health and that is what are willing to do for ourselves and what are willing to face in order to reach that goal we have set for ourselves. And those goals could be different for every individual, for you are free to have your own choices (until we are either born in Afghanistan, Syria or other tyrannical countries) and those choices would very much determine what you could do based on those aspirations and once you take that decision, you will end up realising how even the biggest of mistakes and even the smallest of achievements don't bother much to you, as

    Your Actions Define Your Existence

you have realised how most of time your reaction was not based on what you think about the possible outcome, rather it was based on what you felt somebody else may have thought about it. And once you make the crystal clear to yourself, you are bound to stride no matter how big or small those steps are.

Let's understand how we could make this very basic fact stick in our minds for our entire lifetime and make us capable enough to accept setbacks and victories without being overwhelmed or underwhelmed by them.

You are not the centre of the world

Has it ever happened that you went to a party or an event that you had been excited for a long time and all you could think about was the kind of outfit you should wear in order to be in the limelight of the event and get everyone's attention? You wore an incredible three-piece crisp suit or a dress that you felt would easily make you look extremely charming, handsome and beautiful and everybody's eyes would be fixated on you. And you spray some incredible perfume that you had planned you would be wearing today, some of the guys may have imagined that tonight's the night they finally get a hit with the women of their dreams and the women may have thought tonight is the night they meet the man of their dreams (may not be the case necessarily but that's sometimes what we think). And then you enter the event all hyped up about your presence over there, reimagining particular movie scenes where the lead always takes all the attention and the moment, he/she enters, everybody gets silent and starts admiring you and that's what you keep reimagining about.

But then once you set foot inside the event, Disaster strikes!

Why!

Because you end up seeing almost everybody is well-decked and well-dressed just like you. Everybody is smelling as good as you (some even smell better). Some of them are wearing even more crisp and even more expensive suits than you, yet nobody is complimenting them, how could they do it to you? Yet you end up wondering how every individual in the party is busy in their own world. Some of them are hanging out and having a lot of fun with their friends, some are making new contacts, some are observing everyone as they are either alone or too shy to go say Hi even to somebody they know, and some as usual are hitting (romantically) on the attractive individuals from either sex (male/female). And that's when you end up realising how inconsequential our lives are to everybody and yet we put so much energy and attention into thinking what that other individual might think. We fuss about it, get hyped about it or in some cases get anxious about it, but in reality, none of that matters.

This situation very much explains a regular phenomenon in people's lives. It doesn't necessarily need to be a formal event including suits and dresses, it could be a simple cultural event in our workplace or school as well. But after reading this a lot of you might be thinking, I never ever dress for anybody else, I only dress for myself and my own confidence, well if you do that, then you are somebody I would love to meet and admire, for there is a big difference between what humans really want and what humans say they want (especially women) and based on that I have given the above situation for us as humans always want a compliment, always want somebody something nice about us, as that's what makes us who we are right? That is the reason we often feel low when nobody appreciates our good work or people tend to disregard the amount of effort we have put in.

   Your Actions Define Your Existence

For example, David Hemery, an Olympic gold medalist, embarked on a journey to discover the qualities that distinguish the world's elite athletes. Hemery understood that natural talent and physical attributes, while significant, weren't the entire picture. Many individuals with exceptional genetics never reach the pinnacle of success, while others with seemingly fewer natural advantages do. To explore this, he interviewed over 60 champions, including icons like Wayne Gretzky, Rod Laver, and Edwin Moses. His goal was to uncover the characteristics essential not just for excelling in sports but in any area of life.

One of the most unexpected traits? Sensitivity to others' opinions.

Nine out of ten respondents agreed with the statement, "It's important what other people think of you." An even greater number expressed a desire to please others through their athletic endeavours—whether it be coaches, teammates, family, or friends. Only a small handful admitted that their primary motivation was self-satisfaction.

This study proves how world-class athletes who are given so much admiration and accolades by millions do care about how people perceive them and that's what makes them perform. But having the same attitude of performing to fulfill other's expectations and doing things based on what others say is what causes the downfall of normal folks who end up doing nothing in the hope that people will stop judging or calling them out, and that's where the difference between an Olympic champion and general folk lies.

For the simple reason that the general folk let this feature stop them and prevent them from setting out and doing the things needed to grow, Olympic athletes use this feature to propel themselves way further than any individual could imagine.

Individuals always have a sense of everything and everybody working for them and against them and that's one of the primary reasons behind the fact that why many people aren't able to do the things that they had hoped and had envisioned for themselves. What is really needed in order to gain the necessary qualities and become who you always wanted to become, is the simple fact that you have to accept that every individual in today's day and age is messed up or entangled in their own thoughts and we are all our own heroes in our script, a script known as "**Life**". And this is the script where even the director (you), are not in control of what the other actors (people) do. As every individual is acting according to the basis of their own script. Some of them have somebody else controlling their lives (husband, wife, parents), while others are simply on their own. But the one thing you are in control of is how you view the world and how you do the things needed to get done, to get a life that has a substantial amount of freedom and a life that would enable you to move forward without any attention towards judgements. Although there are some individuals (household aunties, frustrated crooks, predators) whose life would always revolve around how to stop you and how to make sure you never progress, for making you stop would enable them to feel good about their own deficiencies as humans and their inability to make good use of their lives, but remember what you want to do and how you want to do matters. For if tomorrow if you fail to deliver, you will be one facing the brunt of those people who were expecting you to deliver, and that means you are left with absolutely no choice.

It's a brutal world **where if you are not on the table then you would be on the menu**, simple as that. Now the decision that lies in you is whether you would continue to do the things that you wanted to do, or you would hide your incompetence by shifting blame towards someone else. For if you do the former you would feel like you are worthy of being yourself (although people would

 Your Actions Define Your Existence

appreciate but that won't matter as it's basically a temporary event for soon, they would forget your accomplishments) and if you choose the latter you would have to be ready to face the consequences of not delivering for something that you were being counted for, and that's a choice you have to make.

The most important thing that has to be remembered is that since the world does not revolve around you, it's upon you what you choose to make your life off. It's upon you to make the most out of what you have, and all of their energies and thoughts won't necessarily go towards benevolent things, but if your actions and thoughts are able to outweigh benevolence with malevolence, then you have won in life and if you could do that, you are there and you will make sure that you have made a difference. But that intention to make a difference should be first about you, for your intention should be about making a positive difference in your own life, and if you could achieve that with a certain amount of success and if you could do that then most certainly you would make a difference in somebody else's life. But remember that somebody else (apart from a few) will soon forget what you did, but the only person who will always remember is you. And whenever you remember that incredible thing you did, it would propel you on days when darkness has clouded your judgement, and on that day, you would realise it's not them thinking and manifesting bad about you, but rather it's you. It's upon you to wake up and learn how you could change it all and take the right step, for the onus is always on you, it always has been, and it always will be. For you should care what you do, what you think and how you react and behave to the various situations in life. And once you realise all of it, you will become who you want to be, and that would be an individual at ease with his/her actions and that would mean you are there where you are meant to be, not where you were told to be, and that's something to strive for.

Stop magnifying your flaws

Has it ever happened to you that when you were selected for a presentation either during your school and colleges days and you had been informed about it prior to a few days before the day you were meant to do that thing? And the next few days were literal hell for you as you could barely do anything without thinking about what could happen if you mess it up either by forgetting the content or messing up the lines. For some of you, it even gave you sleepless nights and panic attacks as you could not understand how you would do something so big in front of so many people. There is a cloud of emotions and outbursts raging inside of you, and then the big day comes. You are somehow able to muster up the courage and you start speaking and guess what everything becomes easier. There were moments when you stumbled and almost fell ashamed but soon you realised nobody was actually paying attention. You felt people were going to stand up and hurl abuses and do all sorts of things, but once your presentation was over everybody started clapping and soon moved on to the other presenter. You come down the stage and are soon followed by the next speaker, and in the next sixty seconds you end up realising all the mistakes you made and were afraid you would be reprimanded by your teacher then she walks in and almost ignores you, but then simply pats you on the back and says, "well done mate". You are shocked, "Well done" Did she even listen to me? And then you end up thinking the teacher may not have given attention to you and you ask your colleagues what the mistakes you made, and they tell you, "You were amazing", and you are like "what the hell". You soon witness how while the next presenter is speaking individuals on the back are sleeping, some are staring and lost in their own thoughts and barely some are attentive and some are waiting for their turn to speak. And none of them pointed out the flaws that you had imagined and

 Your Actions Define Your Existence

conjured up for yourself, or even if you had done it, nobody cared. And that's when you come to the realisation of how we are all entangled and victimised in our own minds, we end up magnifying our shortcomings by ourselves, as well glorify our existence, but in reality, we are nothing but a specs of dust in the greater scheme of things, and that's when your life changed, and whoever comes to this realisation lives a far some simpler and less anxious life.

Now, this example may have given you an idea regarding how most of the time we end up inflating our own sense of existence and most of the time the hell and misery that we go through are built and developed by our own minds and that's the reason so many of us are unable to make ourselves able and competent individuals for the most of times we are concentrated and deep rooted in our own drawbacks that we aren't able to make our lives worthwhile we are alive. And this begs the question, were our mistakes really that bad?

Well, in order to answer that question first we have to look at the extent of damage you did or made in order to consider how bad those mistakes were. Did somebody die? Did somebody break themselves down? Did you hurt someone really personally? Have you been gaslighting someone? Did you invade another country and massacre millions in the name of religion or other factors? Did you assault somebody? Well, if you haven't done any of these, you need to relax the hell down, because if you haven't done any of these then there are people who are way worse than you could imagine, for people are there and sometimes roaming freely after committing those mistakes that I just mentioned. And the reason I told you to relax is because based on how you are thinking after committing that mistake, and all the worrying you are doing regarding how everybody would judge you because of your flaws and mistakes needs to be suspended. For according to you, your acts might be world shattering, but in the large perspective they haven't done anything substantial and that means you are all right and have got nothing to worry about. Although that doesn't mean you get to go away without holding any responsibility or accountability for the act you did, mostly that responsibility you need to have is, for you and for the ones within your periphery (only if they have been impacted), rest assured you got nothing to fuss about.

And so, the big question that arises is- Will people find it easier once they have understood their place in the world, once they have realised that neither does the world revolve around them and neither is everybody paying enough attention to point out their flaws or appreciate their strengths?

Well, unfortunately no not really, for these realizations are bound to act like an arrow straight into our hearts and force us to question the true purpose of our existence! For who are we if we are not what we had envisioned ourselves to be? It would force us to think that our lives are absolutely useless and our acts are nothing but inconsequential for nobody pays attention to them, Good or Bad. And would make us understand why so many people decide to stay in denial for that's what gives them comfort and would have done to us always, for life was so much simpler when we had not stumble upon this truth.

But then comes the bigger question, Was life really simpler?

Unfortunately, it wasn't either. You lived a life burdened by shame, guilt, and the constant fear of judgment and opinions, making even the earlier years difficult. And now you have to choose which hard you choose, the former of thinking of yourself as truly precious in everyone's life and taking every step with precaution, or the latter where you have truly become an individual who now knows the true measure of your existence and your acts and is content with it, and if you want to live a life with less fear and less miserable you should always choose the latter one.

WHY?

Because now you are well aware of who you are and what your real standing in your world is. You will no longer be oblivious to the truth of our existence. And the truth is that we are all side actors in somebody else's lives, and no matter how big we think our mistakes or flaws are, it's always much smaller than what they deem their flaws as. And once you know that you would become very powerful. For now, you have realised how you would really go and chase those things you had always envisioned but were held back fearing judgement or laughter at your incompetency and your drawbacks. But now you have understood and realised how everybody has drawbacks, and how everybody is flawed and yet they are able to propel towards their visions, so what's stopping you? Although it's true there will always be someone better than you, in some cases, you might be the best, but there will always be someone trying to reclaim your spot and sooner or later that will happen. For the world has seen far too many kings, queens, tyrants, dictators, and superstars, who were once proud of their accomplishments, come and go, for that's the true nature of life, and how nobody ever remembers what they did, until and unless it is needed for our own self needs.

And so this should make you feel like someone who has all the control you need in your life in order to do those things that you dreamt of doing or had planned on doing and now that you are free of fear and judgement, you could do those things without fussing over what could happen if things went south, for there is always a probability of that happening, for that has happened to almost every human who has ever walked on the earth and was willing to do something worthwhile (negative or positive) in their short mortal stay on this rock we call "Earth". Once you realise all of these you come to the realisation your flaws aren't really as giant as you deem them be, rather they are a reflection of your human nature to have drawbacks. The option is what you plan on doing with it, either you work on them and get better at them or you fuss about what you didn't do. Either way, it won't make an impact on anybody else apart from you, and that's the one person whose actions and reactions you could always determine and that's what you should do. For what else would do, if not make yourself less flawed and more strengthened in order to make yourself stronger for the rigours of this world, that's what makes you who you are. A flawed oxygen breathing living organism known as a human.

Deliver or disappear

Do you remember any sportsmen or any actor or any other well-know individual from any sort of field who had once set the world on fire with their incredible and amazing performances? They had literally become the talk of the town with their incredible performances be it on the field or on the stage and they were meant to be the next big thing. But guess what, a few months or a year down the line, barely anybody remembers them and soon they are gone into oblivion, and people forget about who they were and what they had done. And even if they do remember those once great talents, they are remembered for what they could have been rather than what they are. And the simple reason for that is because they stopped delivering on what was expected from them, simple as that.

If it was a sportsman his performances dwindled either because he had lost his way with the incredible amount of adoration and appreciation he received, or either he got injured and never

  Your Actions Define Your Existence

came back. For a singer or an actor, it could be because they lost their way with drugs and alcohol (which happens a lot in the entertainment industry) or they started choosing really bad projects along the way, as they crumbled under the pressure of delivering again and again and that eventually led to their downfall. For whatever reason, they chose to stop living by others' expectations and were soon cast into the wilderness, never to return. Though a few manage to come back, it is rare, as the experience shatters their soul and minds, leaving most without the courage to return.

These instances show how people when they stop performing and stop having the appeal they once had, are abandoned like chewing gum being spat after relishing its real taste. This shows how ruthless the world is and how nobody is really bothered with what you are going through, especially when you are down, for now you no longer serve their best interests and associating with you won't bear any fruits for them and that's the reason you are made to disappear. It is the reason people idealise individuals like Cristiano Ronaldo, Lionel Messi, Tom Cruise, Shah Rukh Khan, Gisele Bundchen and many more. Why because all of them continue to deliver way beyond what they were expected and that's what matters. For if you go through, any of their personal lives, most of them are imperfect and have faced really hard times and many had thought they would disappear, but they didn't, they persevered and continued and continue to deliver and that's what matters. The world knows that they have their own flaws but nobody cares, as long as Ronaldo is scoring goals, Messi is scoring goals, Shah Rukh is giving them great movies, and Gisele is continuing to inspire many upcoming girls to become models, with their continuous and relentless work, nobody really cares. Because through these individuals thousands are getting paid and employed because their work is delivering the right things for their stakeholders and that's what matters. Although people do like them because they are good humans (imperfectly), that attraction mostly comes from what they do, what they have done and what they will continue to do. For the basic fact that what they have done and have been doing is something very few people are able to do consistently for many years, sometimes even a decade or two, and that's delivering upon the expectations bestowed upon them, and making sure they live upon what people expect from them and that's the reason they continue to stay relevant.

On the other hand, those individuals who absolutely rock the stage (or field) with their performances end up losing the way. One of the main reasons for this is that they begin to believe all the appreciation and wealth are meant for them and will remain with them forever. But in reality, these things have been given to them because through their impeccable work (even for a short amount of time) they were able to make other people earn some of the most important things that matter in human lives and that is, a good amount of money, a great deal of happiness, incredible amounts of emotions and make people believe that if they could do it, everybody could. That's the first stage of being great, but in this stage, they end up losing the way, for they already start considering themselves great and think people will keep appreciating them no matter what, no matter how bad they perform people will keep on supporting them, but that's not how the world works. And when they suddenly start finding out they are messing it up, they further fall down the barrel and that's how they end up losing themselves.

What should never be forgotten is that nobody really cares about what you are going through especially if you are a top performer. Some of the legends of every industry continue to get criticised

   Your Actions Define Your Existence

even for one bad game, and the difference between them and others is the fact that they understand why people are angry and turn up the next day and absolutely smash their opponents and continue to deliver and that's how they continue to stay relevant. So many singers or players we once idolised are now dead or going through some sort of a crisis but nobody cares for it no longer bothers them. Everybody was with them during their highs, but now since they can turn up and give them a good time, they are no longer needed and soon they are replaced by somebody else who has outwitted them, and that's the rule of the game, **Either, you turn up and deliver or you don't turn up at all. And if you have turned up, make sure you deliver, for if you don't you will soon be forgotten.** And this may sound really mean and brutal, but unfortunately, that is the rule of the game, for the world isn't sympathetic to anybody, for in your worst times even your biggest of supporters, fans or in some cases even family would turn up against you, for now you no longer give them what they wanted, and what people want could be different for everybody, but it is the want that matters and since now the want is gone, you are gone and unless you create that want again, you will forever be trapped in oblivion and nobody would give a damn, and that's how the world works.

You have to understand how we are all built in the same way, for we expect our heroes to do the same, and the same could be expected from us as well, in fact, it is, and you may not be a superstar or a celebrity but there will always be someone who expects you to deliver every time you are tasked with something and if you fail to deliver you have no right to cry about the reasons you weren't able to succeed, for you did the same to your idols. And if you do cry or sulk over your disappointing result you will come to the realisation regarding how much your idols suffer and persevere in order to become who they have become, and the day you understand you will become a much more empathetic individual, you will become someone who understand how terrible it feels when we fail to deliver and how badly we are judged by it. You will also learn how failing is so very crucial in order to grow and how disappointments are a must in order to strive ahead in life, for what would life be if there was nothing to be disappointed about? But what you will learn along the way that how important it is to deliver and how little or no understanding we have regarding individuals who might be going through a really painful and tough period in their lives. For they all want to deliver as it gives them happiness but when they fail, there isn't anybody more devastated than them, and when you learn to understand that you will become an individual who has gone beyond the realms of a normal human being for you have become someone who expects people to deliver and when they fail, you will lend your hand to help them get up again, for that's when they need you the most. For everybody would lend them a hand when they are at the peak of their performances and are delivering way more than expected, but the scarcity of resources and support happens when you are cornered against the wall.

And if you are brave enough to assist them during those moments, and if they understand how crucial you are (not everybody would understand, especially narcissists) they will forever be behind you as they have now realised what it means to have somebody look out for you, when you have rejected as a finished product, and if you could do that, you could become a person who wants people to deliver and is yet understanding of all their situations and that's what would make you a leader who moves ahead and takes everybody along with you, rather than walking alone to bask in the glory that was never meant for you.

   Your Actions Define Your Existence

And unfortunately, either today or tomorrow times and circumstances will catch up on you, so why wait for that moment, when you have plenty of it?

So, make a difference and make sure everybody delivers and nobody disappears, and even if they do disappear, have the courage to walk in the trenches alone, for the world will be so much better with one less soul residing in misery, desperation and bitterness. And if you could do that, you could do anything.

Reframe your world view

The way you see the world is your worldview, and this worldview is like the lens through which you can get a better understanding of your reality. This reality of yours is more often influenced by various factors such as the culture you witnessed while growing up, the upbringing you were given not necessarily by your parents but all the stakeholders involved and your personal experiences ranging from your childhood to your current age (teenage, adulthood) However, to live a life filled with more contentment and less sorrow, you must learn to reframe your worldview. This reframing doesn't come easily and demands the acceptance of harsh truths about the world and ourselves. And once you accept these harsh truths, you will find yourself empowered to make your existence more meaningful, at least to yourself. For in this brutal world, where most of the individuals you would ever meet or know would be your competition and the margins between success and failure are so razor-thin, you must cultivate a mindset that enables you to survive and thrive, for that is why Charles Darwin had quoted the term of **"Survival of the Fittest"**. Along the way, as you decide this particular worldview as the real way of your life, you will come across instances that would further allow you to believe in this phenomenon and would enforce this harsh but necessary truth more and more into your lives. As stated, before and no matter how harsh or cruel it may sound, the most uncomfortable and difficult truth that you will have to accept is the simple fact that, in the larger scheme of things, everyone around you is, in some way, your competition. Now, this is no way me stating that your mother, father, sibling or even your partner is your competition, but what I am stating is that if you let your guard down in the cutthroat competition of today's day and age, there is a very high probability of your suffering in ways you could have never imagined, and no matter how harsh it sounds, that is something we all have to accept.

This phenomenon I stated above isn't simply limited to the workplace or professional settings; it extends to almost every facet of life. Socially, economically, and even emotionally, people are competing for resources, recognition, and sometimes even affection. It's a grim realization, but necessary.

We have often heard some incredibly powerful individuals who are either millionaires or billionaires say that money doesn't matter. You've likely encountered beautiful women who claim that looks are insignificant. Similarly, the fittest individuals might tell you that the body doesn't matter. While these statements may sound profound and comforting, they often gloss over a critical reality: these people possess the very things they are downplaying. Their words hold weight only because they have achieved a status that allows them to transcend the need for validation through these attributes. A billionaire can afford to say that money doesn't matter because they've already amassed enough wealth to secure their place in society. A stunning woman or a physically fit man can dismiss the importance of looks because they've already benefited from them. This is not to say that their views are disingenuous, but rather to point out the underlying privilege that allows them to make such statements.

    Your Actions Define Your Existence

For most people, however, these things—money, looks, health, and status—do matter. They matter because they often determine how you are perceived and treated by others in society. For the fact that it is the harsh truth in our society wherein until you have those things, you cannot afford to play them down or devalue them to showcase your non-materialistic affections, for the basic fact that those material things give meaning to our lives and those material things define who we are as a person and what kind of treatment we will be given by the society and how we will be treated are all determined by the possession of those things, for without those are lives are as meaningless as a lifeguard in an Olympic swimming competition.

So, what do you do once you realise that the way our society functions, well you forget everything else and bust your ass and work hard to acquire what you need to establish your presence in the world, and only then can you begin to transcend these superficial markers of success? As stated, to work hard and reach that place where you could be making those generalised statements of things that do not matter to you, have to be acknowledged for possessing them and only then you could achieve that place. Although it's true, for sometimes you could get lucky and maybe one day you would wake up to the news of earning a few million dollars or might hear somebody getting rich through some stock suddenly going up where they had invested by mistake, but make no mistake for those are one in a million instances and trust me based on the examples I have seen of people becoming multimillionaires through a lottery or luck, those individuals don't end up doing so well, due to the simple fact that those things came without any sacrifice or any sort of work, and for that reason, those things hold no amount of value for them, until they have lost them. And only then do they realise what they had and how they are back to where they were before.

For that reason, all you can do and all you must do to truly become someone who is competent and yet an individual who conducts and regards himself necessary to the world and himself, and that could only happen when you take up the mantle and proceed towards life as if it's the last day of your life, for by now you may have already realized how nobody cares and how that only strengthens and motivates you to get stronger and do better for yourself.

One of the most empowering and liberating realizations that you can have as you tread along this path, is the absolute necessity of building a self-reliant version of yourself who is capable of withering any storm, who is capable of taking on any task, who is capable of saying yes when he knows it's borderline impossible (everything possible today was once impossible) and who is willing to on the task rather than complaining how hard it is or how unfair it is, come what may. At the same time, you should be aware and mature enough to understand how having a strong support network of your loved ones or well-wishers like your friends, family, and mentors is equally crucial for sometimes their support propels you to finish that last step or take on last battle, for we are all humans and well doubt ourselves, but ultimately you have to train your mind and become bulletproof mentally and understand that you are responsible for your success and your failures cannot be blamed on anybody else. However, this doesn't mean you should withdraw or refuse support from others; rather, it emphasises the importance of taking responsibility for your life, acknowledging the choices that have brought you this far, and making intentional decisions to continue moving forward.

Self-reliance also means accepting the possibility of failure, and accepting that sometimes the result could go sideways in such extreme ways that you would start doubting everything you have

    Your Actions Define Your Existence

ever stood for, and it is at those times that you and your mindset would truly be tested. And it is at that moment that you will come to realise how important failure is and at the same time how bitter it is to fail. For what is life without failure, as it is and will always be a constant at some point in your life? However, how you respond to those events of failure will determine how you proceed with your life, and whether you grow stronger or fall apart.

One of the most intriguing and harshest things that you may have realised and understood by now is how everything you were taught in schools and by society was a lie. And that became permanent in your mind once you realised how harsh the world treats failures and how the world is not kind to those who fail, even though some of the most successful individuals to have graced the world have failed far more than anybody could have ever imagined. At the same time, you have also realised how it rewards those who learn from their failures and keep pushing forward makes them stronger and makes them far more capable enough to take on bigger tasks and become far more competent and dangerous (positively) than they could have ever imagined.

And, you have come to realise how "resilience", therefore, is one of the most important traits you can cultivate within yourself, for sometimes when you feel all is over, it is resilience that would guard you and propel you further. In the journey of Reframing your worldview, you have to start considering failure as a stepping stone rather than a dead end, as that would help you maintain your momentum, even when things get tough. It is resilience that would enable you to make sure that you can negate all those unfortunate happenings and continue striving forward, for that is necessary to achieve things that you set for yourself.

Also, in the pursuit of understanding the true nature of the world and making yourself far more capable of handling it. Another, harsh truth that you must accept is that life is not fair, never was and never will be. You may have heard this line a thousand times, and yet you may have had difficulty accepting it for denial gives us comfort, but understand it and get on with your life by making it laser printed on your brain (hypothetically). The world does not operate on a system of fairness or justice, rather it operates on a system of brutality, where only the ones capable of making themselves dominated and feared are the ones held in high regard although there are a few exceptions, but those are very rare, and most of the times even the individual you had regarded to be benevolent could and would often turn out to have incredible amounts of capability to be malevolent and do some incredibly evil and harsh things to safeguard their ideas and conceptions of reality, and the sooner you accept that reality, the faster you would make yourself less miserable and less frustrated, as in that way anything evil or bitter would create less anger in you and would create an environment for far more mental fortitude and strength within you, no matter how much you have to go through.

Oftentimes, you will encounter situations in your life where people with far less talent than yourself, far less experience and less integrity will end up trumping you and succeeding in their lives, while those who work hard, are honest about their intentions, are empathetic and play by the rules will fail. Such events could be soul-crushing, making you question everything you have known till now and could be incredibly maddening, but it is a reality that you must come to terms with. And to make yourself a far more suitable individual ready to take on the world, you have to let go of the notion that life should be fair. Once you do that you will able to focus more on things that matter, allowing you to

    Your Actions Define Your Existence

make the most of your opportunities and crush your opponents, that is something most of us are not prepared for, for that's the reason those who understand the way the real world works and can be in the top of the food chain. At the same time, you have mindful that in pursuit of your goals, you don't end up becoming the devil you always despised as it's important to understand that accepting the unfairness of life doesn't mean becoming cynical or abandoning your principles. Rather, it would mean that you have recognised that you cannot control everything and that life will oftentimes be arbitrary and unjust. And instead of wasting energy lamenting these facts, you have to use it as motivation to work even harder, smarter, and more strategically.

You have to be able to understand the workings of the modern-day world for that would often give you the edge in various circumstances. To thrive in a world that is constantly changing, you must be willing to learn new things and become a fool, and that is something most of us avoid, and yet that's where true change lies. It's something I have myself faced, for I remember when I started my boxing classes around last year, I hated it as I loved weight training (still do) and being in the gym wearing that compression feeling like a superman made me feel invincible and regarding weight training, I have always known the basics due to almost 5 years of On and Off training and knowledge gaining. But in boxing, I had to suddenly unlearn everything and was taught everything from scratch, and it was ego-shattering especially when my coach would mock my boxing skills, and would surprise me when I wished I could be in the gym. But after six months of training, I became a different man, as my confidence grew and my ability to defend myself and my loved ones grew and that's when I realised how growth often happens when we go and do through things that we know are necessary and yet avoid for it would make us look like a fool and would once again make us look like nobody's, but that's where the real growth lies and that everybody should be striving for, in their ways. And if you continue to cling rigidly to old ways of thinking and doing things the way you have been doing, you are often left behind, while those who can adapt and go through the grinds are the ones who thrive.

Adaptability is not just about being flexible in your actions, but also in your thinking. You must be willing to question your assumptions, challenge your beliefs, and change your mind when you stumble upon things that you once weren't aware of, or denied for that was far easier than accepting and changing yourself. And if you could do that, it means you have integrated humility into your individuality and the fact that you are willing to admit you are wrong, means you are halfway there, for acceptance is the Achilles' heel of far too many people.

You have to understand that competition is and will always be fierce, and for that matter setbacks are inevitable. And yet during those moments how persistent you are, would define whether you failed or succeeded in the task you had set out to carry. There may be times when it is necessary to change your course of action and adjust your goals, and at first, you would resist doing it, but sooner or later you will understand that if your intentions are right and if you are willing to put your faith in it, it will work out. The key is to keep moving forward, even if the direction changes, for sometimes it's necessary to take a curved path to reach our destination, for straight paths are often taken by everybody.

Finally

As a whole what you must understand and accept is the fact that, no matter how big or small your achievements, they will eventually be forgotten. This may sound bleak, but it is a reality that should liberate you from the constant worry over the reaction and drawbacks towards your actions. Once you understand that success is fleeting and that nothing lasts forever, you will be able to free yourself from the pressure to constantly achieve and instead focus on what truly matters to you.

This doesn't mean that you should stop striving for success, but rather that you should redefine what success means to you. Instead of seeking validation from others or chasing after external markers of success, focus on what brings you fulfilment and satisfaction. Success should be about living a life that is meaningful to you, rather than trying to meet society's expectations. Once you grasp it all, you won't just endure the challenges of this world—you will truly thrive.

SEVEN

Beware of the Devil in Human Form

> *"Maybe all the schemes of the devil were nothing compared to what man could think up"*
>
> **Joe Hill**

As children most of us were very well used to hearing stories about Gods and demons, about how they looked. God was often described to us by our elders as somebody who is residing in heaven and everything good about us and about the world is in some or the other way influenced by God itself, for in many ways it is the source of all benevolent things in the world. While the Devil on the other hand is the source of all the bad things that happened in the world and in creation itself. And it told us to be residing in the deep dungeons of hell for that's the way it loves to live, for darkness and cruelty are what it feeds on and when it can't get a good supply of it in hell it comes up onto the surface and creates destruction and pain for that's what makes it survive. In many ways, it is the source of all sorts of malevolent activities in the world.

The devil is the one who creates pain and anarchy in our minds and creates situations where individuals end up acting way beyond any normal human could have acted and that's what makes them the true creators of misery. For it is he who is responsible for the world burning at all times, for when the world burns it creates a sense of pride in his mind, and that's what he strives for and that's what gives meaning to his existence. But as time went humans started evolving more and more and the devil in many ways felt left out, as the humans with their new inventions were now doing much more incredible and amazing things that it wasn't capable of before, and that created a sense of panic in the devil's minds. In ancient times or the times before humans had evolved to such an extent, it used to be a species that considered its life to be revolving around nature, and anything that was beyond its control and anything that seemed unexplainable to it was considered as an act of God. And that consideration also gave rise to the Devil, for whenever anything bad happened or in the occurrence of an unfortunate event the humans ended by interpreting that evil

    Your Actions Define Your Existence

act as the act of the Devil and that's what made the Devil very happy, for it was finally acknowledged. But in modern times, the devil realised if it doesn't adapt to the changing times and needs, it will soon lose its relevance and so what it did, it started creating humans in its own form, and unfortunately, they are very much different to the devil we could be ourselves to be.

The Devil we could all identify with was portrayed as a being who had two horns and was dark coloured and had powers similar to God (although in a negative way) and was the only true rival to all of God's creation. And could easily be identified. But that's where the devil moulded itself in ways that have made it unrecognisable in the modern-day world. And what did it do? It simply created beings in human form and released them into the world, one by one, fully aware of the profound influence a single act of evil can have on an individual. It understood that all it needed was one person in its likeness to carry out its deeds, knowing that such acts would multiply over time. Having witnessed humanity's capacity for darkness, it saw the opportunity to cultivate chaos. By sending a disciple of itself into the world, it gave rise to a reality consumed by malevolence—one filled with suffering, resentment, emotional detachment, hatred, conflict, insecurity, and self-interest. As these destructive forces spread, they reshaped the world into a mirror of its own—a realm of misery beyond imagination. With each act of cruelty, its power grew, and before long, it had assembled an army of its own devoted followers. And the only way he was able to do it was by making them look like all the other humans and by making them show them a world of power with such consequences that they could have never imagined.

These individuals that portray and represent the devil are found in all forms and shapes, and the worst part about them is the fact that they are similar in the way they look and they could be very own dear ones. They are most of the time in the topmost power positions, they are sometimes some of the good-looking individuals and they sometimes seem to be the nicest of individuals, but unfortunately, that is only a sham for what lies beneath those fake masks of their is truly dark and is filled with so much hatred and dark energy, that it could burn any individual with benevolent intentions. And unfortunately, that's what makes them relevant, for that is what they have been doing since ages and that is what has been making them more and more powerful with time.

If we go by what has happened ever since written records have been documented we would be able to get an idea regarding the amounts of malevolent acts that humans have created and how much pain and sorrow it has caused people all around the world. Some of the acts done by them or some of the events that have taken place to date sometimes shiver us from top to bottom as they are beyond the comprehension of a normal being. But that's what the devil is capable of making his disciples do, and unfortunately, those beings continue to leave their mark and make sure more and more individuals following their footsteps come up again and again and continue to cause sorrow and pain to the world.

During these times it often makes us question how somebody could do such horrific and cruel acts to their own human species, and that is where we must understand that these individuals are merely born in the shape of a human, and as they grow along the ways of the world, the traumas, the setbacks, the hurt they faced, makes them susceptible of becoming the very individuals they once despised and soon they end up following in the footsteps of those who came before them and that's how they end up becoming the disciples of the Devil.

    Your Actions Define Your Existence

But what is it that these devils in human form are after?

Well, the answer is simple, **Power**.

It is through their thirst and lust for power that they are willing to go to any extent and make sure their goals and desires are met and they end up epitomising what it means to truly have malevolent intentions and how it could affect everybody around them. For their actions are filled with such incredible amounts of pain and hatred that they have no other option but to continue in their journey, for they know once they stop, they will be consumed by the very beings that they are similar to and in that fear of being avenged by their dear species, they continue on the evil actions towards their human compatriots, and unfortunately there are far too many people who are guided by fear and shame and that is what these beings need to rule and assault them into subjugation in their own ways. These individuals would often come upon as very dominating, malevolent, bitter, resentful, narcissistic, and many more traits, and that is how they are able to make sure more and more people cower under the pressure they are meant by them and that is how they are made to suffer.

And that is where we get it wrong!

These individuals no matter how hateful and evil might be, are some of the most insecure and most fearful individuals. All their displays of bravery and strength are merely a facade, concealing their insecurities and the inefficiencies in how they navigate their lives. Inside they are well aware of the negative implications their actions are having upon the individuals and how they are causing so much suffering. But the bigger problem lies in how the hell do they get away with it all the time. Why the hell do they get elected to such powerful positions, and why the hell are they able to amass such an incredible amount of wealth and power with their evil acts?

It's because of the lack of awareness in the general public.

Most of you often see an individual with any of these personality traits that I mentioned above and the first thing you start doing is avoiding them or either meeting all of their demands. As we often think that they are as strong as they pretend to be and that's one of the main reasons they are able to keep on doing these acts and continue along with their actions. In fact, in many ways, people often get attracted to these traits especially women who get attracted to some of the most evil men, especially the ones with the dark triad traits such as psychopathic, Machiavellianism and narcissism. And when we are ones willing to serve ourselves as well cooked turkey to these non-empathetic monsters, we should not expect our lives to get any better, for that is what we asked for and that is what we have been delivered to.

We often consider their way of life and their perception regarding our lives to be the true way things are decoded and made to be in our lives and that's where we end up giving way more power to these individuals. For in reality even the slightest hint of any sort of rebellion or revolt messes up these individuals and that's what we could say to be the glitch in the matrix. A matrix we all have become used to.

Let me share a real-life story of a man whose way of life and the things he did, were for certain acts no human would ever do if he was not groomed by the devil or had he not been a disciple of it.

Let's call him Nasif.

Nasif is a 77 year old man who I have known in various capacities. His son and I have been close friends since our childhood days and in many ways, he has been involved in various important professional dealings with various members of our family. And so was I, but once I started knowing more and more things about

   Your Actions Define Your Existence

him, it made me realise how not all humans are made by God, rather some are made by the Devil himself, and that is what Nasif is to be associated with.

He was a man who had 4 children, 2 children from his 1st wife, 1 child from his 2nd wife, and 1 child from the affair he had with his housekeeping maid.

From the moment I met him, I had always seen how cruel and bitter he has been towards all of his own children, especially his first two children (my friend was one of them) who in many ways were two of the most responsible and capable individuals I have ever met. And for his other two kids, well he treated them as if they meant the world to him, even though they are two of the most spoiled individuals I have ever met. He had beaten his first wife for almost 30 years something I have witnessed various times during my childhood, and also the fact that he had even done some incredible horrific things to her, some of the things which I can't describe.

He has been charged with beating innocent and young children many times and has even been charged with committing sexual crimes on several of his employees. He had once beaten his own father when his father had come to defend his daughter-in-law. He once even tried to rape his own daughter (something which she escaped thanks to my friend).

These are some of the things that he did and continues to do so and from what I have described here, and any human with the consciousness of a capable and responsible individual would think twice before committing something like this, but alas these things are simply beyond the understanding of people like Nasif for there are many like him out there.

The things individuals like Nasif crave the most are fear and desperation. For these are individuals who have given up every single inch of humanity they ever had in their souls. Pain, terror and suffering are what these people crave the most and that's how I coined the term of **PTS (Pain, Terror and Suffering).**

PTS is something all of us have in some way or another but none of us crave it as much as these devils in human form do. These individuals are the ones who have lost every inch or every single strand of empathy, hope or love that has ever existed in the human world, as these are things that are completely contrary to what these things are known for. As these individuals are some of the most broken and most grief-stricken individuals that anybody has ever met. They don't know what it feels like to be loved, and that's the reason they have no bloody idea of what it feels like to love someone. It is basic human nature that we can only offer others what we ourselves possess. If we lack something, we either seek to acquire it—by asking or learning from others— or we belittle those who have it to mask our own shortcomings. And that is precisely what these individuals do.

These individuals are the ones who would often try to berate you, these individuals are the ones who would often invade countries and make thousands and millions die, all so that they could fulfil and satisfy their fragile and scarred egos. We have many politicians even in the present day and age who have often tried to start wars in order to make sure that they stay in power and these things don't necessarily happen only in autocratic countries, for many democratic countries and their leaders have also started wars and have also committed such horrific crimes in order to make sure their chair of power is safe, and in that process, they end up killing thousands and making millions suffer all so that they could survive all of the things that they feel they could

    Your Actions Define Your Existence

acquire by constantly staying position. A position where many have come before him and many would come after him and yet they feel they will be there constantly for that is what makes us humans think of ourselves as far too grand and bigger than we in reality are.

These sorts of monsters are even found in the most basic of places and even in the schools, something which is unexpected as the schools are known as temples of education, but unfortunately, that's how badly the devils have penetrated our society. Let me share a story about my school days, about an incident which shook me to the core and made me realise how the devil is often everywhere, what matters is how we either avoid him or fight him, for in both ways, it will cost us a lot.

During my school days, mostly on the 2nd Saturday or 4th Saturdays, our school used to get over by noon and then we used to go outside and have some fun by visiting restaurants, cafes or gaming parlours. And we used to have our own set of friends which were about 4-5 of us, and all of us would often go out together and have fun. But on one unfortunate Saturday, everything changed.

So on one Saturday all 4 of us had gathered and were ready to visit a nearby gaming area, and all of us were waiting for a friend of ours who I would like to name Vishal in order to safeguard his real name and privacy. So, Vishal made us wait for almost 2-3 hours and we were worried why the hell he had not arrived till now, for he is literally the most punctual among all of us, and so we were really curious why the hell he had not arrived till now. And then after almost 3.5 hours, he came to us, with a bloodied, bruised and battered face. We were shocked to witness what we had just seen, and then he took off his shirt and there were marks all over his body. We then took him to our friend's place and cleaned his face and asked him what had happened. And then what he told us, shocked the hell out of us.

So, Vishal and I used to study in different schools as I was a humanities student. Vishal was a science student who was doing his coaching in a coaching institution as well, as he was preparing for his engineering exams. The school he studied in allowed students to attend school once a week and do coaching for the rest of the week. And there in his school, Vishal had gone to his school wearing his coaching T-shirt, which was a mistake, which he accepted but what happened afterwards shocked the hell out of him. So, Vishal was called by the director of the school for wearing that T-shirt for which he apologised but then that director started demanding extra money as a fine, something which he refused. And due to his refusal the Director started beating the shit out of him. He slapped him, kicked him and absolutely smashed him. Once Vishal realised he had no other option but to defend himself he started doing exactly that, and then the director called his security guard and driver, and then all of them smashed the shit out of him. This meant a mere 17 year old student got beaten up by almost 5-6 adults and they absolutely smashed him. And then somehow he ran from there and came towards us.

Once we heard this story we quickly went to his home and informed his mother about it and he told the whole story. His mother got so angry that she immediately went to the director of his school and threatened him that she would complain about it to the police. She then sent these clippings to her husband who is a reputed and high ranking government officer and he called up the director and told him that he was going to file a police complaint and also take legal action, which he did as soon as he came back from Delhi.

    Your Actions Define Your Existence

What unfolded next was what made me emphasise how the school director was truly a "Devil in Human Form". So, after Vishal's father filed a police complaint, the director was sent for questioning but then when he was questioned by the police he told them that the Boy had attacked first and that only when he felt provoked he had no other option but to attack that boy and even his employees agreed to those statements (Vishal's father told us everything), and just when we thought he would get away with it, destiny sided with Vishal.

Upon request by Vishal's father, the police went and checked the CCTV footage of Vishal getting physically assaulted by everybody, and that's when the police showed it to Vishal's father, he recorded and showed it to us, and once we saw the footage we literally felt like smashing the shit out of that moron director. And as the footage was found and the investigation went further, more details about the director of that school emerged.

The Director of that school was known to be a notorious womaniser, as he had been implicated a few years on the charges of assaulting his wife. Later on, it was found out, that the woman wasn't really his legal wife rather he had another wife somewhere else and he had married this second woman without divorcing his first wife, which stated how he has always been known for doing illegal things, and the worse part was the fact that he himself was a lawyer. He used to charge useless and fake fees to students under the pretext of exam fees or any other name he felt like giving it and that is how he literally made a mockery of the entire educational system. His school due to all of these things had even been disaffiliated and yet he didn't care. Based on what I have heard from various individuals, he had affairs with various of his employees and would often fire anybody who spoke up against me. His teachers used to be thrown out for no reason at all and he had other children with the women he was staying with, even though he knew the marriage was illegal. There have been so many instances of him and his actions being in the news. A friend of mine was good with his son, and from there he found that the moron director had even raped a family member on his wife's side. And that he used to beat his first wife almost every day, and used to beat her until either she became unconscious or bled so badly that she had to be taken to a hospital. His son had told my friend how his father never ever gave them access to any of his cars or money, but would always give access to his multiple affairs and would splurge money on all those women he was lustfully attracted. He used to beat the shit out of his son as well and in one instance had even beat his daughter so profusely that she had to be hospitalised, and when she was hospitalised his son and his wife caught him having sex with the housekeeping maid in his bedroom.

Hearing all of these things absolutely traumatised me, as I remember the exact moment when I had heard these things, my first reaction to my friend saying these things was,

"Is that Director a human or an evil entity in the form of a human" and trust me as I am writing these things again, I am once again going through all the emotions that I had gone through then and those were of anger and frustration. And yet I chose to write about it as I wanted all of you to get a glimpse of what a devil in human form could look like. And unfortunately, there are individuals worse than him, as that would give you an indication of what the devil is capable of doing even without being here on the surface and by simply sending his disciples to do the things he is known for.

Sometimes there are individuals who aren't necessarily chosen by the devil to represent him and yet they end up finding him and

   Your Actions Define Your Existence

following his path, and the biggest question everybody has is, Why?

Because the devil tempts these individuals with incredible amounts of power, authority, and access to incredible amounts of wealth, and shows them a much easier path to fulfil their lustful needs (all humans have it) and when they look the other way, they see a life filled with way too much responsibility and accountability, and that may mean less wealth and less sexual pleasures and that is why these individuals end up following the devil's path. And unfortunately on that path, they end up losing themselves and become individuals completely contrary to who they were before and that's how the devil ends up sucking more and more humanity out of humans. For ex- In the movie Wonder Woman 84, it was shown how certain individuals got hold of the wish stone that was created by the Greek God Dolos who was known as the God of cunning deception and treachery. Dolos had created the wish stone in order to experiment and see how far the greed of humans could go, although he had also made the stone in such a way that any wish made by the one in possession of the stone could be taken back, but guess what happened, whoever was in possession of that stone got destroyed and became individuals completely contrary to what they were before. Nobody ever took their wish back, rather they got all their wishes met, but unfortunately, the wishes kept on getting worse and worse, the needs kept on getting bigger and bigger and that completely ripped them apart, and caused the entire world into chaos, until "Wonder Woman" saved the world. But unfortunately, the real world won't have any "Wonder women" and the only person who could rescue us from falling into that trap is ourselves.

And so the question is what does it mean to be human, and what defines a human?

Well, to be precise you would get an incredible number of explanations and different versions of the definition of what it means to be human or what humanity is, but in brief,

It is simply the presence of a being who is well aware of his/her actions, someone who is willing to take responsibility for their actions, someone who holds himself and others accountable for their actions and words, someone who is kind and yet stern, somebody who is empathetic and yet understand his priorities, somebody who knows how to exercise self-control in regards to everything in life, somebody who keeps his greed in check, somebody who respects and yet gets their opinions through, somebody who accepts criticism and gives positive criticism, somebody who is willing to fight the ones causing suffering and pain, and somebody who is willing to be as honest he could be for their own good.

If you could be most of it or even half of it, you are bound to stay far away from the clutches of the devil for the life you have chosen may not be as tempting and flashy as the devil had promised you, but it's far better than a life where you end up losing yourself in the pursuit of things that you never wanted but was shown or advertised to in order to fulfil the devil's malevolent needs. And that doesn't mean a human who abstains from sex, or material desires is a holy or clean man, as that's a life where you end up losing the real essence of what it means to be human. But simply by exercising self-control and limiting your malevolent thoughts and lustful needs, you could become a human with humane intentions, and that would mean you are who you are meant to

 Your Actions Define Your Existence

be, and not what you were told to be. We have to understand that in the modern day and age, the Devil won't appear red faced or with two horns on his head. Rather it could come in the form of capitalist and affluent individuals and all we have to do is find our own ways to make sure that the intentions of these malevolent creatures are identified and tackled with great resistance, for that is what would be required to make the world a better place and make it less attractive for the devil and his disciples to influence our lives.

What is important to remember is the fact that being harsh or cruel is easy, being non-empathetic and hurtful to others is easy, destroying somebody to fulfil your selfish needs is easy, buying luxury cars as the boss while underpaying your hardworking staff is easy, staying away from positively impacting the ones around you is easy, making other people submit to your malevolent intentions is easy, hurting others to hide your incompetence is easy, living your trusted and loving partner to fulfil your sexual fantasies is easy, all of these things is incredibly easy. But what is hard is not doing any of these things and simply being who you are meant to be, as for that you have to do the things that I have mentioned above and doing those things in today's day and age of social media show off culture is very hard, but what we have to remember is how we want to be known, during our times on this earth. It doesn't mean doing things to please other people or conforming to their choices, rather it means doing things to regard yourself as higher and better than other humans, and when you could do that you create a chain effect and push more and more people away from the path of becoming or conforming to the needs and desires of the devil, and if you could do that, you could do anything, and that's where you end up becoming someone who is willing to fight the devils in human form, and when you do that, you end up inspiring others and when that happens, you make the world unsustainable for the devil, and that's a world we would all love to live in.

For the devil just like his disciples is shallow and hollow from inside, and all we need to do is recognise that and march through.

 Your Actions Define Your Existence

Your journey should matter to you

"*Your journey is in your own hands and the choices you make*
Over the course of your life will shape your destiny in the future"
Nozer Kanga

On any given day you may have been sitting at your desk either in your office or your classroom and might be thinking, is it really worth it? Is doing these things worth it? Is becoming this person worth it? Is taking up these acts and responsibilities worth it? What the hell am I going to do about it? Who the hell am I going to tell about it? What the hell is going to happen in case everything goes sideways?

These are some of the questions that are often pondered in our minds often times while we messing up our lives and sometimes while we are sacrificing some important things in order to achieve something that could either be incredible or could put us in a place much better than where we are at right now. And so, during these times these questions start getting in our minds in ways we may not have imagined for maybe things aren't the way we had planned them to be. And so, what is the journey?

The Journey of life is nothing more than the encapsulation of all the events in our lives. The type of events could be either good or bad, but ultimately they get registered as a part of what we call the journey of life. And in this journey family, friends, our actions, and reactions are all equally important, for it is them that give meaning to our lives. But what do they mean to us? Well, the meaning of all of it is basically what we construct and consider it to be, based on how we interpret them to be in order to fit them into our lives. We end up encountering various situations where we start doubting whether our existence means anything at all in the larger scheme of things, although we also encounter situations where we start considering our actions as world-changing, all of it based on how we interpret it and based on how they impact those around us. But the one thing that we often fail to question is- How does it affect us (ourselves)? How could those actions push us towards something that we had never thought possible

     Your Actions Define Your Existence

and yet we are now seeing glimpses of things turning around, all because we started considering how those actions could impact us, and that is where we were able to make the big change.

Let me share another great quote by Chris Williamson

"There is a period in everybody's journey where they are so different because they have started to do new things that they no longer fit in with the old set of friends, but they are not sufficiently developed to gain a new set of friends and they are unsure, should I go back, should I lean back into the boys on the weekend. Is that the highest way I can live my life forward for that's what everybody else does, and my friends are taking a piss, "Oh, not drinking again" too good for us are we, not going out again this week, "Oh enjoy staying at home and reading, fucking nerd", and so now you are stuck in the middle place where you don't know who you are going to be on the other side of this. And it is that lonely chapter that's in the middle of something and is crucial for a person who has gone from a place to where they are to where they want to be."

The first I heard this quote it gave me chills as it very much gave an answer to all my doubts and fears I had regarding all the thoughts I had in my mind and the discussions I had with my friends and many other people who were either going through the same things or were either having this question once they had decided to make that big leap.

Such moments and such times are incredibly crucial if we want to make our lives much more nourishing and at the same time be much more grateful about our lives for that's all we want.

Today, if we could go around and ask people what they want, most of us would say a stable income, a stable family and a good amount of money where we don't have to go and face up to somebody else or be reprimanded by somebody else to earn our livelihoods, for that's what most of us strive for. Very few individuals would actually say that they want a billion dollars as most individuals would want a life that makes them feel less bitter about themselves and the situations of their lives, for that is all they want. And yet it is at that moment we have to understand how precious our lives are and how we could do so much out of it, if we decide to do it in order to make ourselves competent, capable and secure enough to judge the journey based on what we interpret it to be, and not based on what others interpret it to be.

Our life and its happening are never ever truly in our hands, for we have to consider the fact that they are truly in the hands of something or someone we could interpret in our own ways, as religiously inclined individuals would say it is in God's hands, spiritually inclined individuals would say it is in the universe's hands, and those away from all these stuff would say it is destiny, and so all have of us have our own interpretation of everything that happens in our lives, but the one thing that would matter the most in between all of this is how we react to those happenings, how we react to them and what we make out of them, as that's the way we would be able to remember it unless we have caused considerable harm to others through our actions, for then our version would no longer matter as enough damage would have been done.

One thing that often bothers us at most of the time is our insistence on the fact that how life would be so much better if we were in that particular place where we wish to be, and that particular place could vary people-people, but deep down wanting to be in that place has the same meaning- peace and purpose. These are the two things that most of us are often chasing in our lives,

    Your Actions Define Your Existence

and yet find it very rare to avail until and unless we haven't been pushed to the corner, or have a situation in our lives where we end up losing access to things that we currently have, for it is in those moments that we truly realise how grateful we were to have those things in our possession and yet were wishing for things that we could have lived without or could have stopped bothering us, but unfortunately that could never happen, for that's what makes us human. It is our desire to scale that next big thing or scale that next mountain peak that gives us purpose in our lives, but the thing that we often get it wrong is considering the fact that once we have achieved that particular goal or target of ours, we would have fulfilled our purpose and that would make our lives so much better and would make us incredibly happy and proud of ourselves, although that is rarely the case.

As individuals, we must understand that our happiness, our sorrow, our moments of anger, despair and our moments of triumph are all short lived and we will never ever be able to understand and cherish those moments if we don't learn how to enjoy the process that we had to go through to achieve that particular thing that we were so determined to achieve, and the process that starts from initiating the plan all the way to the execution of it is the journey that I have been talking about, and yet we judge the entire journey based on the outcome, something which ends up making even some incredible progress made during that process seem like they were nothing noteworthy, and that is where we end up making mistakes. As it is important to consider the simple fact that all those learnings, mistakes and successes that we endured during our time while aiming for that goal, should matter to us, for one day those actions would bear the fruit we had hoped for it bear, and even if it doesn't, it would make us individuals who know a thing or two by something other than living just for the sake of living.

In order to make sure that what you do matters to you, you have to learn some very basic fundamentals about life, as it is those things that will lay the foundation for a life where you would be so much in content with what you are doing rather than waiting for that one day when you would achieve all of it to be content. As when you do that, you end up losing the simple and the basic aspect of your life, and that is embracing what is happening right now rather than sulking and being bitter about why you are not at that particular place. And in order to do that you have to change the way you go about things in your life, for it is those changes that would end up making you far more grateful and far more appreciative about everything that is happening to you, and that would inevitably allow you to appreciate things that are happening around you. And that could only happen when you understand how precious every moment is, for you never know when that moment will ever happen again. For example- sometimes when we are spending time with our family we are often reminiscing about how beautiful our life would have been, had our friends been there. But by doing that you are creating two types of sorrows. The first one is happening to you right now where you are sulking about things, regarding how they used to be. The second type of sorrow would happen in the future, when you would remember about today and regret, regarding how you simply missed the chance of enjoying some incredible moments with your family, sometimes which is hard to come by as all of them are busy in their own ways. So it becomes imperative that we understand these two important things, one is how crucial and beautiful these moments are in the grand scheme of things for ourselves, and the second is the fact that we have to accept that we are all side parts in somebody else's lives, and only when we are able to accept both these things we would be able to cherish our life and its moments unhinged, and that is when we

   Your Actions Define Your Existence

would realise how grateful and how lucky we were when we had it, or how lucky we are when we have it.

Time is something none of us have in our control whatsoever, and yet we spend most of our time on this planet thinking about how we could do everything that we had planned out to be, as even that isn't in our hands, and when you realise these things, you will find how precious your existence is in this world. And the moment that preciousness regarding your existence hits you, you will end up realising how you have been spending far too much time thinking about things that are neither in your control nor neither would have any sort of substantive impact upon your lives.

During that moment you will also realise how you have been far too critical of everything you have done until now and way too fixated on what you are going to do in the future, for that is the reason you haven't been able to do things that truly matter, and that is: Patting yourself on the back for the things that you have done, and the day you would be able to do that, you would realise how important it is to enjoy this incredible journey on this planet, while it lasts. During this process you would also become wary of how life is short and so very unpredictable and how sometimes it's so important to just sit back and relax and realise you have always lived up to what you could, and even if you haven't you should be grateful that your intentions have always been to deliver the best you could for things that matter to you and to your dear ones, and if you could do that you are truly on the verge of becoming someone who would always look at world with a much broader aspect and with much more open eyes, and that would enable you to view yourself and your life in a much more grateful way.

Now some of you might be thinking, what about the ones with malevolent intentions?

Well first of all, most of you no matter how much harm your actions might have brought about or no matter how cruel your actions might have been, there is very little chance of you accepting the evil things you did, for according to you were well within your rights to do that and you have a valid reason for that as well, for that's what makes us human. But just take a moment and deep down ask yourself what you have done, and be absolutely honest with yourself. Remember you don't have to go out and tell people how you feel sorry for what you have done, just take a deep pause and ask yourself the things you know weren't right. Well, I guess by now most of you might have done it, and so now think how you could make a difference and make sure that you don't end up doing something similar again. But remember there is a very high probability that you could end up doing it all over again, for it's much easier to do what you know rather than make a change and do what you don't know. But just take a deep breath and ask how you could make the change, and if you are absolutely honest with yourself, trust me you will find a way, to make sure that doesn't happen again, although the chances of it happening again are very high, if you could understand and remember how bitter it made you feel, when you had to realise the repercussions of what you had done, you will end up realising how it's better not to do it ever again, at least there will be some sort of a hesitancy in your mind to make sure that you don't repeat it again. And if you could do that, life would feel so much better and so much more beautiful in the eyes of the beholder, which would be you, as it has always been you.

What you did here by making this change, is that you have made your journey far more crucial and far more important for your life in the greater scheme of things. And why did you do that?

  Your Actions Define Your Existence

Well by gaining the courage to ask yourself and interrogate yourself about some of the things that you know you did wrong, and yet weren't willing to accept, you have created a chain ripple in which every good or every noble or even every non-malevolent act that you do in order to make sure that there is less malevolence in your life and the world, you are creating far more importance for all the malevolent acts that you did in the past. For it is the

Procrastination regarding the result of those acts that has led to you becoming an individual who is far less resentful towards yourself and the world and is far more grateful for the things that have happened around you and around your dear ones. For whenever the memory of those acts and the action of yours comes to your mind you end up realising how you should avoid them and how you could be an inspiration and hope for those who feel it's too late to change and get their act together, for once they have seen you they get the motivation to push themselves further and when they do that, they become individuals even they had never thought was possible but has become possible, and when an individual goes through that process, it makes them realise how being bitter and unaccountable is so easy, while being content and satisfied is hard. But by taking the hard path, you have made your journey even more special, and also of those who have followed you, and when that happens we create beings who are no longer anxious about what happened and the things they did, rather they are happy that it happened and gaining the courage to introspect has allowed them to realise how important every moment in our lives are, and when that happens it means the world has one less resentful individual and the world has one more grateful individual, who has now understood the true essence of every moment in his life and is far more generous to himself and the things that has happened as that is what makes us truly being proud and be content with every moment of our life.

Once this happens, all those things that have often caused pain, and sorrow and have caused a lot of contemplation in your mind end up making you feel grateful for the very same things. For now you have realised how much those action of yours have mattered into making you the person you are today, for had you not done that during those times, you would have done them today, and once you have realised how dark that place was that you called home, you also end up realising how incredible grateful you are that you decided to ask yourself the tough questions, introspect and make the required change, and that has allowed to start doing things and start planning for things you had thought could never be initiated but now have been initiated all because you took that jump and you are now far more appreciative of every little moment in your life, for you have understood how fungible you are to this world and to time itself, and that mean most of worries are nothing but dark energy compelling us to feel sad and bitter about ourselves and criticising every step of our journey, while in many ways your journey was the journey that has enabled you to take shape in the way you have taken shape and that means your life is now filled with much more solitude and appreciation of everything that happened, while also being appreciative of everything that is going to happen, for that's what moments of our lives are about and that's what life should be all about.

There would be moments in your life when nothing would be going your way. There are moments in your life when no matter what you do and how much do, your parents, friends, partners, or even your loved ones are not satisfied with you. Some would call you lazy, some would call you an embarrassment while some would call you arrogant, depending on what fits their dictionary of words. And at that point, you would feel so pathetic and bitter about yourself and your situation, that you will feel a deep sense of grief and anger within you.

    Your Actions Define Your Existence

For that's what any human would do. However, the distinction lies in how you perceive that situation moving forward. Suppose something occurred to you or happened to you a few years down the line and you felt real pain because of the things that had happened in the past, it would cause you a lot more pain than it should have. But what if you start thinking about those moments the other way around? What if you started regarding those moments as crucial and incredibly beneficial in making you the individual that you are today? What if you started reminiscing about those moments of grief and started being grateful for how much they have taught you? And once you start taking that viewpoint in your life, your life will truly change in an incredible way. As what happened that day is no longer a cause of pain for you, rather it's a cause for reflection and introspection in a positive way.

When things start mattering to you, it inevitably starts mattering to all those around you, or to all those linked to you, for it is you who holds power to place the price of our worth and live your life in a way where you no longer crib about the things that have happened, and rather look at the things in a way that enables you to cherish them. You have to understand the simple fact that, not every problem is out to make your life hard, for some of them are there to make you and shape you into a far more competent and able person. Once you look at life through that viewpoint, you start becoming less harsh towards your problems and start being more enthusiastic about what comes next. Although in between those days, there would be moments when you would mess up really badly, succeed really highly, cry really badly, laugh really loudly, get sleepless nights while sometimes sleeping like a baby, all of these things are going to come and sometimes would come unexpected and if at the end of all, once it's all over you look at those things with a smile on your face, you would understand how you have changed and in many ways grown in between all those moments, and it is in those moments that the true treasure of our life lies and that's what would make us who we are.

"Value each moment and cherish your time on this earth, for only in recognizing their worth will you grasp the true significance of your journey, becoming someone deeply grateful for the path you have walked."

 Your Actions Define Your Existence

EIGHT

Everything is a Transaction

> *"Life is a series of transactions*
> *We all give to receive"*
>
> ***David Hair***

Has it ever happened to you that you might be either the older or younger sibling in your family, and somehow for some other reason your parents seem to always favour the other individual? You are always taunted for not becoming as good as your sibling is, you are told or given speeches about how either your brother/sister is so focused in their lives, and no matter how much you try to do, they are always disappointed with you. You have witnessed how just because your sibling gives your parents the required things to live a comfortable life, they target you. Your brother/sister is doing everything they can to support the family, but perhaps you're different. You've recognised your own talents and found your own way to help your parents—one that differs from your sibling's. Yet, instead of appreciating you for who you are, they constantly compare you to him. You have realised how your brother/sister is given so much preferential treatment and almost all their mistakes are often ignored, while on the other when you make any of those mistakes they had committed you are vilified and crucified and you are made to feel like a villain while your sibling is often given a free pass. It is during these moments you ask yourself the question, why the hell are my parents so indifferent to me? What the hell have I done wrong? Why can't they see the good qualities I have? Why can't they accept me for who I am? Why can't they give me some time, as no matter how talented my sibling might be, maybe I will also shine like him/her in my given time! They are my parents and should treat me equally, and rather than insult and criticise me for who I am, they should support me for who I am!

These are some of the questions that cross everyone's mind, especially those suffering. And if somebody says I am not bothered by such things, then either they are lying or they belong to those group of individuals are that child who is doing everything they can for their family, and that's something we should all appreciate,

    Your Actions Define Your Existence

but that does not mean we should devalue the other ones, who simply may not be capable of enough of doing what their other sibling is doing.

This situation should help you all understand what I'm talking about and give you insight into how relationships—and life itself—are fundamentally about give and take. Let me explain further!

You see in life, when we are babies we are often scolded and reprimanded by some and cuddled and loved by others. And during that time, we get an idea of who are the people who would love me no matter what and who are the ones who are harsh on me, and so we mould our behaviours in order to fit that particular narrative to live our lives. And that is where we should understand how the very reason we behave differently and act differently based on different sorts of individuals is because of what we have been given by one set of individuals and what we have been given by the other set of individuals and so we shape our entire reality based on that. And that is how we treat them as well.

Similarly, when we grow up and our parents get old (based on the above example) and they are no longer who they used to be, can no longer do the tasks they used to do, they look towards somebody who could give them some sort of meaning or assistance towards living their lives. And when they see a child of theirs taking up the responsibilities they once held, see them hold the fort and do everything possible to give them a good life, sacrifice his own time and happiness to give them what they could, they automatically garner a soft place for that child of theirs, as they understand how much they are giving up of themselves in order to make sure that they could live their lives, with less pain and suffering, and at that age when they can no longer give other things, the least they could give back is love, support and adoration. Similarly, when they see that the other child is not doing anything in order to make their lives, or isn't contributing in any considerable way they feel disappointed and even though they love him/her as much as their other sibling (in many cases) they think they have no other option but to criticise and tell him how he isn't contributing (giving) anything positive into their lives, and so why should do. They feel he is of no use to them and in pursuit of making him/her become better they constantly put pressure on him/her to become like the other sibling. During such times, the individual is confused and feels a lot of pain in his heart, as he feels he is being given undue criticism for no falls of his, and that is when he misses the point of how everything in life is based on the transaction value of that particular relationship, and the sooner you understand that the better your life would become. It would be really tough and bitter to accept such a harsh truth, but in time it will only make your life better.

What you have to understand during such moments is the fact that the way you had your own favourite individuals while growing up, all because of what you received from them which necessarily may not have been material and simply could have been love and support. And that's how you have your own set of individuals who are like minded individuals for you, similarly even for your parents, even though they may not have anything necessarily against you, they simply have nothing for you, as you have failed to understand the fact that when they call you a disappointment, they are saying it based on what they interpret your actions in relation to them. Now, at the same time, you could be a brilliant employee for your company or could be an amazing boyfriend, but those things are not what they are concerned about. Yes, they would like you to stay safe and be

   Your Actions Define Your Existence

healthy, but when you aren't giving them anything, why should they give you anything, for it is based on your contribution that you would get the things that your other sibling is getting, and that is the fact that he is giving them his time, his money and his effort. He is getting the things he is getting as a consequence to that. And if tomorrow, suddenly, he stops doing all those things, he would face the same amount of criticism and be a witness to the same sort of treatment from them. For instance, if your brother goes away and now you look after them, then you will be given the same treatment that he has been given all this money, and at that time you have to understand the fact that the love, adoration and applaud you are suddenly getting from them isn't necessarily for you as a person but is based on what you could do as a person for them and that's what they are treating you for, and if tomorrow you once again go back to your old ways, you would once again be recipient of the same treatment that you once were, and it has nothing to do who you are, but has everything to do with who they perceive you to be and that is what you will be given.

For example- I visit the gym every alternate day and in the morning I do, I take my dog out for a walk. The next morning I wake up at around 6:30 AM, while on the day I go to the gym I wake up at 4:30 AM. And so based on that I take my dog for a walk thrice a week and hit the gym thrice a week. If you ask me I would love to do both at least 5 times a week but I can't as for that I would have to sleep around 5 hours thrice a week which means my body won't recover well and in pursuit of taking my dog out for a walk 5 days a week and hit the gym 5 days a week I would sacrifice on my much needed sleep and that would affect my mental and physical health and that would affect my work and all my activities would be affected and so I have no option but to continue on this schedule until one day hilariously

God comes and tells me that I would be able to control time, something I know is unlikely happen.

So, what I did in this instance is that I traded an additional two days of workout and two days of dog walk, for what is very important to me, and that is sleep and recovery. As having a good night's sleep can make a world of difference especially training as hard as I do. In this instance even though I would love to go for those workouts get those incredible pumps and take those amazing walks with my dog, I won't, as I chose to focus on what is more important in my life, and that is how every transaction in our lives takes place.

Winston Churchill, a former Prime Minister of the United Kingdom and also a historic figure in terms of modern history, had quoted a famous line,

"We make a living by what we get, but we make a life by what we give"

This quote should affirm this simple and yet often ignored truth about life. As humans we often ignore the most basic realities and the truth about them, for accepting them requires a lot of courage and is very painful. As who would want to accept that their parents gave them so much admiration only because of their usefulness, the rich individuals would want to accept that they are only liked and honoured because of their money, while beautiful women or models would want to accept that people and brands report to her based on what they can gain from her body and looks. In many instances, most of you may already know this truth but we simply refuse to accept it, as accepting it means because as humans we are all but equal, as individuals we have traded something for other things, And we are all fungible, for whoever is willing to contribute more to the other side will inevitably oust us and that means all our laurels and value aren't

   Your Actions Define Your Existence

necessarily for us, but is based on what we are able to do for them in order for them to gain what they can through us, and no matter how harsh, cruel and inhuman it sounds, that is the truth and reality regarding how the world function, and even though many of us are well aware of it we simply refuse to budge or accept it.

One of the main reasons many people refuse to accept it is that, no matter how much they have accomplished, a single misstep can negatively undo everything. You would begin to question the true purpose of our lives and our actual value within it all. At that time, you have to understand that simple fact that your value and how you will be perceived and treated by others will be based on what sort of output they could derive from you, and the day that output has been overshadowed by some other individual you would be pushed down the pecking order. For instance, we have seen how some incredible sportsmen who have made such incredible contributions to their sport and who had been once considered as demigods, suddenly get treated harshly for the very fact that they may not be performing based on how and what they used to perform earlier and when they can't do that they are sidelined by new talents. But what did they do wrong, it's the same guy. Well, the simple answer is that when he plays, a lot of people gain different things in their own ways. When he plays well and wins, fans gain happiness, exuberance and excitement, while the broadcasters get more engagement which means more people would go and watch their channel, which means their advertisements would get more coverage, which means they would be able to charge more for their advertisements and that would inevitably lead to more profit.

Similarly, when the once loving son/daughter given such preferential treatment in the house suddenly stops doing what he once did, they have to face the wrath of what his other sibling has been used to facing. And no matter how harsh it sounds, our values and how we are perceived in this world are based on what we are able to give to the other side and how we are able to contribute to the other side, in order to make sure it is worth it.

At the same time, the transaction between the broadcaster or fan and a parent or spouse would be very different, but ultimately it would all come down to what they are able to get from you. Although no parent would ever hate their child for not living upon their expectations (until and unless they are evil) they would definitely make sure that they are made to feel as incompetent as they are felt by either their parent or by their spouse, for how could they expect special things when they are offering nothing special in return.

In life, once you understand this basic truth you will understand how cruel and yet how real and ruthless this world is. Although at the same time, you will find some very rare instances where your value is no longer based on what you do and is based equally as a human, but those instances are very rare and with time as the world becomes more and more socialised, inter-connected and globalised those moments would become rarer and rarer, and the only way you could prepare yourself to understand the basic truth about this world is by making yourself aware about the harsh and yet the real way the world functions. Once you do that, neither would you ask yourself those questions that I had stated in the first paragraph and neither would be feel bitter and resentful. As you would come to the realisation that that is how the world works, and if you can't contribute you won't be given a share of the pie and it is the pie that everything is fighting for, and everybody has their own pies in their lives, the only thing that varies is its size and its way of workings.

     Your Actions Define Your Existence

Understanding such basic notions of the way the humans work can make your eyes open up to a lot many things that you had always known for and yet had not accepted them. It's similar to stopping expecting love and compassion from a narcissist, no matter how dear they might mean to you, but that is simply beyond their ways of workings, and the only down you would get their acceptance is when you bow down yourself to their cruel and selfish needs and that is something you should not do, in order to safeguard your interests and protect your mental health, and that is another type of transaction, where you avoid them for your own well-being, no matter how close they are or they once were.

It's also similar to people buying a Husky dog in extremely warm conditions, knowing it's not suitable for the climate, but they are well aware of how expensive it is to have one. And they know how having that dog alleviates their social status and so, they trade their social status for an animal's life, and that is what people are willing to trade for in order to gain what they deem to be right based on their perception. As we are well aware of how many local Indian dog breeds there are but we aren't interested in any of them, as there is no value attached to them and unfortunately that is what we want in our lives in order to fill the void left in our hearts, due to the lack of a proper and larger purpose to make sure our lives on this planet is, worth it.

You have to understand and accept the most basic fact that your position and your chair are easily replaceable, for your company could find somebody else, even if you are a self-made entrepreneur your employees would often hope that one day you are replaced (not all of them), especially when your ideas don't incline to theirs. You have to understand that if you have siblings and if they started becoming competent and taking on the responsibility that had been born by you, all along that even you are replaceable and you could fall down the pecking order. If you are not a good partner, you could be replaced by someone who is far more empathetic, kind, good-looking and richer than you. It may sound harsh but that is how the world works. Your value is based upon your output and if you can't keep up to their demands and somebody better is around the horizon, you will be replaced, by somebody better, and the sooner you understand it, the better is.

Although during all of this, you have to understand that just because they disregarded you, and discarded you for somebody better, they are evil, as that is rarely the case. As, it's based on the simple fact that if they can't get what they want from you, either they will criticise you and in case of a better alternative they would replace you, simple as that. You have to accept that in most cases your colleagues or higher-ups aren't necessarily evil, neither are your parents/partner/friend's evil and neither are all those who made you face such a situation in their lives. It's just that they were looking out for something in you, and until and unless they couldn't find somebody better they hung onto you and tried to propel you, but once they realised you aren't capable of meeting their expectations and somebody better has arrived and that somebody could give more value to their lives, they decided to accept it, as that is the game of life and that is the reason I stated, how **"everything is a transaction"** based on the value of our output and if we can't give it, we can't get or accept anything in better, as that is the way of workings of the world, and the sooner you accept and understand the better it is for you.

Very rarely would you find individuals with truly malevolent intentions going out of their way, and making your life miserable. Unfortunately, certain individuals want to reflect the failings of

 Your Actions Define Your Existence

their lives upon you. But most of the time you are nothing but a simple casualty of a transaction that didn't go in their favour, as the trader found somebody with a better market and individual value than what they could derive from you, and that is what you had to go through what you want through, simple as that.

And so, the question is, what do you do about it?

Well, the answer is simple, you work your ass off to make yourself way more valuable than you had ever thought and make yourself so valuable that your competitors have no other option but to accept how you are simply better than them, as that is the only way you could deal with this real situation of your lives. Although at the same time you have to be humble and aware enough to accept the basic fact that no matter how good you are and no matter how valuable you are at the present moment and no matter how incredible you are at your work, a day will come when you will be upstaged by somebody who has arrived newly and is better than you at your craft. Somebody who is younger, who is hungrier, who is stronger, who is more good looking, and who is capable of delivering more for the stakeholders, more than what you have till now. And at that time, you have to be smart enough to assess the situation and if you feel you have the last dance in you, go for it, or else the cruel and grim reality that your throne has been taken by someone else, as that is what human lives is about. Nobody is young, fresh, smart and intellectual forever. But what you cannot do is not make the most of what you were capable of during the time that was allotted by destiny itself to shine. For you could use that argument that one day it will be all over, as unfortunately, that is the truth of life, we are all hounded by mortality but that is no reason for you to sit back and let others have the fun, when it could be you, initiating the fun during that time of yours, and yet taking a step back when you realised your time is up. And any individual who realises this would become an individual who is far more content and far less miserable with the things they did, rather than fuss about the things they didn't do. For we all have our own time, our own value and our own space in this world. Our job is to make the most of it and then pass it along, rather than fight it with our fragile egos and destroy what we have built for many greats have done and continue to do so. As it takes courage to accept our fragilities after witnessing such strengths. And any individual who is able to do it is far more-stronger of a human than we have ever witnessed and that is what is needed to embrace the essence of life.

"Life is a series of transactions, each moment shaped by the value we bring and the exchanges we make. Understanding this truth allows us to navigate the impermanence of existence with grace. When our time comes to move on, we must let go without resistance, for every encounter and action reflects our transactional worth. Embrace this wisdom, and find fulfilment not in clinging, but in knowing when to give and step back. In this lies the path to true solitude and peace."

NINE

There is No Fairytale Ending

> *"Life has no fairy-tale endings.*
> *But it has fairy tale moments."*
> **Tracy Winegar**

As humans, it is our expectations related to everything that give hope to our lives and what and how we decode our lives and how we frame our lives in many ways in relation to the expectation we have in regards to what the outcome is to be. And it is in that process that we end up having the biggest and the most consistent expectation of our lives, and that is

"The expectation of having a happy/fairytale ending to our lives", which in most situations is never really the case.

You might be a government employee or could be a budding entrepreneur or could be working 9-5 in a big or small corporation and most of you might be dreaming of that day when all the savings and investments you had made, would accumulate to be the figure you had been promised to or you have hoped it to be. And then on the day you would retire, all that money would get credited into your account, and by then you would be happily married with the love of your life and you would have your children and once you retire you would all sit down and have dinner together every night and the money you have accumulated by working so hard all these years would now be used to fund all the desires that you have not fulfilled when you were young since you were so overburdened by responsibilities. And now that your job is over, your kids have grown up and have married, you are free. And you will wake up every morning and see the grateful sun and then plan on what to do for the rest of the day and your wife will cook you some amazing breakfast and then you will travel the world, buying things that would make you happy, and then you would live from the age of 60-90 like this, and then on any given day, after enjoying 30 years of freedom, you would one day have a nice meal and go to bed and never wake up again, for that's how most of you would want your death to be right? A nice and peaceful one after enjoying and relishing all of life's

  Your Actions Define Your Existence

riches. And once you are dead, your kids will always remember you, if you were a rich man everybody would remember you and talk about you and your legend will stay forever. People will talk about how good you are, and your soul and your work will forever be immortal. You will be remembered for ages and the endings of your life would be so good, that everybody would want to live like you. Now, some of you may not want such a perfect ending but most of you wait for the one day when all your troubles and obstacles will be over and you will be literally waking up with a smile on your face and free to do whatever the hell want to do. Right?

Unfortunately, that is very rarely the case, as life as we all know is filled with things we had never imagined and sometimes it takes us towards a path that was filled with so much pain and trauma that even our imagination would take a backseat. But why is it that some of you may be thinking, if there are no perfect endings, what is life about?

Let's talk about it.

Life as we all know is something that has never really been in our control especially the events and circumstances that surround the periphery of our existence. As the biggest events in our lives, the real big events, often happen at times, and we were completely unprepared for it. This has likely happened to almost all of you in one way or another, as it is an inherent part of life. I often term life as nothing else but a short duration that we have on this planet, and in that duration there would be some incredible ups and some incredible downs and there would be days of incredible calm, at the same time there would be days of incredible hostility. There would be days when everything would just click and there would be days when no matter how hard you try nothing would ever come together, as every step that you might have taken would have ended up further deteriorating the current situation, and no matter how hard you try, that is the reality and the unfortunate truth about life. And yet after going through so many unfortunate and unexpected events in our lives we gather the courage and also have the foresight to expect that in the end it will all be over and our lives will be free of all these troubles and we will be able to live your life free of any obligation, and having these hopes even after going through the miserable of circumstances is what makes us humans, and no matter how much we go through we always have that glimmer of hope that one day you would be on your own and your life would be filled with what you may deem as happiness and freedom, But alas that is never really what happens.

Unforeseen troubles are always on the horizon

Troubles and obstacles are what make our life what we deem it to be, for how we recover from that is in truth defines our legacy. You may be 60 and may have happily retired and the enormous corpus that you have accumulated over time in order to live a happy retired life might have been credited into your account, and you may have been really excited for the days to come, but unfortunately, disaster struck. And that disaster could be in many ways, your wife/husband or your kids may have gotten seriously ill and may have been diagnosed with a serious illness. And all that money you had saved so hard in order to live the life you always wanted is now being spent on an illness you had never ever prepared for and yet life has thrown it upon you and all you could do is sit down and ask God what have you done wrong, for you felt you deserved this break from life, and yet nothing happens. Sometimes in the worst of situations, you may die, or any of your family members could die, either way, your entire life could turn upside down in a few moments and that would

   Your Actions Define Your Existence

completely shatter you, as everything that you had hoped for has now been completely shattered and your life post-retirement has actually gotten worse. In many cases, all the money you had accumulated is now being used on things that you had never expected, and now at this old age you have no other option but to look for a job again, and in many cases, you end up taking one that pays lesser than what you were paid for and is no longer giving you the job satisfaction that you have always been used to.

These circumstances and challenges would once again reinstate the fact that the happy ending that you had wished and hoped for never really comes. Rather we are born in this world to face challenges, and the ones who overcome them, end up making a mark for themselves, while the ones who cower up to them remain unfulfilled, bitter and resentful. But unfortunately, even the ones who end up making a mark for themselves are forgotten as that is the reality and yet the beauty of life. For everything that once was is often replaced by everything that now is, and yet we have no other option but to continue to live our lives with the goals and motives that we have set ourselves with, for what else would you do?

In order to make yourself far less disappointed with the things that could happen in your life, you have to understand that life is unpredictable and short in many ways, and having the foresight to have a life free of any obligation would be highly risky on your part as more than often times, that happy ending would never come, and instead of that some incredible disasters could happen in your lives, and those disasters could change your entire course of your life, and could even make your ending far more miserable and could make your ending shorter and much more dreadful and that is the reason your mind and your soul should always be prepared for an ending that would be similar to what you have been used to. And that would be moments filled with sadness, happiness, trouble, escape, joy and sorrow, as that is what would make you expect even the most disastrous of events as a welcome event for you knew and well aware that there is no happily ever after and believing in that notion would only cause you far more harm and far more sorrow than you could have ever imagined, and that is not how you would want your life to end by, for you are well aware of how precious life is, so why not do what you can, when you can and leave the rest upon fate.

Your end could be nearer than you had imagined

A friend of mine lives in Delhi, and his father is one of the most disciplined, sober and intelligent men I have ever met. He worked in Europe as a mechanic for almost 20 years, and through his grit and determination, he worked so hard from such humble beginnings, that with the sheer power of his grit, he ended up starting his own family and bought a house for them in Mumbai and then left Europe and came back to look after his family. His wife often used to tell me how he has never ever touched a cigarette in his life and has neither drank alcohol, and every day no matter how hard the day was he would leave the house at 5 am to go and work in his newly launched business and would come back home by 8 pm, and then have dinner and go to sleep. He never ever stayed till late and was one of the most disciplined men that I have ever met. He had also amassed a good enough corpus through various investments and was all set to use some of it during his son's wedding (something which we all were excited for). I mean in many ways I have never ever met a more meticulous man than him in my entire life. I have never ever met a more strict and more disciplined and more punctual man in my entire life.

 Your Actions Define Your Existence

And yet a month back I received a call from my friend, who was crying and sobbing so loud that I had to ask him again and again what had happened, and that's when he told me how his father had a heart attack while driving to work, and instantly passed away at around 7 am in the morning.

The moment I heard the news I couldn't believe what had happened. As my first reaction, how could something like this happen to a man who had been so disciplined and so strict about everything in life, men like him are usually attached to habits leading to longevity but unfortunately, he died at the age of 57 and that is no age to die. He had planned so much for his son's wedding and was so excited for him and yet he couldn't witness any of it, and the ending was way more disastrous than he could have ever imagined as neither was his son nor his wife near him when he took his last breath. Rather it was the security in his office building that was the last person to witness him take his last breath and that is far sad than any of us could have ever imagined.

Such stories and such moments should be more than enough to make all of you understand that you never really when it could be your last day on this planet, you never really know when you could meet or see someone for the last time in their lives, you never really know when it could be the last time you are hearing someone's voice, and so make sure you make the most out of what you can, for its understandable that there would be moments when you would be angry, sad, bitter, depressed and frustrated, as that's what life is about, but often times our problems are created out of artificial and superficial needs and these are the problems that we should always avoid as they suck the life out of the limited number of days we have in this planet, and takes the joy out of the life that we are so incredible to witness.

Some individuals who plan to live till 90 with their incredible habits die by 45, and some who are meant to die by 40 due to their bad habits die by 80. And that shows how life and death are the only true constant and no matter how tech savvy we become, we can never ever control our lives and what happens with it. For what is meant to happen will happen when it's meant to happen, and the only thing you can do is live and love while you or they are alive, for once death occurs those tears won't mean anything and those sorry's would be unheard of and so make the most of what you can, in between all the obstacles and troubles, for that's what makes our lives worthwhile. Don't wait to reach your deathbed and make up for your faults, rather do what you can when you still can, or else the pain will remain forever while the life will be lost forever.

The goodbye and the farewells that you had planned for in a perfect way would never really happen the way you had hoped for. For example- I remember going to Mumbai for my graduation with my mother and staying at my sister's place in Bandra, Mumbai. During that time's we had a parrot who had been staying with us for almost 10 years in Guwahati. But since even Mom was travelling this time, we had no other option but to hand him over to our neighbours. And guess what two days into my graduation journey we received a call from my friend that our parrot who we had named "Archie" had stopped eating any food and would often faint and fall down from his cage. Then I asked my friend to take him to a nearby Vet and there the Vet declared that he was badly depressed due to us not being there, and then he also stated that he had indigestion, so he inserted a pipe inside the throat and then Archie choked and sadly passed away. I mean once we heard the news we were absolutely distraught and it is not something everybody could relate to but the animal lovers would.

   Your Actions Define Your Existence

What I am trying to tell you and emphasise is that all of us are living in this world on borrowed time and we never really know what the borrower would be like "Enough is enough, it's time for you to pay your debt", and unfortunately very rarely do we get prior notices as the bank of life and its ways of workings is completely opposite to what the conventional bank in our world does, and so it becomes imperative that in between all the struggles, obstacles, conflicts and hatred, we are able to make ourselves and inevitably our lives worth-while and make ourselves willing to live our lives in ways that wouldn't surprise us is our lives ended today. And what we must understand is most people spend their lives thinking of that perfect moment or time when they would implement what they have been planning to do, in regard to life. Unfortunately, that perfect moment never really comes, rather it is upon us to create it and make our lives far less bitter and far less resentful than they already are, for we never know when that last breadth of ours is to be taken, and once we do it's all over and nothing is left for we came without nothing and will leave without nothing so why spend it in resentment and bitterness when the alternative is so much better and those alternative are for sure going to give you a life that would mean far more peace and way more solitude than you could have ever imagined, and that is what you all should be striving for, although conflicts and troubles will come, depends upon how you react to it and how you allow it to affect your lives, for you never know that could be the end or beginning of something you could have never hoped for.

Do things for yourself

It's true that you never really know when your end could be for that's what life is about and at the same time, what's also true is that you have a responsibility for yourself. As you have to remember the simple fact no matter how much you do, no matter how much you sacrifice and no matter how amazing of a person you become, all of this will be forgotten one day. And the people you are trying to impress would be dead one day, so you have no option but to make the most of what you can when you can and make yourself capable enough to live the moments you could live and do the things that are within your control.

At the same time you have understood to have peace, for the fact no matter how incredible your house may be and no matter how much of incredible wealth you may have earned, there will come a time when all of this will be either enjoyed by someone else and you would be forgotten in many ways. And many times as I have stated before you may not be even alive to enjoy the fruits of your sacrifices and long hours and so what do you do in such an instance? Well, it's very simple, you do it for yourself and for what you believe in, for now that you are well aware of what things will be like once you are gone, you have the license to make sure you make your lives worthwhile, without any fear of what could happen if in case things go sideways.

As you do things for yourself, you inadvertently create a ripple effect that ends up benefiting a lot of people, they could be your family, friends, colleagues or anybody who has seen you become who you have become and that is what makes them understand the fickleness and the preciousness of what we call life. Because living and doing things for yourself without causing harm to others means you live authentically and pursue your passions, and that inevitably inspires those around you to do the same. Your life becomes an example of what it means to live fully, without fear of the unknown or regret for what might have been, as it is the fear of the unknown that often clouds human judgment. And when you do that, those who come after you may not necessarily

    Your Actions Define Your Existence

remember your name or the grandiose of your achievements, but they will feel the impact of your actions in the legacy you leave behind—a legacy not of material wealth or fame, but of a life well-lived. And that is the greatest gift of life. When deciding to live for yourself after knowing how all those grand plans could come to a halt at one go, you contribute to the well-being of others in ways that are often unseen and unacknowledged. When you focus on your growth and happiness, you become a source of positivity and strength for those around you. You show them that it's possible to live without the constant worry of the future and rather concentrate on the present and accept the ups and downs that come with it.

Moreover, doing things for yourself aligns you with your true purpose. It allows you to discover what genuinely makes you happy, and what fulfils you on a deep, personal level, as that is what we all had planned for the future, but these are the same things that could be gained in the present at various considerable means, so why wait and delay them for a future we have no control over. And that's where true happiness lies—not in waiting to enjoy or savouring the moment at the perfect time, but rather doing what you can when you can, without too much contemplation of the future.

In this way, when you live for yourself, you start recognising the basic fact that your time on this planet is limited and choosing to spend it in a way that brings you joy and fulfilment while embracing the sorrows and failures is what's going to count. You have to reiterate the simple fact that the perfect ending everybody seeks doesn't exist and that the only way to create meaning in your life is to live it fully, with all its imperfections and uncertainties.

There's a certain freedom in this understanding—a freedom from the need to control every outcome, to ensure that everything turns out just right, as none of this was ever in your control and will never be at least in the foreseeable future. So what do you do about it?

Well, you accept that life is unpredictable and that there's no perfect ending and once you can let go of the fear that holds you back and embrace the unknown with open arms, You become an individual who is willing to take risks, make mistakes, and learn from them, knowing it's all part of the journey. And in the end, that's what life is about. It's these series of moments, each one fleeting and precious, and the only way to truly live is to be present in each of those moments. When you do things for yourself, you're not just living for today; you're creating a life that reflects your true self, which you can look back on with pride and satisfaction. So do things for yourself, not because it's easy, but because it's necessary. Do them because your life is your own, and you deserve to live it in a way that brings you happiness and fulfilment. Do them because, in the end, it's not about what you leave behind, but about how you lived. And when you live for yourself, you live fully, without regret, and with the knowledge that you made the most of the time you were given.

The understanding that life has no perfect ending should not be a source of despair, but rather a call to action and an honest admission about how the tomorrow is never going to come, so make the today count. It's a reminder that the only time we have is now and that the only life we can truly control is our own. So embrace this truth, and let it guide you in everything you do. Make your life your masterpiece, not by trying to please others or meet some impossible standard, but by living authentically, fearlessly, and with a deep appreciation for the present moment.

    Your Actions Define Your Existence

Be grateful and appreciate life's unpredictability

It is imperative that rather than wait for that perfect ending and be so busy finding that day when all your troubles would be over, you should concentrate on the moments that are happening every day in your day to day lives. For it is these moments that eventually make your life what it is. And yet that is what most of you don't do.

As humans, we are so fixated on having everything under our control and wanting everything to work according to our plans, that we often forget that the happenings of life and mostly the major and biggest happenings are very often never really in our hands. They happen when they have to happen. And so what do you do in such times? Well, you form a balanced approach to living your lives in a way that is very different to the way you may be living right now.

Some of you may be incredibly disciplined and unwilling to make time for even your dear and loved ones as that is the need of the hour. But god or universe (whatever you call it) makes sure that we are given time to make our dear ones feel loved and wanted cause no matter what you do and no matter who you become, your journey and your story would only be half-fulfilled if you are unable to bring some people along with you on your journey, for very rarely does it happen that individuals who were successful or made it big, did it all by themselves. And that individual could be 1 person or 2 people, but when you make some time and allocate it towards them and then get along with the goal that you have, you end up realising that you are far more focussed and having even 1 individual by your side, in your journey only makes the experience far more memorable and makes your journey and time on this planet far more cherishing and that is what most of you want.

There would be times when that moment might as well have been the last time you had the chance to hear from them, and if you can, and until and unless what you are doing has your life or your company's life at stake, you should make sure that you pick up the call or meet them, for you should accept the incredible unpredictability of life and how it could all go south and end in one go, and all those plannings of yours to make time for them once it has all settled down may go up in flames. This is something I learned the hard way when a family member went through a similar situation, let me share the story.

A family member of mine who was an amazingly calm and loving husband but was an enraging alcoholic had come to our house. He told us how he is so sad that his wife has cheated on him and yet he is willing to take her back as he still loves her, but she is always showing tantrums towards her even though she is the one who cheated and due to that he is now contemplating suicide. An uncle of mine calmed him down and then dropped him to the house once he had come out of the idea of taking his life. Then around 5 hours at around 11 PM in the night, we received the news that he had committed suicide. My mother and I could not describe how something like that could have happened knowing the fact that a few hours ago we had met him. Then his eldest son came to our house and told us the story regarding why his father took that step.

So, apparently, once his father was dropped off at his house by my uncle, he got into a fight with a neighbour for some reason, and due to that he started drinking and due to that he left the house as he scolded his father for drinking once again. His father then called him in order to ask him to come back home and even apologised to him, but after receiving the first call he stopped receiving the other calls, that kept on coming (his father called

   Your Actions Define Your Existence

28 times). Then based on his father's phone record he called his mother in law in order to tell her how because of her daughter he was going through all of it but even she didn't pick up (he called her 12 times), by now he was absolutely sloshed as he had downed an entire bottle, and then in order to create a scene he tied a rope around his neck and tied it to the ceiling fan and called his wife to tell her how because of her he is doing all of this. At first, his wife told him to stop the drama, but then her husband slipped and got accidentally tied to the fan and then he could take himself out of that grip and died on the spot. At that moment, his wife fainted as she saw her husband die (accidentally committed suicide) in front of her, and then after an hour when his son came back home, he saw his father tied and hanging from the ceiling fan and then he called all his neighbours and then they called the police.

His son to date regrets why he didn't receive the calls and so does his grandmother (father's mother in law), and his wife ever since stopped her affairs and is now taking care of her sons and is often posting emotional posts about her husband and her faults and often shares stories about him with his pictures.

Through this story, I learned how unpredictable life and its happenings are and how often we don't give enough thought to how every moment is so precious and how being enraged and being pre-occupied with things that could have been avoided makes our life filled with issues that could easily be avoided. For instance- had that wife learned the true value of her husband and known how she had indulged in such disgusting acts, she would have had her husband and her son would have had a father. In a similar way, we should all be always grateful for the things, the moments and the people that we have in our lives, for it is the moments with them that make our life way better than anything else could. As appreciation or non-appreciation from them could either make our days better or worse, and even if they don't do that, having such people who genuinely care for us, has the ability to make our lives far better than we could have ever imagined.

That goal you have is incredible and absolutely amazing for that makes you a top-tier individual but always be prepared for the bargain, as you can't have loads of people and also chase your dream, for that's the price you pay for excellence and if you are somebody who truly understands how beautiful and celebrating this thing called "life" is, you will understand how important it is to appreciate those little moments and accept that, all of this could be over in a single snap of a second. And that should make you far more humble and make you accept how everything could become better or worse in a few moments and when you accept that, you will end up realising how most of our worries are often formed out of what I call "abundance problems". This means the things, the tools and the technologies that we all have access to would make individuals in the past feel like God made them for that's how incredible and crucial they are, and yet we are often hell-bent on keeping our minds focused on things that aren't really problems but rather coming out from our constant need to find a purpose in our lives, especially in such a fast paced and non-responsive world, where everybody is centred on their own selves, with little or no concern for the ones moving along with them.

The next time you get sad at not being able to buy those sneakers or complain about the phone you couldn't buy, take a second and think about those individuals who have lost their limbs and would never ever be able to take a walk. Think about those individuals who can't even afford two meals for their kids, think about those soldiers who end up leaving their families and fighting for their

 Your Actions Define Your Existence

country, sometimes to fulfil many selfish politicians' needs, who are willing to go to war to satisfy their ego. And when you think about all of these you would realise how grateful you are to live a life where neither are bullets whizzing past your ears and neither are you sleeping on the pavements and eating leftover food. While you are scrolling through your phone, ordering pizza and complaining about the world, regarding how the world has been so cruel and bitter to you in so many ways, while completely ignoring the incredible ways it has been so kind and loving to you. You have to understand that if you keep on cribbing or keep on chasing things by placing too much thought on the future, then one day your present may end up looking so dark and bleak that you forget what living is like. And that day you will realise how grateful you are to be who you are and live where you are living, with all of it having its own sets of comforts and discomforts, for it is those features that make our lives what it is today and the sooner you accept it the better your life would become and more expecting you would become of the world and its features. You have to understand how so many millionaires and billionaires have lost all of their wealth in an instant never to recover from there again, so many actors who once ruled the world got pushed to the sidelines, and so many individuals who were planning for retirement never ever reached that age, as fate took their life away sooner than they had thought, and when you end up realising and observing all of it, you end up regarding how crucial life is and how being grateful for what it has given now, while staying focussed on your goals and ambitions is what is needed to live a life filled with content and purpose. And unpredictability and lack of structure are what life is about, even though you should try to be as disciplined and focused as possible, you should also be humble enough to accept how all your structure could be dismantled in an instant without any prior warnings, and when you become that individual you become an individual who enjoys the present for its imperfections rather than strive for a perfect future, something which, none of us will ever receive, for that is something that never existed and never would, and that's the order of nature and life in itself. Sooner you accept it, the better your life becomes.

"Embrace the uncertainty of life with gratitude, for in its unpredictability lies the essence of existence. Live for yourself first, for in doing so, you inevitably uplift others, creating a ripple of fulfilment and inspiration. Accept that the end may come sooner than you expect and that unforeseen challenges will always loom on the horizon. If you can grasp these truths, your life will be filled with profound solitude and imperfect yet beautiful moments, far richer than any illusion of a flawless finale."

 Your Actions Define Your Existence

TEN

You Become Who You Spend Your Time With

"Change your life consciously, choosing to surround yourself with people with higher standards"

Tony Robbins

As Darren Hardy writes in The Compound Effect:

"According to research by social psychologist Dr. David McClelland of Harvard, [the people you habitually associate with] determine as much as 95 percent of your success or failure in life."

A NASA study on airline accidents stated that 75% of all airline accidents occur when crews are flying together for the first time. Furthermore, the study showed a well-rested, freshly trained crew working together for the first time consistently under-performed a tired crew who just pulled an all-nighter, but who had regularly served together.

The people you surround yourself with really matter!

These two highly researched and proven statistics should form the benchmark regarding how most of the time, as individuals we are nothing but an end-product of the individuals we spend our time with. And these very individuals could belong to any aspect of our lives. They could be our parents, siblings, friends, or even our colleagues. As the power these individuals hold over our lives is far more powerful than most could have ever realised.

In today's day and age we are largely consuming information through the internet and mostly in the form of social media, and what we make of that information is largely dependent on the people we share that particular information with.

For instance, you might be overweight and depressed, due to which you end up stumbling upon a reel or a video where you get to know the incredible benefits of physical activity and so you finally decide to start moving your body from tomorrow onwards, and also be mindful of what you eat. You chalk up all the plans and goals you have in your mind and promise yourself that you are going to do it no matter what and that within the

    Your Actions Define Your Existence

particular time frame you have given yourself you are going to change yourself for good, and you decide that you are no longer going to feel bad and anxious about your existence, rather you will take ownership of your life. And so you get all pumped up, excited and absolutely elated to share the news with your family or friend, and that is when your destiny is meant to be made.

The very decision that you took to share this amazing plan of yours with somebody that matters to you, would very much state as to how far you could go far with the plan. And then as you share the plan with them, you are met with all sorts of negative impressions and roadblocks. You are either given a smirk or laughed at, or you are told how it's an absolutely shit plan and why there is no point in doing all of these things and rather you should continue living your life the way you have been living all this while. And once you hear these words, all the excitement and elation that had built up within you fizzles out. After which your hype is dead and you are made to realize how being where you are is so much better than doing things that you had never done, and once you realise that you could also live your life the same way you had been living all this while, gives you a sense of comfort and makes you believe that it was really a shitty and a delusional plan and that you don't need to be fit, healthy and be mindful of what you eat. Rather you should continue devouring on all sorts of foods, continue with your negative vices and continue to live your life pathetically and miserably.

Then you go to your friend, who further tells you how your parents are right and that you should stay the way you are and that you are already so stressed in your life, so why take up extra tasks and use extra effort when what you are doing is more than enough in your life. And once you hear these words you forget all those amazing plans of yours and you make the words of your parent, sibling and your friends, as the right one, and you end up believing that what they are saying is right, also the fact that you no longer have to do something different and stick to your current schedule makes you feel, good for the short term and then you continue to live along your life the way you have been living, and soon one day you wake up, and you realise you are a 50 year old miserable moron, who neither loves his job, neither loves where you are at in your live, neither likes the way you look, neither loves the people you are with, and soon you end up becoming so traumatised and vengeful that you continue the same cycle with your children (if you have any) and make sure none of them fulfil their dreams or reach their true potential, for you didn't have the guts to do it, why would you let others do it, and slowly and steadily, one day you lie on your deathbed, with a life full of regrets, and nobody at your bedside, for in the effort to please other and stay where you are, you made yourself so miserable and hateful, that you ended up pushing everything and everybody away from you.

Now let's consider another scenario.

After making those ambitious plans and lofty goals you go to your parent, and your parent listens to you carefully once you finish talking about your plans, they pat you on the back or your shoulder and tell you, all the best son, there is nothing that one cannot do, and I believe if you are able to pull it off, you will inspire a lot of other people to take their health and how they want to deal with it on their own hands. The parent tells you how they are proud of what you have decided to set out to achieve, and then tells you that you can do it.

Once you hear these words the fire within you grows even faster and your intensity and hype are now on an absolutely different level, as you realised how you could achieve anything you want in

 Your Actions Define Your Existence

life. You are made to think about how these things that you had never ever done or even planned to execute in your life, could be done. And so you are absolutely pumped up and you feel like you could achieve it all. While speaking with your parents, you express that you have never done anything like this before and are afraid of failing.

At that time your parent tells you how he/she never ever dared to do something like that, and the fact that you are even planning to take on such a task is far more than what they could have ever planned for. And even if you fail, you will learn various things on the way, and those things could be setbacks, trials and tribulations, but if you continue to focus on your goal no matter what, you will soon start seeing changes and those changes will further motivate you to push even harder and stronger, and that is far more than what you could have ever imagined.

Hearing all of these things make you feel so good and so happy about your new plan, that you go to your friend, who then tells you that you are doing the right things by taking this crucial step in your life. He tells you how he was planning to work on himself and his health, but simply lacked the needed push to implement it. But now that you have taken this step, he is going to join you in this pursuit of changing himself, and he tells you how he is so happy that both of you have finally decided to take charge of your lives. Soon you are doing things that you always wanted to do, you are in a shape that you could have never ever imagined to be in, and just by being in shape, you realise how your entire worldview has changed and how everything that you thought about the world, and the world had thought about you, was now on a completely different level in a positive way. And one day you wake up as a 50 year old individual with a smile on your face. As now you are doing things you love to do, you are doing something you look forward to most mornings, the reason I stated "**most**" instead of "**every**" is that even the most successful individuals sometimes feel like not doing it as motivation comes and goes, but it is here that discipline comes into the picture and it is discipline that is now an integral and important part of your life. Due to discipline, you are now living your life with a far more positive outlook, and irrespective of the problems that come and go, you are looking forward to facing them in a far more courageous way, rather than fearing them and cowering to them.

As an individual, you are content with your partner, and your children (if you have them) look forward to seeing you and spending time with you, as your very presence makes them feel assured and confident about their lives, and their very presence makes you feel fulfilled and valued in your own life. That's what we get when we positively trade our energies and share each other's spaces with content, trust and respect. You are far less bitter than your other friends are, and you and your other friend who had taken that decision of working on yourselves two decades back are now absolutely enthralled and far more at peace with where you both are.

The parents who had motivated you into taking that step, 20 years back, are now being looked after by you, and they are far more proud of you than you could have ever imagined, and taking care of them gives you far more peace than you could have ever imagined.

Now when you compare these two hypothetical scenarios, you would be able to figure out how in the first instance you became absolutely miserable and vengeful with our lives. And that is because the people whose words mattered to you the most, or the people around whom you spend your lives the most, pushed you away from your plans to work on yourself. They talked you out of

   Your Actions Define Your Existence

your ambitious plans to do something worthwhile for yourself in your life. For they were too insecure to let you become somebody they could have never envisioned becoming, for they were too afraid and scared to take that big leap in their lives, that would have meant temporary suffering but would have pushed them towards a life, where they would have been far more content and less miserable with their lives.

In the second instance, the parent and the friends' positive encouragement forces the belief in you that what you had envisioned for yourself could be done. And that enforcement allowed you to take the steps that meant temporary discomfort, but in hindsight, those steps meant taking a path where you walk down a road, you had never taken but was necessary for you to make something out of your life. And when you end up becoming the competent, disciplined, gracious and benevolent individual you ended up becoming, you should realise how it was because of the push given by those who matter to you that you are where you are, and that meant living a life where you look forward to waking up most mornings and spend your time, doing things that are far more than what you could have ever envisioned.

These two instances would give you an example regarding how often what we make out of our lives, is in many ways who surround ourselves with, and what we make of our reality is in many ways dependent on a lot of other things rather than the simple work that needs to be put in. although that doesn't mean that we always need people motivating us to fulfil our goals, for even without them we could achieve them with a strong mental fortitude, but having someone besides us during such times really helps, and makes us less traumatised when we achieve them.

Let me share a real-life story in order to explain, how our company and who we spend time with truly matter.

Let's call him, Matt.

Matt and I have been friends and have known each other for nearly nine years. We have hung out a lot during my college days and at one point he was one of the closest individuals I have ever met. But with time and as the circumstances and situations of our lives started changing we started going our distant ways, but even in those rare and distant times, we made sure to meet at least maybe once or twice a year, sometimes maybe once in two years, but whenever we meet we make sure that we go out on a long road trip somewhere and spend some quality times with each other. And that is exactly what I had recently.

It was a Monday morning and at around 10 am I received a call from an unknown number, when I received It was known other than Matt on the other side. He then told me how he was in town for about 2 weeks and he would love to catch up and meet me. I told him how we could go somewhere for a single night trip and have some fun somewhere, as the last few weeks had been really hectic for me as well, in fact, they had been so hectic that I worked almost 49 days on the go without any single day off, due to certain government examinations being held in my school, due to which even on Sunday's I had to wake up at 2 AM in the morning to go for my examination related work and would reach home by 9 PM, and by then I was really cooked. And so for that reason, I told Matt how I would not really prefer driving back and forth for hours on the same day, as that way I would feel even more tired and would rather stay for a night somewhere peaceful and a bit secluded. And so based on these requests of mine, he chose a place and we both went on that one day trip.

For me, the trip was meant to make me feel relaxed and make me feel far more grateful for the things that have happened, but

  Your Actions Define Your Existence

turns out everything was absolutely different from what I had expected.

From the beginning Matt started the trip cribbing about his environment at home, which was quite understandable as often times when you don't have understanding parents or family members at home it creates an environment of unfulfillment and creates an environment of uneasiness within yourself, due to which you often feel sad, guilty and feel anxious for most parts of the time you spend over there. At that time I told him how it's normal for him to feel the way he has been feeling of late, and so I told him how he should rather concentrate on the good things that have happened to him in recent times. I told him how his new job is so amazing and I am happy that he is now working in a place, where he is no longer guided by fear and anxiety, but rather has an environment of appreciation and calmness. Hearing that Matt then went about almost 20 minutes cribbing how he is not grateful for his workplace and he would rather do something else than work there. To which, I told him that he has to be patient and to which he stated that how there is no point in being so optimistic and ambitious about our lives, and how even I should not be willing to dream so big and all that bullshit. Things which I completely ignored.

Then he told me how he hasn't been doing any sort of physical activity of late, as he is too busy and then he looked at my physique (which is great, possibly best this year) and told me how I am so privileged and that's why I am able to maintain my physique and told me how we all die one day and there is no point in being in such great shape. He then told me how he is no longer attracted to his girlfriend the way he used to be and yet he is going to marry her as he doesn't really want to go anywhere else, or meet anybody else now in his life and will settle for what he has. Then he told me how his girlfriend and his mother and sister don't get along, to which I told him that he should rent someplace else until he could afford a place of his own, to which he stated that he would stay where he is now, as even though he could afford a house, he won't go anywhere else, even if he hates his family he will stay with them, for he wants to his own share of the property.

And while we were having this conversation, we stopped by for a cup of tea, and I was thinking who the hell is this guy, I don't even know him anymore. Being with me has suddenly turned me into having such pathetic feelings about my own self. I started having thoughts about myself and my family and my circumstances that barely came into my mind. I started feeling guilty and angry for being ambitious and for being so happy and grateful for my life, and even the bad things that happened which I was grateful for, suddenly now I was feeling angry about them and cribbing about them. And then as I sat in the car, all I did was crib and crib about my issues, something which I realised only when I came back home the next night. And the morning I woke up on a Monday, I was no longer willing to go to work or to the gym, as I had fallen into this state of self inflicted hell. Matt was telling me how he dreads waking up on Monday mornings because he hates his job. And it was only around in the evening on the same day, that after work feeling dejected, down and low for no reason that I decided to do some yoga and meditate for some time, and guess what an hour passed by with my eyes shut and I didn't even realise, and I when I got up I came to the realisation that nothing had really changed in my life, rather most of the things were in my head, and had been planted in my head through those negative and pessimistic conversations that I had with Matt during the trip, and that's when I realised that I really need to choose Who I travel with from next time. And I decided that before travelling

    Your Actions Define Your Existence

with somebody I had not met in a while, I would at least meet them for sometimes somewhere in order to get an idea of where they are at mentally or as a person, for I don't want to destroy my own mental sanity for a night of experience.

This Example that I just shared with you should give you an idea regarding how often times even when everything is going in the right direction, all it takes is spending some time, with the wrong sort of individual or individuals, and that could be anybody, and that time that you spend with them will make sure that life becomes nothing else, but a living hell.

Their words and their actions will make sure that your subconscious is filled with some much more doubt and non-clarity that would start forgetting about all the incredible things that you have witnessed until now in your life. Sometimes you have understood that these sorts of individuals could belong to your so-called closest circle of individuals and so you have to be very careful, in regards to whom your share information with.

For instance, I remember when I launched my clothing brand (Toxci) along with one of my closest buddies, our posts and stories on all the social media platforms reached numbers that we had never ever witnessed in a long time, but what surprised us was the basic fact that individuals from whom we were expecting to get some well wishes or at least some congratulations or even reshares or virtual supports, were nowhere to be seen. But rather individuals with whom we have had no or barely any contact ended up giving some incredible good wishes. I received calls from individuals I had even forgotten used to exist in my life, and so did my friend. And the next morning we both discussed how people are so insecure and so frail in their minds, and at that time I told him how "everybody just wants us to survive or if they are suffering even we should suffer, but the moment we somehow get our life together and do something different or take a life-changing step, they hate us. Why? Not because we did something wrong, but because we did something or at least took a step towards something which could change our life, and because they were too scared or incompetent about it, means unless they take that step, they will stay there forever, and most of the time, they do stay there forever".

These lines or words are not meant to demean or show disregard towards any individual's life situation but are rather a truth of human nature. Wherein because of our own inadequacies and inefficiencies we choose to hate on that person who took that first step to change their lives, and rather than learning from them or even assisting them in doing what they planned out on doing, we try to bring them down, forgetting how this way we are spending our lives on such a pathetic and malevolent activity while the other one is hell bent on changing their life, while we are still where we are.

So, it becomes imperative that you decide who you want to be. Be the one taking that step, be the one assisting the ones taking that step, or be the one who is hating them for taking that step. Whoever you decide to be, will end up determining who you are going to be in the future, who your kids are going to be and how your family is going to be. And if you want a life that is fulfilled and makes you less vengeful and less miserable then you should choose the first two steps, for why would you decide to take the third step, as you have every right to live your life with morality and with a sense of fulfilment and solitude, and choosing not to do that is a betrayal to your soul and to your life itself. And why would you decide to be bitter, resentful and miserable your whole life, when there is such an amazing place to be on the other side?

 Your Actions Define Your Existence

Your life and your existence should matter to you, more than it might matter to anybody else. You should understand how as an individual you are capable of doing such incredible and honourable things, and how powerful you are. And yet none of these things would matter if you end up spending your lives with people who wear a mask to be your supporters, while beneath that mask is a vengeful and miserable individual who wants nothing but you to stay where you are. All of these things are only possible when you decide not to give them the power to make a considerable impact on your lives, for that is only possible when you decide to let go of those who make you feel alone even while being together. And that is worse than being lonely on your own.

So choose wisely and make your life a worthwhile experience and not a hellish one, for you owe to yourself to make the most of your life, and trust me you are truly capable of that, everybody is.

ELEVEN

Appreciate What You Have Before It's Too Late

> *"Once it's too late, you appreciate what a miracle life is"*
>
> **Bill Watterson**

Around 11 PM on the final day of Durga Puja—a festival in which Hindus worship Goddess Durga—just after finishing dinner, my sister, my cousin Alakesh, and I went to bid farewell to our grandmother. She had travelled from her village to our city specifically to attend the Durga Puja organized by her eldest son—my father. Hosting a puja independently is an expensive endeavour, and she deeply understood the struggles of poverty that she and her elder children had endured in the early years of their lives. Watching her son successfully organize the puja on his own was a moment of immense pride for her, which is why she never missed the occasion.

However, what happened next would remain etched in my memory forever.

And so, as the 3 of us went to say goodbye to her, we noticed that she had forgotten the way to her bedroom and was lost in the hall of the house. Then it was my sister who showed her the way and assisted her in reaching her bedroom. And even then she kept on asking us again and again whether she kitchen? And we were shocked for it was the very same place where she was sitting and having her late night tea a few minutes back. Once again my sister assisted her to the kitchen where she consumed her favourite betelnut and pan (an Indian post meal food). And then as she was brought back to her room, while me and my cousin were sharing a laugh about something, my sister said something that literally pierced through my heart, "Make sure you make the most out of these moments as this might be the last time you see her attending this puja", and then I completely zoned out. As I sat in the chair, staring at the ceiling of the room absolutely numb and quiet, my cousin kept on saying how due to the lack of sleep in the last 72 hours (12 hours of sleep in the last 72 hours) my body had given up and that's why I had zoned out, but

 Your Actions Define Your Existence

the reality was something else. As we all stood up to hug her and say goodbye to her, I completely broke down and both my cousin and my sister were shocked as their reaction said only one thing, "Does Neel even cry"! And unfortunately, that is what happened. I simply could not control my tears and my grandmother looked at me and even her eyes got filled with tears, as she knew why I was crying.

In reality, a lot of things had built up over time, ultimately leading to the moment when I completely broke down, gave up, and surrendered to my emotions.

Our grandmother has always been known for being one with a strong will and one with grit and perseverance that very few people can be compared to, and seeing her become so frail and weak really made me question everything that our lives comprise. Our achievements, our bodies, our goals, our inspirations, our fight, our misunderstandings, our financial gains, our material possessions and even our loving family members. Seeing her made me realise how nature is the most beautiful and yet the most brutal thing that the creator has ever created. Because our lives are made in such a way, we are oftentimes surrounded and bothered by so many things all around that we end up failing to appreciate the true beauty of our lives. My grandmother was the very woman who once used to roam around the entire village bare-footed and never really gave a fuck regarding how people perceived her, as that's the attitude she has carried all her life, and that is what she has instilled in her children as well, and seeing her becoming so frail, to the point that she can't even identify her own room barely 5 steps away, made me realise how eventually we are all bound to face these days in our lives, and no matter what we achieve, gain or possess at the peak of our powers, one day all of these things will be gone and somebody else would posses these things that we feel so proud and arrogant about. And once I realised that it made me understand how, as humans we are always going after our next conquest one after the other, going after those next goals as soon as one is completed and in the process we end up forgetting the reason why we had set that very first goal of ours in the first place, why we had chosen to take up that journey, why we chose that particular path in our lives, and when we ask that question, often times we will all end up coming up with different answers to those questions, as for some it was to become happy, for some it was to find a purpose in life, for others it would be to prove yourself and others about your capabilities and yet once we reach those goals, we end up forgetting these reasons and keeping on going after the next conquest one after the other, which is needed as that is what makes us win the game of life, but equally important is taking a step back and cherishing those amazing moments that led up to this moment and realise and at the same time be grateful for what an amazing and incredible gift that we have known as life, and how it should be cherished whenever the opportunity arise, as that makes us incredibly fulfilled as individuals and makes us live our lives with far less regret and not have any qualms about what we could have done, once we get old, and that's the reason why appreciation is the cornerstone if we truly want to cherish and enjoy the amazing gift of life.

In terms of my grandmother, she even visited our house that day and had lunch at our house after almost a decade. She went around the entire house and inspected each and every room and sat over there for a few minutes as if she wanted to embrace this house for one last time, she sat in the corner of the kitchen which always used to be her favourite place to sit and relax, and sipped a cup of tea while sitting there. Then she came to sit in the hall of our house and watched the television and at the same time sat

    Your Actions Define Your Existence

down for some amazing conversations with us cousins, in many ways, it was really such a fulfilling and incredible experience, something that would forever stay with me my entire life. Even these moments made me realise the fragility of our existence and the moments that oftentimes we give far more importance than it should have been.

"Reflecting on my younger days, I remember how my mother and grandmother would often find themselves in clashes of egos—a common and universal struggle between a daughter-in-law and mother-in-law. But when I look at them now, it's nothing short of magical. I've seen them sitting together, engaging in the most beautiful and meaningful conversations, as they've both come to understand that all those past conflicts were insignificant. Time has shown them that such things hold no weight in the grand scheme of life. Even now, my grandmother occasionally scolds my mother's youngest sister, who is married to my father's youngest brother, and sometimes she even reprimands my father. Yet, no one takes offence anymore. They all see her as a sheltering tree—providing comfort, protection, and, yes, occasional scolding. But they know that when she's gone, no one will be there to guide them, even if it's with a stern word. Over the years, everyone has realised that what truly matters are those fleeting moments that bring joy and laughter, and it's from these small experiences we should learn the essence of life."

Life, as we all know, is a dynamic and ever-changing experience filled with both joys and challenges. At its core, it is meant to be lived with a sense of purpose—something that drives us to wake up every morning and strive for more as our ambitions and goals give structure and direction to our lives. In many ways, they are the fuel that keeps our engines (lives) running, ensuring that we remain motivated, focused, and engaged in pursuing something meaningful. Whether it is the goal of personal growth, professional success, artistic expression, or simply the pursuit of happiness, these aspirations shape our paths and define our journeys. However, while it is crucial to have ambitions and goals, it is equally essential to develop the courage and peace of mind to pause, take a step back, and reflect on the journey we have taken thus far, for if not, we end up losing the very reason we first set out on this vision of ours. Often, in the constant hustle of life, we forget the value of taking a step back and reflecting on what we have done thus far. During these moments of reflection, we can truly appreciate how far we have come. By slowing down, we allow ourselves the time to reconnect with our inner selves, evaluate our experiences, and understand the lessons life has taught us. This introspection helps us gain clarity and opens our eyes to the blessings we often overlook.

When we take the time to pause and reflect, gratitude becomes a natural outcome. We start to recognise and cherish the incredible moments we have experienced and the people who have touched our lives along the way. In the rush of daily life, it's easy to take these blessings for granted. But when we allow ourselves to become still, we gain a deeper appreciation for the simple things—those small acts of kindness, the support from loved ones, or even the opportunity to wake up each day and witness the sunrise. As it is in these moments of gratitude, we are reminded how blessed we are to be alive and share this journey with such remarkable individuals.

However, adopting this mindset of gratitude and appreciation does not necessarily guarantee a life free from conflicts, sadness, or bitterness. Life is, after all, a complicated and unpredictable experience. As individuals, no matter how stoic your way of life might have become, you will eventually encounter difficult

     Your Actions Define Your Existence

and untoward situations, face loss, or deal with moments of disappointment, as these challenges are inevitable in our short and mortal lives. Yet, when we cultivate an attitude of gratitude and openness, we become better equipped to handle these difficulties. We develop resilience and inner strength, allowing us to navigate life's storms with greater ease and composure.

Understanding that having this outlook does not mean avoiding or denying negative emotions is essential. Instead, it involves accepting them as a part of life's rich experience as a whole. Embracing the full spectrum of our positive and negative feelings enables us to grow and learn. When we encounter sadness, it becomes an opportunity for self-reflection and healing. When we face conflict, it presents a chance to develop understanding, empathy, and compromise. By accepting that life will have its ups and downs, we gain a more balanced perspective, which helps us navigate challenges without being overwhelmed.

Furthermore, adopting a mindset of living in the present, as if every moment could be our last, enhances our ability to savour the simple joys of life. When we live with the awareness that time is fleeting and that we may not have as much time as we think, we value the present more. Something that I understand far more from spending those moments with my grandmother and the way she interacted with her family. It made me realise the importance of cherishing the laughter shared with friends, the quiet moments of solitude, and even the mundane routines that form the fabric of our everyday lives. This awareness allowed me to approach life with a sense of urgency, not frantically or anxiously, but mindfully and appreciatively. Similarly, it should encourage others to make the most of each moment, connect deeply with those around us, and express love, gratitude, and kindness whenever possible.

Living with this sense of presence and appreciation also shifts our perspective on the future. Many of us spend significant time worrying about what lies ahead. We plan meticulously, attempting to control every detail to secure a future that aligns with our expectations. While planning and preparation are necessary, an excessive focus on maintaining the future can lead to anxiety and stress. It can prevent us from fully experiencing the present moment, as we are constantly preoccupied with what might or might not happen. It is at this moment that acceptance and letting go becomes crucial. When we become capable enough to accept life's unpredictability, we liberate ourselves from needing to control everything. We begin to see the beauty in uncertainty, recognising that life's unpredictability brings excitement and wonder. By embracing the unknown, we open ourselves up to the endless possibilities. We begin to trust that life will unfold in ways we may not have anticipated, but that could bring unexpected joys and opportunities.

This openness to the future also helps us let go of regrets from the past. Mind you, regret is a powerful emotion that can weigh heavily on our hearts, preventing us from moving forward. But when we shift our focus to the present and the future, we realise that the past is a chapter that has already been written. While it may hold valuable lessons, it does not define our present or dictate our future. By accepting the past as it is, we free ourselves from its hold, allowing us to focus on the beauty and potential of the present moment. Life demands growth, resilience, and a willingness to adapt to change. Yet, when we approach life with an open heart, a sense of gratitude, and a desire to embrace the present, we begin to see that the true treasures of life are not found in controlling every aspect of our journey but in appreciating the simple, beautiful moments that we encounter along the way. In doing so, we can create a life that is not only filled with ambition

  Your Actions Define Your Existence

and achievement but also with peace, fulfilment, and a deep sense of gratitude for the gift of being alive.

Here are some moments I captured from that day we spent with my grandmother—a day that profoundly changed my perspective, making me truly appreciate the value of life and its delicate, fleeting, yet unforgiving nature.

Most of these pictures were taken while we were in the worst state of tiredness as we had slept only 12 hours in the last 72 hours, and we are celebrating one of the biggest festivals in our state of Assam, India. But in the middle of all of this chaos and celebrations, I found out how truly life is oftentimes giving us such wonderful and amazing things and at the same time also filling our lives with such incredibly subtle signs to stop fussing about what has not happened, and rather focus on what has happened and what we have done, and taking that approach often times bring far more peace and solitude into our lives, than we could have ever imagined.

Below are two pictures of my grandmother with my sister, my cousins and a friend of mine.

As a whole what we must all understand that life is a gift that very few of us truly appreciate in its true form, and the reason for that is most of us often times wrapped up in our own little world, due to which we are never able to go out and push towards or pursue the things that truly matter, and buy the time we realise it's too

Your Actions Define Your Existence

late. As I mentioned earlier, ambition is important—whether it's dreaming of a luxury sports car or dating a stunning model, if that's what motivates you. However, just as crucial is the ability to appreciate and find fulfilment once you've achieved those dreams. For if you can't appreciate those things, you will never ever be able to appreciate anything, and that would make you bitter, broken and resentful of everything about life, and that's no way to live and cherish such a wonderful existence known as "Life", for the life you are living could be a dream for many, so why not live it with appreciation and gratitude.

As that's what life is about and that's what living should be about.

TWELVE

Life Will Make You Humble

> *"Humility is the key to success the moment you think you have achieved it all, that's the moment you're most vulnerable."*
>
> ***Lou Holtz***

Has it ever happened to you that you felt you could do anything you wanted to, as every step that you were taking was inevitably leading to incredible amounts of success? You became so cocky about your abilities that you felt invincible. You often showed disdain at what other people felt or believed, and showed little or no remorse to what others believed in. Always regarded what you did as the absolute right way of action. You disregarded that there is something stronger than all of us, you thought there is nothing that you can't achieve and take yourself to the top which is good as that means that you have a strong belief regarding your abilities. But there is always a thin line between **self-belief** and **arrogance**.

And that's when shit hits the fan!

Just when you thought the riches are going to stay forever, your beliefs and your way of living is the ultimate way of doing things, you decisions are always right, and you are forever going to stay atop that mountain, all of that goes downhill, as an incident happened out of nowhere , and that led to absolutely catastrophic results and all of the things that you felt so proud of and were so arrogant about goes downhill and you end up losing everything, and everything and every individual that you once disregarded and were warned about comes to haunt you, and soon you find yourself at the bottom of the mountain, while in some cases you have even gone beyond that, and that's when you are stripped of all the glory and achievements that you were once proud of, and that's when you realise how miniscule and small you are in the larger scheme of things and how minute your achievements were, and how all that grandiose you once felt made you invincible has pushed you the periphery of vulnerability, and that's when you realise that you have come across the most powerful occurrence in the universe, and that occurrence is none other than, **"Life"** itself.

 Your Actions Define Your Existence

In order to explain this better, let me share my own story of how I came to this realisation and how most of us often go through such stages in life, that change us completely.

So, around 4 years back I was at my absolute peak. I was able to lift a decent amount of weight across various exercises, including bench presses, dumbbell presses, squats, and deadlifts. And I was so cocky and so proud of how fit and strong I was. I used to wear a compression, have a cup of black coffee along with a banana and used to have amazing training sessions. Even though the weights weren't as heavy as professional athletes would do, for somebody who always focused on athletic performance and looks, I was really proud of myself. During that time, I also started boxing and so my confidence really peaked and really felt I could smash anybody who came, which no matter what should not have been the case as there is always somebody better than you, but it was that mentality that has always allowed me to do things that I loved. That is the reason I adore individuals such as Cristiano, Virat and Djokovic so much, as none of them were really as supremely talented individual as some of the other players in many ways, but their discipline and work ethic led them to do the incredible things they have done.

And just when I had thought I was untouchable, disaster struck.

It was a Saturday evening, which usually is my favourite day of the week to work, as most individuals are out partying, the gym has half the people it usually has, and I could sleep in on Sunday, and it was leg day, which meant I could recover well, as I could sleep in. As I began my warm-up lunges, I felt a slight, itching pain in my back, but I brushed it off. However, when I moved on to leg presses, the pain became noticeably strange. I put on a belt, hoping it would help, but it made no difference. Then I loaded up 100 kgs in the power squat machine and did the first set, and by now I could feel something was off but I continued, and then as I did my second set and paused for extra muscle contraction, I could hear a loud sound in my back and as I went up the belt by itself came out and I could feel numb and almost felt paralysed in the lower part of my body. Then I somehow gained the courage to stretch a bit and then left the gym midway through workout and the journey back home was hell, as I couldn't feel the brake and accelerator but somehow I reached home and lay down, and the next morning I literally had the worst pain of my life. Due to that, instead of going to the office I straight away went for an MRI as advised by my Physiotherapist. There it was found that four of the lower back discs had been damaged and I had an internal tear in it, and the liquid the holds the back together had come out. Then my physio told me, how I wouldn't be able to workout for the next 6 months and even after that I won't be able to go back to my usual self for some time. Hearing all of these almost gave me depression and I couldn't believe what had happened, then in the evening when I realised I could no longer hit the gym, I realised how big of a fool I was to think so much about myself by overestimating everything about my abilities.

Then in a few months, I ended up losing a good amount of my size, my chests stopped being so pumped and my shoulders were neither upright and that's when I realised how fickle and small we humans are in the larger scheme of things. And then as time went by, I started doing things I often made fun of and became someone I never thought would be possible.

So, as a guy, I was always a non-believer in doing yoga or any sort of these blood flow and breathing exercises and would often mock those who believed in them, as I always believed in those hard and grind sort of things, but life wanted to teach me how everything is important. And so as suggested by many

    Your Actions Define Your Existence

I started doing Yoga regularly along with undergoing the Physio-treatment as through that I was building strength and flexibility at the same time. During this time, I also started getting panic attacks and would frequently become anxious as fitness was such a crucial part of my life, and so I had to seek counselling through a wonderful therapist who I still talk to occasionally as I found her through an amazing platform known as Amaha, and she is an absolutely amazing individual who has really helped me whenever I needed something to do or get a solution to any roadblock I felt was hindering my progress. It all started when one day due to not being able to sleep and getting all sorts of negative thoughts into my mind and staring at the ceiling fan I realised I needed help, and that's when reached out to her. Something I could have never imagined a year back, as I used to regard people who would seek counselling as cowards, but then life had something else in the story for me. And with Yoga, counselling, physiotherapy and meditation I became and felt so powerful from inside I could have never imagined. My fitness was no longer the level it used to be, but by doing these things, I had opened a side of me that I had never thought was possible. All my mindset regarding how being fit and having muscles was my only identity absolutely changed and in many ways that injury was like a blessing in disguise. Through meditation, I unlocked extraordinary levels of mental strength that once seemed unimaginable. In many ways, I was no longer the Neel of the past, yet this transformed version of myself—despite my resistance—was someone I had to embrace. And the first person to accept this new me was none other than myself. Through these changes, I discovered the profound power of inner happiness and compassion. When we cultivate these qualities within, we evolve into versions of ourselves we never thought possible. Self-acceptance, once elusive to me, became a lesson I fully grasped during this transformative period.

Today I am an author with 2 books under my name (this is 2nd one), I have my own clothing brand, something I could have never imagined, And I have taken my mom on a foreign trip (something I always dreamt about). As a person, I have become so much calm and composed and all of this was only possible because of that injury and how it forced me to do and accept things that I once considered weak and feminine. Fortunately, these challenges gave me a vision of myself and revealed a path that had always been within me—one I had simply been in denial about following. Today, I am fitter than ever, though the back pain lingers. Yet, my mind has grown significantly calmer. Arrogance has been replaced with gratitude, and every workout, every action in my life, is now carried out with a deeper sense of calm and solitude. This shift has made me realize that our true strength lies not in what we think we possess but in the limitless potential of our minds. And all of this became possible because I chose to heal my mind. That choice itself was only made possible because life, in its way, showed me how everything we take pride in—everything we are arrogant about—can be taken away in an instant. It taught me that true power lies in gratitude and respect for our abilities, for only then can we become individuals capable of making the world a better place—far beyond what we ever imagined.

This is a lesson we must all learn: nothing has ever been more supreme than life itself. The sooner we understand this and humble ourselves before it, the better. We start appreciating life's gifts to us instead of focusing on others' fortunes or our own shortcomings. If we choose to dwell in resentment, we will forever despise life. And when life eventually leaves our bodies, what remains is nothing more than an empty shell—a body without a soul. That is not the path any of us should walk. Instead, we should strive for a life of purpose, fulfilment, and a vision that honours the gift of existence.

    Your Actions Define Your Existence

These are some of the things that even the movies have showcased to us in different ways, and one of the biggest examples we could gather is from the movie Thor.

So, Thor as you all know is known as the God of Thunder based on Norse mythology, who is extremely strong and is an extremely powerful being. And right from his youth, he has been known as someone who has always shown an incredible amount of arrogance regarding his powers. And then on the day of his coronation as King, the frost giants who are another species residing in Jotunheim, sneak into their planet to get access to the space stone. And then Odin (Thor's father and king of gods) kills them and ever since then, Thor has been seeking vengeance against the Frost giants for ruining his special day. Then one day Thor gathers his core group of friends and attacks them, and there he kills an incredible number of frost giants but then Odin shows up to stop the fight and to rescue them as he knows they would be overwhelmed by the sheer number of Frost giants. Then Odin takes them back with him to their planet and scolds Thor for being arrogant and creating instability and for starting a war and disrupting the galaxy. But then Thor calls Odin a coward, an old man and a fool with a cowardly heart for staying quiet even after seeing the frost giants penetrate their planet. It is then that Odin loses his cool and takes away all his powers, throws his hammer away and banishes him away to outer space until he falls to earth. And on Earth, Thor realises that he no longer has the powers he had before and he is no longer a God and is as simple as a human. And it is during that time that Thor truly changes as he has to embrace life with his riches and powers, and he ends up becoming a man he could have never thought was possible and during that time he also falls in love with an earthling.

And then once he goes back to his planet (Asgard) he is no longer the same man, as he is much more calm, composed and much more grateful for the things that life has bestowed upon him. By banishing Thor, Odin taught him a lesson that if you truly want to be the ones holding and exercising power, the first thing you have to learn is how to live your life without your powers and how to become a better and much more grateful individual, for only a man who has control over his lusts, desires and emotions is truly made to rule and show the people around them a better path.

During his exile, Thor discovered that his true essence remained intact even without his godly powers or his mighty hammer—an artefact that could only be wielded by one deemed worthy. Through this journey, he realized he had entirely misunderstood the meaning of power. His perception of what it meant to wield authority had been deeply flawed, a lesson that holds significance for all of us.

He came to understand that life itself is the greatest equalizer, capable of humbling even the mightiest while also lifting the most unassuming. Everything we experience as individuals is ultimately governed by life, and we are all merely playing our roles within its grand design. Even though Thor's lifespan of 5,000 years far exceeds that of an ordinary human, in the vast expanse of existence, even his time is fleeting. This realization underscores the undeniable truth that nothing is more supreme than life itself. The sooner we embrace this wisdom, the more we can grow and evolve as individuals.

Kindness costs nothing

Indeed, the world we live in today day and age is undoubtedly an absolutely brutal and challenging place to be, as it is something I have myself talked about in detail in the previous sections of my book, it is precisely in these trying times and this sort of an age of humankind that kindness becomes even more crucial.

 Your Actions Define Your Existence

Kindness, as a concept, might seem almost trivial when we compare it to the things that we as humans are going through, especially the unbelievably sad and dark things that are often ravaging our world. And yet it is in these times that we must not get overwhelmed by our possessions and rather start to acknowledge and be grateful for the things that surround us. We have to understand the basic notion of kindness, which is simplicity and accessibility; having these things costs nothing and is often well within the reach of everyone, regardless of their circumstances. Especially in a world that often feels cold and unyielding, kindness is a warm, glowing light that can cut through the darkness, offering comfort, hope, and connection. And the ones who are kind enough to appreciate life and also encourage others to do so make a world where individuals are humbled and bowing towards what life is capable of doing as, once you become that and aspire others to become that, you create a world with far less harshness, arrogance and

You could be a celebrity, a footballer, or even a famous social media influencer, just see how amazing it feels when a fan or anybody runs towards you and greets you and you move aside your arrogance and feeling of grandiose and treat them with a welcoming smile and respect their wishes. It is at that moment you will see how the power of kindness could overpower any sort of malevolent act. You have to understand that this fame or influence you are holding today could be gone in an instant, so why use that time and make a lasting impact on those, based on whose good wishes and followings you have become who you have become? The satisfaction derived from being kind whether through a thoughtful gesture, or a listening ear can be immeasurable. It fosters a sense of connection, deepens relationships, and nurtures a sense of belonging essential to our well-being.

Kindness stands in stark contrast to the destructive mindset of feeling that what you have today, the fort that you are holding today and the possession you are in charge of today will stay forever. It affirms the value of each person and their dreams, encouraging them to persevere even in the face of adversity. The power of kindness also lies in its ability to transcend barriers. In a world often divided by race, religion, politics, and socioeconomic status, kindness serves as a universal language that can bridge these divides. When we choose to act kindly, we demonstrate a shared humanity that transcends our differences. Although in truth, kindness won't go around and solve all of the world's problems, it can certainly make the burden of these problems easier to bear. Even science has proven how, the simple act of giving—whether it be time, resources, or a kind word—triggers the release of feel-good hormones like oxytocin and endorphins. These hormones help to combat the effects of stress and anxiety, something which an incredible number of individuals are facing in today's day and age. At the same time, you have to understand that to be kind, humble and grateful you have to be a strong individual, because when you are at the top of your prowess everything seems correct and good, but once you come down you realise what all you had doing wrong, and then the ones you once showed disdain towards celebrate your fallings, and that is not who you should aim to become no matter how big you become. At the same time, you have to understand that there will always be haters and people wanting your downfall, but the best you can do is not increase their strength with your ungrateful and arrogant habits. It's important to note that kindness does not always come easily.

You have to understand that being vulnerable in a positive way is the first step towards becoming somebody willing to be

 Your Actions Define Your Existence

kind. You need to have the strength to reciprocate and truly acknowledge the things that are happening around the world no matter how good or bad. To be truly kind, you must be willing to open yourself up to others, let down your guard, and become an individual who is willing to engage with the world in a meaningful way. Doing something and becoming someone like that could be an absolutely daunting task, especially in a world where vulnerability is often seen as a weakness. But it is through this vulnerability that you would be able to forge genuine connections and create a sense of oneness with the ones that truly matter. By choosing to act as you did and striving for positive change, you unintentionally challenge the status quo and present an alternative vision of a world where people treat each other with greater kindness, gratitude, and respect for life's forces. For it is that fear that would allow you to stay humble, it is the gratefulness that would allow you to love your journey, and it is your appreciative behaviour that would allow you to go towards your goals and understand how beautiful life is. It is a conscious decision to approach life with an open heart and a generous spirit. It is about recognising the inherent worth of every individual and treating them with the dignity and respect they deserve. Kindness is about seeing beyond the surface, beyond our own needs and desires, and responding to the needs of others with compassion and understanding.

You have to accept that the biggest superpower life has given you is being kind and when you are willing to use that you become twice the person you could have ever hoped to become and that is truly magnificent and incredible in so many ways. When you do that, you grow along the way and that's what we should all be aiming for.

Be Competent by being Kind

In the pursuit of achieving our goals and aspirations, there is an underlying truth that you all may have come to realise and that is the fact that to achieve things that you have set out for yourself, for your motives and your wishes, you have to do things that the ordinary individuals aren't willing to do. You have to be competent, resilient and steadfast on what your goals and accordingly approach them and race towards, as Competence, resilience, and a steadfast commitment to your goals are essential, and yet the one things that would truly make you far more appreciative of your life and be accepting of what life is capable of is being **"Kind"** and being accepting of what and how things have happened and could happen if life decides to do so. And this balance between being strong and kind is not only a powerful tool in personal development but also a means of attaining lasting success.

To begin with, let's consider what it means to be competent. Competence is more than having the skills or knowledge to perform and fulfil our tasks to the best of our abilities. Rather it's also about being confident in your abilities and making decisions with conviction. However, competence without courage often leads to mediocrity. If you are too timid or too afraid of making mistakes or being on the wrong side of things, even with the best intentions and goals, you are unlikely to achieve your full potential. This fear of failure can trap you in a state of resentment and unfulfillment, as the opportunities to reach your goals slip away, paralysed by indecision and doubt. To achieve your goals, you have to be willing to do what is wrong without causing irreversible harm to anybody for that's the price you pay for being competent and able to do what is right.

 Your Actions Define Your Existence

Because in many, the world can be a harsh place, filled with challenges and setbacks that can test your resolve. Sometimes, these trials can be so overwhelming that they change you fundamentally. When you are repeatedly battered by the world, and subjected to unimaginable hardships, it can erode your belief in the goodness around you. The darkness you experience can breed a desire to inflict the same pain on others, leading to a destructive cycle where you wish for the world to burn, just as you have been burned. As you no longer have any sense of empathy towards anybody that is living. This descent into a mindset of vengeance and bitterness slowly pushes you to become an individual who is no longer appreciative and grateful for the things that you have received in life, rather you become somebody who despises life itself and slowly and steadily you become someone who is no longer aware of the things that you are doing or the damage you are inflicting and even if you do, you don't seem to be bothered by it as you start seeking and regarding yourself far more superior and far more powerful than life itself and when you do that, you inevitably create a situation where sooner or later you are going to face the repercussions of your actions, but unfortunately, by the time you do it, it rips you apart and makes you somebody who is no longer what life would have liked you to be and in many ways you become Anti-life and that's where you start getting it wrong.

What I am talking about has been illustrated incredibly well, in the story of Black Panther, where the characters grapple with loss, anger, and the desire for retribution and yet one small decision changes everything.

In the fictional world of Wakanda (as portrayed in movies), a hidden African nation rich in vibranium, the narrative unfolds around the death of the Black Panther, the nation's protector and king. Following his death, his sister Shuri takes up the mantle of the Black Panther, only to face further tragedy when their mother is killed by Namor, the ruler of an underwater civilisation called Talokan. Namor, who is seen as a god by his people and is referred to as Kukulkan (serpent God), becomes the target of Shuri's wrath. As Shuri seeks revenge, a brutal war erupts between Wakanda and Talokan. The conflict escalates to a point where Shuri, in her rage and grief, overpowers Namor and is on the brink of killing him. At this critical moment, Shuri is haunted by her mother's voice, urging her to reconsider the path she is about to take. This moment is pivotal, as it underscores the theme that seeking vengeance can lead to a never-ending cycle of violence and destruction. Killing Namor, the god of his people, would undoubtedly provoke a full-scale war between the two nations, leading to countless deaths and suffering on both sides. However, Shuri's decision to spare Namor is a testament to the strength that comes from kindness and compassion. In choosing not to kill him, she not only prevents further bloodshed but also demonstrates her inner strength and wisdom. Forgiveness, as Shuri's actions illustrate, is a trait that only the truly strong possess. It is easy to be consumed by anger and hatred, but it takes far greater strength to rise above those emotions and choose a path of mercy.

Through this act of mercy, Shuri achieves something extraordinary—she proves that it is possible to be both kind and competent, to be powerful without being ruthless. By sparing Namor, she sends a message to her people and her enemies: she is a leader who can be trusted to make the right decisions, even in the most challenging circumstances. This duality of strength and kindness elevates her in the eyes of her people and solidifies her position as a formidable and respected leader.

   Your Actions Define Your Existence

The story of Shuri and Namor serves as a powerful metaphor for real life. We all face situations where we must choose between being harsh or being kind, between pursuing our goals at any cost or considering the broader impact of our actions. The world is unpredictable, and today's victories can turn into tomorrow's defeats if we do not navigate life with both strength and compassion. The tables may turn, and those we spare today could become allies in the future, just as those we defeat could rise again.

Kindness, therefore, is not a sign of weakness, but a strategic choice that can lead to lasting success and fulfilment. It allows us to build bridges rather than burn them, to create a legacy of respect and trust rather than fear and resentment. By being kind, we open ourselves to opportunities that might not be immediately apparent, but which can lead to even greater achievements in the long run. As the true path to competence is not just about mastering skills or achieving goals; it is also about mastering oneself while accepting the strength of life. It requires a balance of strength and kindness, decisiveness and compassion. This balance is what allows us to achieve incredible things while remaining true to our values and principles and bowing down to what could be and what would be. Just as Shuri's choice to spare Namor made her stronger and more respected, our choices to act with kindness can lead us to greater success and fulfilment. By embracing kindness as a core part of our competence, we not only achieve our goals but also create a positive impact on the world around us, leaving a legacy of strength, wisdom, and compassion.

Accept the presence of divine powers

In today's world, it is undeniable that people prefer to operate on their terms. Many expect others to conform to their will, and this tendency is especially prevalent among those in positions of power and influence. Once a person reaches such heights, they often begin to see themselves as invincible, believing they are destined to hold onto their authority indefinitely. This mindset explains why so many first-generation entrepreneurs and business leaders refuse to step aside, often clinging to control well into their 70s and 80s. By the time they finally consider relinquishing power, it is often too late—the damage has been done, and the business struggles to survive, leading to the frequent failure of second-generation enterprises.

The same pattern emerges in politics. Many leaders who rise to power through democratic means eventually grow to resent the very system that placed them there. Over time, they become far too powerful, deeply corrupt, and, ironically, morph into the very figures they once opposed. But this phenomenon is not limited to business tycoons or politicians; it applies to anyone who is elevated to a position of authority. Even an ordinary person, when given a taste of power, can easily lose themselves, forgetting the fine line between being competent and being dictatorial. The ability to recognize this distinction—and to demand the same awareness from others—is what sets apart those who are truly fit to lead from those who are not.

This timeless struggle was powerfully depicted in Exodus: Gods and Kings, a film that masterfully illustrates how power, if unchecked, can transform even the most well-intentioned individuals into the very tyrants they once stood against.

In this movie, King Seti gives one of the best lines ever-

"Men who crave power are best fitted to acquire it and least fitted to exercise it".

This line very much states how once a man reaches the positions of powers he had so badly wanted, ends up losing himself,

 Your Actions Define Your Existence

thinking of himself as the all in all, and it is during this time we see divine intervention in many forms.

When I speak of divine intervention, I am not referring to the kind described in holy books or tied exclusively to religious beliefs, as not everyone may be a devout follower of religion. Instead, divine intervention can manifest in various ways, interpreted differently by different people. Some might say, "**The universe has decided this**," while others may call it **"destiny," "fate,"** or **"karma."** Regardless of how one perceives it, there is an undeniable force beyond human comprehension—one that reveals its presence through the events and experiences of our lives, demonstrating its power in ways we may never fully understand.

You have to understand that some forces and things are out there you simply cannot comprehend and all your grandiose achievements could turn into dust in a single second, for that reason, you should be mindful of your actions and think again for the actions that you carry out when you are at the prime of your prowess, for that's not where you will be every day. For ex- I once knew a man who had an incredible amount of wealth and money and had a great amount of influence. And during his days he was known for committing adultery, rape, domestic violence, sexual assaults on women, and physical assaults on various individuals, but now he has been caught with liver disease and due to that he has abstained from all sorts of things he once loved to eat. He has to walk every day to keep himself alive, as his condition is so bad that he is barely a few steps away from liver cirrhosis. Today he can't sleep in as he has always been a paranoid and fearful man, and that's why he walks extra every morning to keep himself and his liver healthy. He can't eat any of the things he once ate, and so no matter what we say, he is facing hell even after having everything that he once desired, and yet all of his acts have now started to catch up with him and due to that he is becoming more and more resentful for his life and due to that he is forcing himself to show that he is still the same person, and due to that he is making even more mistakes with the passing of each and every day. This man is deeply religious, constantly invoking God's name even after committing crimes. But no matter what we say or believe, our actions will inevitably catch up with us—whether today or tomorrow. We must face the consequences of our deeds, and the concepts of heaven and hell we often imagine may, in many ways, manifest right here on Earth.

Countless men like him are now suffering the repercussions of the choices they made when they believed themselves to be invincible. Yet, life itself has a way of demonstrating the true power of the divine. It can offer both heavenly bliss and unbearable suffering within a single lifetime. As for what lies beyond, in the afterlife— that remains beyond human understanding, leaving us only with our imaginations and interpretations to make sense.

To live your life in a way where you end up becoming less resentful as time passes, you have to be well aware of what you are doing. You have to understand the difference between someone who is confident has an incredible work ethic is highly successful and yet is kind and willing to be helpful to the ones he/she can as that is what would turn you into an individual who is making a difference not just in your own life but in other people's lives as well. Or you could choose to become someone who is absolutely cocky and arrogant about your achievements and consider everybody to be beneath you and anybody who comes to you for assistance is met with your unhelpful and sinful demeanour. Because if you become the latter you have to be well aware of how you will end up getting the same treatment from others the day you are no longer as good as you are today, and it is only on

   Your Actions Define Your Existence

that day you will realise how weak and small you are, and how big and powerful "Life" is.

"Choices have consequences", and the sooner you make yourselves aware of that the less resentful and the less painful your life will be when you lose all these powers of yours.

So, choose wisely, because either today or tomorrow life is going to catch up with you. You won't be young and ripe forever. Once you gain this wisdom and implement it in your life, your life would become so much better and you would so much more than the person that you are right now, and that's something you should all strive to become and wish to do. That's how you would make your life a life where your actions would positively have far-reaching consequences, and that's when you will understand what happiness truly is.

And that's when life would be a little bit less bitter towards you, because no matter what you do, bitterness will always follow you and will sometimes swallow you up, and so when you have the opportunity to be kind, be understanding and yet be ambitious, that's when you would realise that you have been able to hold of various malevolent things that could have appeared in your life, through the divine force. If you could eliminate that, it would mean a life that is much better than what many individuals could have ever witnessed or hoped for, and that's what would make your existence less painful and so much better than what could have happened had you taken the other way around, and that's how you make your existence a formidable and memorable one, even if it meant only a few remember and talk about you in fondness rather than despising you and your soul even in death, for that's what you did to them and that's what you are getting.

So, choose better and strive to be remembered for the things that you did, rather than the pain you caused and the suffering you unleashed upon those who may or may not have wanted you to succeed depending upon their needs, but your actions and your choice were in your control, and all you have to do is choose the path you want to take, for either or tomorrow they will catch up with you, so why not let life catch upon on some benevolent actions and their consequences if the choice is there and if that's what life has bestowed upon you, and no matter what you say, life bestows the choices upon everybody, depends on what we choose and depends on what you do about it, for that's what you will be known for.

"Ambition and hard work are the fuel to achieve greatness, but let them be guided by kindness and understanding. For in life's many twists, you may one day need the same compassion you once had the chance to offer. Strive to reach your goals, but never lose sight of the human connections that make success meaningful. In doing so, you craft a life not marred by bitterness, but enriched by empathy and wisdom. That is the true essence of a fulfilled life."

What Next

And so here we are, it's been an absolutely fabulous and incredible journey. Life is way more strange and far more mysterious than I had ever thought. Because it was about 10 months after I had finished writing and editing my first book that I wasn't able to write a single word for my 2nd book as I had hit, what they say the "writer's block". By the 4th month, I was deeply frustrated and was really on tenterhooks as I was so desperate not to be known as an author who was a "One Book Wonder" or a "One Book writer", as that's not how I wanted to be known if not for anybody else but myself. But slowly and steadily I realised that in life we cannot really achieve anything if we are so desperate to gain and do the things that we want to do, as that's not how life works. Rather it works in a way where we could either achieve our goals or fail terribly in them as that has never been in our hands, but what is there in our hands, is what we choose to do with what we can and what we have and that's where the difference is made, and so I decided to let things rest and started seeing, exploring, meeting different people in order to understand what really goes on in people's lives, plus working in the education sector is an added plus as through that I am able to meet countless numbers of individuals every day, and meeting both the parents and the students on everyday basis allows me to get the way and get an insight into how the lives of two completely different generations go around, and that's when I realised how complex and how complicated human lives and how we are so deeply immersed into our own inner battles of finding solutions to our problems, that we have forgotten how to live and what life is all about.

We have created a world where we are differentiated, judged and treated based on how big our squares are. For example- an individual who owns a penthouse at the top of an apartment building feels he or she is superior to the ones staying on the lower floors of the house, and that's how we have created a world so indifferent and so away from what it means to be human, that we are perpetually caught in the state of chasing. This is good in many ways, as that is what gives us purpose, for what would humans do without these things, that is what motivates them to truly live through their lives, but unfortunately, it is those things that have ended up defining us as individuals for who we are, and that's not the right way to live our lives.

We often judge others based on our perceptions of right and wrong, believing that we are driving the world toward a greater good. Yet, in reality, society is filled with individuals struggling to escape misery, with many walking a path burdened by growing mental distress.

Depression, for instance, has reached alarming levels. In the U.S., the percentage of adults diagnosed with depression at some point in their lives has surged to 29.0%, nearly 10 percentage points higher than in 2015. Meanwhile, the proportion of Americans currently experiencing or receiving treatment for depression has risen to 17.8%, marking a seven-point increase over the same period. These figures, recorded by Gallup, are the highest since it began using its current data collection method. Similarly, stress and depression are escalating in India, with 43% of Indians now suffering from depression, according to a study conducted by GOQii, a smart-tech-enabled preventive healthcare platform.

The study, which surveyed over 10,000 individuals, examined how people are coping with the "new normal."

These statistics are deeply concerning and should compel us to reflect on where we are truly headed as a society. If our progress is leading to such widespread suffering, we must ask ourselves: what are we striving for? While pain is an unavoidable part of life and suffering may seem inevitable, we have the power to eliminate the smaller burdens that unnecessarily intensify our struggles. It is for this very reason that I wrote this book—to shed light on these issues and explore ways to create a life that is less consumed by misery.

Complexity is what makes our lives far more difficult than they should have been, and as individuals we have the power to change that narrative and truly usher in an era and in a world where our lives are far more appreciative of what we have, rather than staying in constant agony of what others have, as with that mindset and way of life we could and would never ever be able to live what is so rare, imperfect and beautiful in its own ways, and that is "**Life**" itself.

Striving to make an impact, improve your life, and showcase your skills—while proving yourself to those who doubted you—sets a truly successful individual apart from an unsuccessful one. But at the same time if your life purpose is about competing and defeating others and flaunting it in a malevolent way then you are completely missing the point about winning in life, for that's not what life is about. Your job is to make sure that you understand how imperfect you are and how complicated life is, but what you can do is to make sure that you can tone down those difficulties and make sure life becomes less complex than it already is. And if you could do that you could do so many things that you may have never ever imagined, and that's what life should be about.

You have to understand that there will always be somebody better than you, stronger than you and smarter than you and even if there isn't there will be a time when your spot will be reclaimed by somebody who you may have never considered a threat, but that's life is about. **For what goes up would eventually come down**. And it doesn't matter how good you were at one point or how good you are, right now! Eventually, you will be outsmarted and outshone by somebody else, and these are some little acceptances that we must have in life because if we do, we end up creating far less cohesion, conflict and far less pain in our lives. The more you contemplate over what could have been and what must have been, the more you will be drowning in desperation and the more you will be creating a far more unfulfilled life. You have to understand that sometimes in order to win and to do things that we so desperately do, we end up committing horrific things and that makes our lives far more comparable to the hell we once despised. For example- In Mahabharat (Indian mythology) Aswathama during the Kurukshetra war ends up killing unborn babies and innocent children due to which Lord Krishan becomes so enraged and angry that he curses him with immortality. Through that, Ashwathama would have to live his life living and reminiscing the evil act he did and now he has to pay for the choices he made.

Similarly, we have the simple choice to make our lives better for ourselves and for the ones who so desperately are in need of a bit of assistance in order to make their lives better as that's what we all strive for each and every day and that's what we should do, for what else we would do.

We must strive to make our brief existence more meaningful, creating lives that are far more fulfilling than what most people typically experience. When we achieve this, we begin to see life's

   Your Actions Define Your Existence

trials and hardships as temporary—neither overwhelming nor insignificant, but simply phases that will eventually pass. To reach this state of mind, one must seek knowledge, cultivate wisdom, and uncover the deeper truths of the world. Only then can we perceive life through eyes and a mind capable of shaping it into what we truly desire. This transformation, however, requires stepping beyond our comfort zones—doing what we have never done before—because only by embracing the unfamiliar can we attain the things we have long wished for and dreamed of.

A few years ago, if someone had told me I would be the author of two books, with many more to come, and that I would co-own a clothing brand with one of my best friends, I would have found it hard to believe. At the time, I was often ridiculed for my imagination and writing. Despite this, I chose to focus on personal development and resilience. I am grateful for the experiences that shaped me, whether challenging or rewarding, as they all contribute to the journey of life.

After publishing my first book, an individual I had known for almost 29 years belittled my efforts, claiming I would never achieve anything independently. This criticism motivated me to prove him wrong. My plans for the clothing brand were initially set for the following year, but his words sparked a determination within me to accelerate those plans.

Today, I am proud to say I have authored two books and successfully launched a clothing company. Rather than harboring bitterness toward that individual, I feel gratitude for the motivation he inadvertently provided. I take pride in my accomplishments and growth, understanding that our responses to life's challenges define who we become.

To my readers, I am beyond thankful that this journey has barely begun and with time incredible memories and incredible stories are all waiting for us in our lives. Some would make those moments hard and complicated while others would make them easy and abundant, and all we could do is accept them and cherish them in whatever form they come. It is an acceptance, that would make your lives far better and far more likeable than what you may have envisioned in a positive way. And if you could do that, you could do anything and that's the beauty of life.

So, thank you for coming along with me on this journey, and until next time take care, look after your family, love those who were never loved and be someone who you always wanted to become, as that is the hero you should all aspire to be, and that is what makes life unbelievably amazing, challenging and cherish at the same time. I am hopeful I will see you soon.

     Your Actions Define Your Existence

Hard times create strong men
Strong men create good times
Good times create weak men
Weak men create hard times

G. Michael Hopf

References

- How to Say No to People, (2023, December 6) Elizabeth Scott

- **How to say no to others and why you shouldn't feel guilty (2022, December 7) Elizabeth Perry** https://www.betterup.com/blog/how-to-say-no

- https://centreforemotionaleducation.com/why-cant-i-say-no-to-anyone/

- **How to set boundaries in your relationship, (2023, August 6) Jennifer Litner,** https://psychcentral.com/relationships/why-healthy-relationships-always-have-boundaries

- **Mark Manson,** https://markmanson.net/boundaries

- **A guide for setting boundaries in relationships, (2023, March7) Ainhoa Indurain,** https://www.lyrahealth.com/blog/boundaries-in-relationships/

- **Be the Mirror, negative person perspective (2022, December 10) Harvey Llyod,** https://www.linkedin.com/pulse/mirror-negative-person-perspective-harvey-lloyd/

- **How to stop other people's opinions guide your life, Andrea Still,** https://tinybuddha.com/blog/how-to-stop-letting-other-peoples-opinions-guide-your-life/

- **The Psychology of Negative People, (2020, December 30)** https://tinybuddha.com/blog/how-to-stop-letting-other-peoples-opinions-guide-your-life/

- **How not to be bothered by other's negative opinions about you, (2021, October 19) Nayaswami Hriman,** https://www.ananda.org/ask/how-to-not-be-bothered-by-others-negative-opinions-of-you/

- **What is negativity Bias and how can it be overcome, (2019, December 30) Catherine Moore** https://positivepsychology.com/3-steps-negativity-bias/

- **7 things that will likely happen when you take a leap of faith in yourself, (2018, March 10) Mo Seetubin,** https://thehappinessplanner.com/blogs/wisdom/7-things-that-will-likely-happen-when-you-take-a-leap-of-faith-in-yourself

- **Sometimes all you need is a leap of faith, (2017, May26) Aditya Vats,** https://medium.com/@adityavats/sometimes-all-you-need-is-a-leap-of-faith-c1ec918d3ca8

- **Self-efficacy and why believing in yourself matters (2024, June 25) Amy Morin,** https://www.verywellmind.com/what-is-self-efficacy-2795954#:~:text=Because%20individuals%20with%20high%20self,for%20new%20ways%20to%20overcome.

- **8 things, super confident people believe about themselves (2015, March 2nd) John Brandon,** https://www.inc.com/john-brandon/8-things-super-confident-people-believe-about-themselves.html

- **The power Of believing in yourself, (2022, July 22) Marianna Pogosyan,** https://www.psychologytoday.com/intl/blog/between-cultures/202207/the-power-believing-in-yourself

- What makes high achievers different from low achievers? Self-regulated learners in the context of a high-stakes academic long-term task (Received April 2021, Revised 20 September 2021, Accepted 24 September 2021) , Carmen Nadja, Yves Karlan, Katharina Maag, Francesca Suter, https://www.sciencedirect.com/science/article/pii/S1041608021001229

- Mccoach, D. Betsy & Siegle, Del. (2001). A comparison of high achievers' and low achievers' attitudes, perceptions, and motivations. Academic Exchange Quarterly. 5. 71-76., https://www.researchgate.net/publication/292324738_A_comparison_of_high_achievers'_and_low_achievers'_attitudes_perceptions_and_motivations

- Harvard Business Review, Don't let your parents disapproval derail your dream, (2020, September 28), Ron Carucci, https://hbr.org/2020/09/dont-let-your-parents-disapproval-derail-your-dreams

- Why you shouldn't care what your parents think, Warren Wong, https://warrenwong.blog/parents/

- Why you shouldn't believe everything your parents tell you, (2020, October 5) East Coast radio, https://www.ecr.co.za/shows/various-/why-you-shouldnt-believe-everything-your-parents-tell-you/

- CNBC, A psychotherapist shares the 5 phrases parents should never say to their kids—and what to use instead, (2019, November 1), Amy Morin, https://www.cnbc.com/2019/11/01/5-phrases-parents-should-never-say-to-their-kids-according-to-a-psychologist.html

- Jeremy Godwin, https://letstalkaboutmentalhealth.com.au/2023/06/11/validation/

- What is Validation in Therapy and why is it important, (2021, September 1) Jeremy Sutton, Ph.D, https://positivepsychology.com/validation-in-therapy/

- What is the Negative Bias, (2023, November 13), Kendra Cherry, https://www.verywellmind.com/negative-bias-4589618

- What is Negative Bias and how can it be overcome, (2019, December 19), Catherine Moore, https://positivepsychology.com/3-steps-negativity-bias/

- Using Social Media for reassurance and happiness, (2021, November 26), Bonnie Zucker, https://www.psychologytoday.com/us/blog/liberate-yourself/202111/using-social-media-reassurance-and-validation

- Onifade, Titoluwanimi. (2022). Effects of Social Media Validation. 1. https://www.researchgate.net/publication/357606313_Effects_of_Social_Media_Validation

- Stop seeking validation from your family, (2014, December 21), Graham Stoney, https://confidentman.net/family/stop-seeking-validation-family

- What if your parents are toxic in your life, Rebecca Ray, https://rebeccaray.com.au/what-if-your-parents-are-toxic-in-your-life/

- Approval- Seeking behaviours, (2022, October 27) Joslyn Jelinek, https://psychcentral.com/blog/what-drives-our-need-for-approval

- TOP 3 REASONS TO RELEASE CONTROL OF YOUR LIFE – Kissy Denise | The Masterpiece. https://www.kissydenise.com/top-3-reasons-release-control-life/

- 9 signs you have been neglecting your needs for far too long, (2024, march19), Eliza Hartley, https://geediting.com/subtle-signs-youve-been-neglecting-your-own-needs-for-too-long-without-even-realizing-it/

- M.J. Lawler, E.B. Talbot, in **Encyclopedia of Human Behavior (Second Edition)**, 2012, https://www.sciencedirect.com/topics/psychology/emotional-neglect

- 5 signs you are neglecting yourself, Sharron Grossman PHD, https://drsharongrossman.com/5-signs-youre-neglecting-yourself/

- Trends That Will Move the Art World Forward – – tribuned. http://tribunedc.com/trends-that-will-move-the-art-world-forwa. Lilius J, Kanov J, Dutton J, Worline M, Maitlis S. *Compassion Revealed: What We Know About Compassion at Work (and Where We Need to Know More)*. Oxford University Press; 2011. doi:10.1093/oxfordhb/9780199734610.013.0021,

- What is Compassion, (2021, November1) Kendra Cherry MSED, https://www.verywellmind.com/what-is-compassion-5207366

 Your Actions Define Your Existence

- When is it right to trust your gut instincts, (2022, April 4) David Robson, https://www.bbc.com/worklife/article/20220401-intuition-when-is-it-right-to-trust-your-gut-instincts

- 10 clear reasons why you shouldn't care what others think, (2020, December 11), Teddy Lim, https://www.lifehack.org/articles/productivity/10-clear-reasons-why-you-shouldnt-care-what-others-think.html

- Denial- How it hurts, how it helps and how to cope, (2023, July 26), Heidi Godman, https://www.health.harvard.edu/blog/denial-how-it-hurts-how-it-helps-and-how-to-cope-202307262958#:~:text=Denial%20can%20shield%20us%20from,the%20thought%20of%20being%20together.

- Denial as a defence mechanism, (2023, November 14), Kendra Cherry, MSED, https://www.verywellmind.com/denial-as-a-defense-mechanism-5114461

- How denial affects your life, (2021, September 14), Melina Retini, Liliana Hogan, https://www.webmd.com/mental-health/features/how-denial-affects-your-life

- Suffering in Silence isn't heroic, (2023, August 4), Rhoberta Shaler, PHD, https://www.yourtango.com/heartbreak/why-suffering-in-silence-ruins-good-relationships

- Ending the silence of quiet suffering, (2022, July 10), Gina Payne, https://adaa.org/living-with-anxiety/personal-stories/ending-silence-quiet-suffering

- What are your regrets? Most people regret not becoming their ideal self, (2018, May 13), Alice G Walton, https://www.forbes.com/sites/alicegwalton/2018/05/30/what-are-your-regrets-most-people-regret-not-becoming-ideal-self-study-finds/

- 10 ways to help other that lead you to success, (2018, January 17), John Hall, https://www.forbes.com/sites/johnhall/2013/05/26/10-ways-to-help-others-that-will-lead-you-to-success/

- What does it mean to be yourself? Carly Sotas, Ted X Youth, https://www.youtube.com/watch?v=Ptvwrfftziw

- The pain of hiding your true self, Ruth Clare, Ted X Youth, https://www.youtube.com/watch?v=orOJb8MDaGk

- Chris Williamson, Modern Wisdom Podcast, https://www.youtube.com/@ChrisWillx

- Care Too Much About What Other People Think? Research Shows That Trait Can Become Your Success Superpower, Especially, as a study of dozens of elite performers shows, when you reframe that emotion to make it work for you,

  (September 25, 2023) Jeff Haden, https://www.inc.com/jeff-haden/care-too-much-about-what-other-people-think-research-shows-that-trait-can-become-your-success-superpower.html

- You Are Not the Centre of the Universe. Admit It and You'll Be More Confident Than Ever, According to Science People don't pay attention to your 'flaws' as much as you think. (July 21, 2019) Carmine Gallo, Harvard instructor, https://www.inc.com/carmine-gallo/you-are-not-center-of-universe-admit-it-youll-be-more-confident-than-ever-according-to-science.html

- Forbes, Three Brutal Truths about success you need to know, (July 27, 2021), Thomas Griffin, (July 27, 2021), https://www.forbes.com/councils/theyec/2021/07/27/three-brutal-truths-about-success-you-need-to-know-now/

- Is being ruthless the key to career success, (2016, January 4), Jillian Kramer, Glamour, https://www.glamour.com/story/ruthless-attitude-career

- The New role model, Amber Valleta, (16 Aug, 2017), The Business of Fashion,

  https://www.youtube.com/watch?app=desktop&v=mSkceh5pNq4

- Why humans are cruel, Sean Illing (Dec 1, 2019) https://www.vox.com/science-and-health/2017/12/14/16687388/cruelty-border-immigration-psychology-human-nature

- The Psychology of the nature of the evil: Evaluating the evil within us all, (October 2023) Tiffany Ann Bickett, https://digitalcommons.cwu.edu/cgi/viewcontent.cgi?article=1263&context=ijurca

- Wonder women 1984

- The Desire for Money it killed our planet and now it is killing our planet,

  (Dec 19, 2023) Shan Shi, https://sites.manchester.ac.uk/global-social-challenges/2023/12/19/the-desire-for-money-it-killed-our-humanity-and-now-it-is-killing-our-planet/

- All relationships are transactional, even the unconditional ones,

  (Dec 22, 2022), Jeff Hayward, https://goodmenproject.com/featured-content/all-relationships-are-transactional/

- I believe all relationships are transactional, https://www.youtube.com/watch?v=HQKIzdig5To

- Transactional Relationships: The Link Between Reciprocity and Connection

  Is it bad when the give-and-take drives everything? (February 24, 2024),

  Kendra Cherry, MSED, https://www.verywellmind.com/transactional-relationships-8580613

- Be Consciously Transactional. Why Every Relationship is Transactional,

  Teal Swan, https://www.youtube.com/watch?v=RRWKNtbmg00

- What if there is no happy ending, (January 15, 2019) Heather Plett,

  https://heatherplett.com/2019/01/no-happy-ending/

- Why I prefer sad endings over happy ones, (November 5, 2019) https://dailyfreepress.com/2021/11/02/why-i-prefer-sad-endings-over-happy-ones/

- In praise of the unhappy, happy ending, (May 23, 2022) Natalie Jenner, https://lithub.com/in-praise-of-the-unhappy-happy-ending/

- 12 reasons to embrace chaos and move ahead in life, Bob Miglani,

  https://grateful.org/resource/12-reasons-embrace-chaos-move-forward-life/

- Forbes, Good Things Don't Come To Those Who Wait -- Good Things Come To Those Who Hustle, (October 29, 2018) Terrina Allen, https://www.forbes.com/sites/terinaallen/2018/10/27/good-things-dont-come-to-those-who-wait-good-things-come-to-those-who-hustle/

- CNBC, You will regret these 10 choices in 10 years, Thomas Oppong,

  (Feb 24, 2017) https://www.cnbc.com/2017/02/24/you-will-regret-these-choices-in-10-years.html

- Why Is It Important to Stay Humble? The Benefits of Humility,

  (April 30, 2024) Tiara Blain, https://www.verywellmind.com/why-is-it-important-to-be-humble-5223266

- Forbes- 13 Habits Of Humble People, (December 10, 2021), Jeff Boss, https://www.forbes.com/sites/jeffboss/2015/03/01/13-habits-of-humble-people/

- US depression rates reach new heights, (17 May, 2023) Dan Witters, https://news.gallup.com/poll/505745/depression-rates-reach-new-highs.aspx

- 43% Indians suffering from depression, Times Of India, https://timesofindia.indiatimes.com/india/43-indians-suffering-from-depression-study/articleshow/77220895.cms#:~:text=Representational%20photo.,according%20to%20a%20new%20study.

- Warren B. The Top Five Regrets of the Dying: A Life Transformed by the Dearly Departing by Bronnie Ware. Proc (Bayl Univ Med Cent). 2012 Jul;25(3):299–300. PMCID: PMC3377309. https://www.ncbi.nlm.nih.gov/pmc/articles/PMC3377309/

- The people you surround yourself with really matters, (August 21, 2019),

  https://pittsburghexperiment.org/the-doorkeepers-blog/2019/8/21/cte1msssodn1td90ge346o64iz9rj7

- Forbes, Chris Myers, Remember that who you spend time with is who you become, (May 30, 2018), https://www.forbes.com/sites/chrismyers/2018/05/30/entrepreneurs-remember-that-who-you-spend-time-with-is-who-you-become/

- Drew Mclean, https://agencymanagementinstitute.com/who-you-spend-time-with-critical-to-success/#:~:text=But%20most%20business%20leaders%20won,that%20fill%20you%20with%20joy

 Your Actions Define Your Existence

- Top 5 regrets people have when they die, says ex-hospice care worker—many don't realize them 'until the end', (June 7, 2024), Ashton Jackson, https://www.cnbc.com/2024/06/07/phrases-that-are-often-peoples-last-regrets-says-author-what-we-can-learn.html

- It's Never Too Late to Say Thank You, (March 6, 2024) Caroline Leavitt, https://www.psychologytoday.com/intl/blog/runs-in-the-family/202403/its-never-too-late-to-say-thank-you

- Express that appreciation now before it's too late, (11 April, 2021) https://thesun.ng/express-that-appreciation-now-before-its-too-late/

- How to Appreciate What You Have Already, (July 2, 2019), Dr. Illene Strauss Cohen, Phd, https://www.psychologytoday.com/intl/blog/your-emotional-meter/201907/how-to-appreciate-what-you-have-already

www.ingramcontent.com/pod-product-compliance
Lightning Source LLC
LaVergne TN
LVHW041451170726
843492LV00005B/1175